The Coast of Maine

The Coast of Maine

An Informal History and Guide / Updated Edition

LOUISE DICKINSON RICH

Photographs by Samuel Chamberlain

THOMAS Y. CROWELL COMPANY
New York / Established 1834

Manufactured in the United States of America

ISBN 0-690-00698-5
      0-690-00957-7 (pbk.)

Library of Congress Cataloging in Publication Data

Rich, Louise Dickinson, date
    The coast of Maine.

    Includes index.
    1. Maine—History. 2. Maine—Description and
travel—1951–   I. Title.
F19.R5   1975   974.1   75-6662
ISBN 0-690-00698-5
ISBN 0-690-00957-7 (pbk.)

1   2   3   4   5   6   7   8   9   10

To Edith Ames and Bertha Cameron

Contents

Illustrations

Introduction

WELL OVER two decades ago, I first went Down-East by highway. I followed old U.S. Route 1 to Lincolnville, Maine, the embarkation point of the ferry to Dark Harbour on an island in Penobscot Bay. There my children and I were to spend the summer. We had never visited the Maine coast before, but we'd heard a lot about Down-East from my mother and grandmother.

My grandmother's family originated on the coast of Nova Scotia, and throughout my childhood I listened to her talk about Down-East. She was as happy in her Massachusetts home as is the average human lot, I am sure; yet her tone was that of an exile when she spoke of the little saltwater farm on which she was raised, with scrub sheep cropping the sparse grass among sea-looking ledges and her brothers building lobster traps in the barnyard and launching boats in the shingle cove below the house. She told of digging clams on the flats and picking blueberries "up-back-a-piece" and gathering dulse—a seaweed—along the shore to chew or to make into a type of milk pudding. She described epic fogs and surf as high as houses the crashing of which rattled the windows and coated them thick with salt; and of northern lights that sent wavering streamers of fire a thousand miles long into the sky. It all sounded to us children like something made up—as she would say—out of whole cloth.

So did the people she re-created; people who said and did the most outlandish things imaginable. There was a woman, for example, who threatened to sit on a half-tide ledge—a ledge exposed only at half-tide or less—until her husband apologized for criticizing her cooking. He was stubborn, too, and refused to say he was sorry. So she sat there as the water rose icily around her until she drowned.

We didn't believe this tale at the time. Nobody could be that cross-grained and ornery. I believe it now, though. Now I've come to know well many Down-Easters, and I wouldn't put the most quixotic behavior past them. They are a strange, independent breed, tough on others, but just as tough on themselves. Perhaps that's the secret of their survival in a land where everything—the climate, the soil, the sea, the lack of opportunity—is against them.

They come by their distinguishing traits honestly. They are descended from a long line of the eccentric, the dogged, the independent and inventive. As far back as 1745, William Vaughn, a Damariscotta fisherman, made up his mind that the French of Canada should be taught not to meddle with Maine affairs. The thing to do, he said, was to capture their impregnable fortress at Louisbourg. This was impossible; but a motley crew of Maine men did it.

Or consider Samuel Clough, as level-headed, practical, and hardbitten a sea captain as any along the coast. He undertook and almost succeeded in the dangerous mission of saving Marie Antoinette from the guillotine by spiriting her away to his home in Edgecomb; not for money, not for fame, not even for love, but just because the notion struck his fancy. Or the widow Alice Greeley, who in 1775 ran a tavern in Portland. When the city was set afire by a British bombardment, she saved her establishment by tucking up her skirts, lugging pails of water up a ladder to douse the flames on the roof, and cracking bitter jokes all the while.

I know men and women on the Maine coast today who I am sure would be capable of any or all of these actions. They are almost the rule rather than the exception. Some say that the Down-East character is the result of the environment, of the constant battle against adversity in the form of the weather, submarginal soil, difficult means of livelihood, and continual economic pressure. I think that this is putting the cart before the horse. The environment didn't make Down-Easters the way they are. Instead, it weeded out the weaklings, who either died or moved to easier-living climes. Those who remain are like their ancestors. They do what they please, say what they think and, if they feel like it, cut off their noses to spite their faces.

Down-East is very hard to pinpoint. To my grandmother it was Nova Scotia. To various acquaintances it is as variously Portland, Bailey's Island, Blue Hill, or Jonesport, Maine. There is some disparity here. It's a far cry, not only geographically but culturally and spiritually as well, from Portland to Nova Scotia. They both can't be Down-East.

Or can they? Where is Down-East? To me it is the little village beyond Ellsworth where I have lived for many years; and to my cousin it is Boothbay Harbor, where she spends summers. We are both right. Down-East is where you find it, the place where a curve of beach or the loom of a headland lifts your spirits inexplicably, where the smiles and greetings of the people on a busy street or on a narrow dirt road winding through fields of blowing daisies to the sea warm the cockles of your heart. Each of us must find his own Down-East.

All writers, I think, are imbued to some extent with missionary zeal. They are not happy until they have aired their opinions and observations as widely as possible. So after having lived on the coast of Maine for a few years and become completely enthralled with it and its people and way of life, both past and present, I was twitching like a witch to write a book on the subject. That was pretty pretentious of me, I now realize. There was an awful lot I didn't know at the time; an awful lot I still don't know.

How much I didn't appreciate until the last time I

traversed the coast, this time in my son's small Cessna. When I climbed into the plane at the Trenton airport, which serves Bar Harbor, I was confident of my expertise. I'd lived on the coast for years, eaten goosegrass greens, gone out with the lobster fleet at dawn, explored dozens of islands and capes and hundreds of backroads. I'd learned to speak of "sailing under bare poles" rather than being financially embarrassed, and "oiling up" instead of putting on my raincoat. I thought I knew the subject well.

We flew at about two thousand feet, high enough to permit an all-encompassing view, low enough to inspect details like hidden farms at the ends of secret lanes and small island coves sheltering tiny boats. The whole fantastic coastline lay below us—the tattered shore with its deep indentations and bold promontories, its salt marshes and small towns, its reefs and islands, all fringed white by breaking surf, all floating on a vast ocean that shaded from green to turquoise to deep, deep blue. I saw places that I never knew existed and that I could have been persuaded against reason no one else knew about, either. If so much of simple coastal geography lay outside my knowledge, how much greater must be my ignorance of the intangibles—of coastal thought and customs and beliefs. The rest of my life would not be long enough to learn all I should know.

So I will not pretend that this revision is the final and definitive word on the coast of Maine. I doubt if that word is possible ever on so vast, varied and flexible a subject. Rather its purpose is to give additional and updated information, and, more especially, to make some suggestions on procedure for those who wish to do their own exploring and perhaps, happily, to find their own private and individual Down-Easts.

PART I

The candy-striped West Quoddy Head Light, near Lubec, marks the point farthest east in the United States.

1 · Geographical Background

IT IS POSSIBLE, of course, to visit and to delight in a beautiful country without possessing any knowledge of its history; but without that knowledge it is not possible to experience the deeper and more lasting satisfaction arising from an understanding of the forces that made the land and the people what they are today. A village may impress the eye by the graciousness of its old houses and the peace of its tree-arched streets; but only familiarity with the struggles that shaped that village can impress the mind and heart. Today is just a moment in Time, a bridge between the long past and the veiled future. Observing a locality in ignorance of the past is seeing only to the ends of the bridge. The future we cannot surely foretell; but if we know the past, we can at least appreciate the import of the bridge of Time on which we stand, and perhaps find some clue of what is to come. To ignore history is deliberately to blind the intelligence to all that makes a territory significant and to deprive the imagination of food on which to feed.

Perhaps there are those who don't care, who are not moved by the certainty, "Right here where my feet are now, Champlain's feet once were planted"; or "A thousand years ago the Vikings sailed along this coast and saw the surf break on these rocks as I am seeing it." Perhaps there are people like that—but I can't imagine who they

• 3

may be. I cannot imagine the type of mind that does not quicken to the realization of a continuance in itself of a great adventure, of a brotherhood that has extended down the centuries. For those who do care, I would like to tell briefly the story of what happened along the Maine coast in bygone days, so that they may read the meanings of the places of today which we will explore.

All history is determined by geography, by the nature of a country—by its topography and climate, by its latitude and longitude, by its soil and natural resources, by the hundreds of other conditions that contribute to its own special character. Nowhere has this been more clearly demonstrated than along the coast of Maine, because nowhere is there an area of more strongly marked traits.

In the first place, almost nowhere in the world is there a more irregular coastline. Although the distance from Kittery at the southwest to Eastport at the northeast is only 225 miles as the gull flies, the line of the coast is actually 2500 miles long. It is only three miles from Lubec to Eastport by water, but the shortest road between the two covers forty miles, and the shoreline proper measures a hundred miles. This is the result of Maine's having what is known geologically as a *drowned coastline,* and the scientific term describes it very well to a lay mind such as mine.

Once the entire territory was a mountain range rising well above the sea; but during the Ice Age the inconceivable weight of the great icecap creeping down from the Pole bore on it with such tremendous pressure that it sank beneath the ocean. Water rushed up the long valleys, forming winding bays and deep coves and fjords, and turning the river mouths into wide estuaries. After the glacier retreated, mountains that had been near the shore were islands, and those that had been inland now discovered themselves to be bold headlands looking out to sea. The land never lifted to its old level, although apparently it did rise a little after the pressure was relieved. At Isle au

Haut and on Mt. Desert, beach gravels and clay containing marine fossils have been found as high as the 225-foot level, plain evidence that once the surf broke there. With this rise, a few of the mountain tops that had been covered with water regained the light and open air, so that now there are about two thousand islands off the Maine coast, some large and well-populated townships, some just a few acres of barren rock, and many, many in-between that are just the right size to take to your heart.

If you will pick up a large piece of stiff paper, crumple it into folds and hollows, peaks and depressions, sink it in a tub of water, and then raise it a little, you will see what happened to the coast of Maine way back before the memory of man.

The result of this prehistoric ordeal is not only a coast-line of such infinite variety and beauty that it has to be seen to be believed, but also so many safe harbors, deep-water approaches, and sheltered inside passages that you might almost say Maine men were forced to become a breed of shipbuilders and traders to the far corners of the world. The drowned coastline made them into fishermen, too. The wide sunken shelf of the continent with its banks and submerged ledges and cold, pure water was and is the natural home and breeding ground of the cod, the haddock, the lobster, and many other edible and market-able species. The first Europeans to spend any time at all in Maine waters came for the fishing.

The Maine coast has the most spectacular fogs in the world, if such a quiet and insidious thing as fog can be called spectacular. They're caused by the confluence of the warm Gulf Stream and the icy Laborador Current somewhere offshore, and they march down silently from the direction of the Bay of Fundy or in from the sea. Rainbows play along their faces before they move in to engulf the land and blot out everything except sound— which seems to be sharpened by them—so that the world is reduced to the small circle of dripping blueberry bushes in which you happen to be standing. The farther Down-

East you go, the more likely you are to find yourself fog-bound. Last summer I was way Down, almost at the Canadian border, when a wall of fog moved in from the ocean, and for eight days I saw the ledges in front of the cabin, a few rods offshore, only twice for periods of about two minutes each, through chance rifts.

It was then that I said to the keeper of the general store and post office, "I'll bet this area has more fog than any place on earth except possibly the Aleutians." I'd heard about the terrific fogs blanketing those lonely Pacific islands from servicemen who had been stationed there during the war.

The storekeeper looked hurt and affronted, and I thought I'd wounded him by an implied criticism of his native heath. But not at all. He told me firmly that the Coast Guard station on Great Wass Island—"Off thataway a short piece," he said, gesturing into the murk—was obliged to keep a record of weather conditions, and almost every year they came out ahead of the Aleutians in the Foggy-Day Count. "We have the *most* fog in the world," he said with quiet pride. "A hunerd-eighty-odd days last year." There's nothing like the Yankee talent for turning a local (or personal) vice into a virtue; and it's the philosophical attitude, after all, if the vice is something you can't do anything about, like fog.

It's the fogs that permit the flowers to grow so luxuriantly and bloom so prodigally and brilliantly in what look like unpromising rootholds amid the ledges; and the fogs protect them from the nip of the early winters, so that I have seen wild roses flowering with abandon in Stonington on Deer Isle in late October.

And the fog has played its part in Maine history, too. To give just one example, Jesuit missionaries established themselves on Mt. Desert in 1612 because they'd become lost in a fog. They hadn't intended to go there at all; but, when the fog lifted after several days, that's where they found themselves. They decided that this was the will of God, and went ashore and built cabins and an altar; and so it came about that as natural a thing as a Maine pea-souper led eventually to the first clash and bloodshed between the French and the British in the New World, and the beginning of a century-and-a-half-long struggle for supremacy. But we'll go into that affair in more detail later on.

What of the land that lies behind this ragged coastline? Well, it's a beautiful land, strong and rock-ribbed, with nothing of the soft and lush about it. Rough ledges thrust out into the sea, shedding from their backs great rollers that pound in from the North Atlantic in smothers of foam and spray. Between the capes and promontories there are beaches of white sand, or sometimes pink, if the granite of the locality happens to be the pink Cadillac type; and I know a little purple beach, where the sand is composed of clam and mussel shells, pulverized by the hammering of the waves. It's lovely between the pink rocks with wild roses and daisies and sea lavender all around, just as lovely today as it was when only the Indians knew it. The water is cold all along the shore, which is good for the lobsters but a little daunting to all but hardy swimmers.

Back of the rocks and beaches lies a country that was once largely covered with forest. Now it is mostly fir and spruce, black tips pointing stiffly to the heavens, with an intermingling of oak and birch and maple, which blaze in autumn. When the white man discovered the coast of Maine, however, the tall white pine grew abundantly on the hillsides, the best trees in the world for the masts of the old sailing ships. So superior were they that the King of England claimed for the use of the Royal Navy all that measured over twenty-four inches in diameter a foot from the ground. He sent out cruisers and surveyors to mark them with the broad arrow that indicated royal property, whether it was found on a tree, a ship's bucket, or the shirt of a prisoner in a dungeon; and anyone caught cutting one of the King's masts was fined and punished.

The settlers cut them just the same, when they thought they could get away with it. I know a house in which some of the boards of the pine paneling are a yard wide and must have come from one of His Majesty's trees, in spite of the Royal edict; and I know another house where the ancient pine floor boards all measure exactly twenty-one and three-quarters inches. They came off the saw wider, so the story goes, but were trimmed down to legal width in case the King's mast agent should drop in some fine day.

A lively business in the cutting and shipping of masts to England went on at one period, and Samuel Pepys remarks in his diary the arrival of a shipment of the long sticks, which he says occasioned great joy and relief, as they were sorely needed by the royal shipyards, held up in production by lack of masts. Consequently, the old white or "punkin" pine is almost extinct today in Maine. What white pine there is is small stuff, although once in a while you'll see one of the old giants towering above the surrounding forest; and there is a stand of them near Brunswick, owned by Bowdoin College and preserved as a monument to the old days. Some of the trees in that little grove are older than the white man in America.

In the shadow of the forests, moving secretly and busily, was wealth in another form—the fox and the mink and the otter and especially the beaver. The pelts of these animals were primed by the cold winters, and the European demand for them was insatiable. This was particularly true in the case of the beaver, because of a great and sweeping vogue in beaver hats. Many of the Maine towns of today started life as fur trapping and trading posts, before anyone had any notion of permanent settlements. Deer and moose and bear roamed the woods and furnished fresh meat for the taking and hides for boots and clothing and robes. There were clams and oysters and fish to be had from the sea, and the streams abounded in fresh-water varieties. The wild land had plenty to offer a man who had the will to work for it and the stamina to undergo hardship. The Plymouth Pilgrims paid for the *Mayflower*, for which they'd gone deeply in debt when they set sail for the New World, in furs trapped or traded at an outpost they established in 1628 on the Kennebec.

Another of Maine's natural resources lay under the surface of the land. There was limestone, the basis of the lime burning business, and slate, and granite in a dozen shades from almost white to black, and in tints of green and rose. Maine granite adorns buildings all over the world and cobbles the streets of cities far from the sound of surf breaking on reefs. It filled the holds of many an outbound ship of Maine construction, and sunk many of those ships, too. A vessel loaded with Maine lumber could often ride out a storm because of the natural buoyancy of its cargo, while the same storm could prove fatal to a granite ship, in spite of the superb seamanship of Maine-bred sailors.

The soil that covered the bedrock of the coast was good soil. Even before the white man came, Indians farmed the land and raised their crops of corn and beans and squash, using rotted fish for fertilizer and seaweed as a mulch. They taught the whites a great deal about local methods. Yet even without the fish and kelp, the soil was fertile. One of the very earliest explorers, Captain George Weymouth, reported back to England in 1605 that he'd planted barley and peas, and in sixteen days they were eight inches tall; but that I rather doubt. However, the land was good enough so that as soon as they had pushed back the forest far enough from their cabins to let in a little sunlight and air, the pioneers had no trouble in raising enough produce to more than meet their needs.

Maine lies halfway between the equator and the North Pole. In fact, there is a granite marker beside the Eastport-Perry road indicating the point where the forty-fifth parallel crosses the thoroughfare. So the climate is theoretically temperate, although as a survivor of a great many Maine winters I must say that there have been times when it seemed a lot colder than that to me. I'm not the first to have found it so.

In the early 1600's, the Maine climate had a very bad reputation in Europe, various reports having filtered back that it would be impossible for civilized man to withstand the rigors of a Maine winter, and that therefore colonization was not feasible. Sir Ferdinando Gorges and Sir John Popham, the Lord Chief Justice of England, had become interested in the settling of Maine, so they sent out an expedition under George Popham and Raleigh Gilbert, son of Sir Humphrey Gilbert, to establish a settlement chiefly for the purpose of testing the climate.

They landed near the end of the summer and formed a little colony of about a hundred and twenty men at Hunniwell or Popham's Point, at the mouth of the Kennebec. It happened that Maine had one of its really tough winters that year, much more severe than usual. George Popham and many others died; and, in an effort to keep warm, the colonists heaped so much wood on the fireplace that they burned down the building. When Captain Davis' ship returned in the spring to check on the party's well-being, he found its members in a bad way. They were only too eager to give up the whole idea and go home; and the tales they took back with them about the severity of the Maine climate discouraged further attempts at colonization by the English for quite a while.

I don't know whether those who settled Maine were naturally of an ingenious turn, or whether living there developed ingenuity. Probably it was a little of both. At any rate, even the bitterness of the winters was turned to account in time. In 1815, a young man inherited a fleet of windjammers. He had no cargo with which to fill them, so he conceived the notion of going into the ice business. Ice was plentiful and free for the cutting on any of the Maine ponds and rivers for months of the year. He filled his ships with ice and peddled it all over the hotter portions of the globe. So successful was he that many others followed his example and, for a long time, until the development of electric refrigeration, huge icehouses were a feature of the landscape all along the coast of Maine.

Many a respectable Maine fortune was founded on frozen Kennebec or Penobscot water. Myself, I find it rather fascinating to think of men and women in broiling Cuba and Africa and sultry Singapore happily cooling their tongues with clear ice from streams whose names they may never have heard and whose shores they almost certainly never would see. That water was a long way from home, but perhaps it took some of its virtue with it.

Maine is not only the northernmost of the United States; it is also the most easterly. The first soil of the nation that the sun touches as it rises each day is the summit of Mt. Katahdin, so that Maine natives say, "We pry up the sun in the mornin' "; and West Quoddy Head, near Lubec, is the point farthest east in the whole country. Maine stretches out its capes and peninsulas like arms toward Europe. And the first landfall made by the adventurous Vikings, by John Cabot for the English, by Verrazano, an Italian in the service of France, by the Spaniard Gómez, was Maine. It must have looked beautiful after the long weeks at sea, and more than one of the early explorers— who seem to have been men of letters and poets at heart —have commented on the delicious smell of the land, a perfume compounded of flowers and grass and the resinous odor of pine and spruce, drifting out on the westerly stir of air.

But like many proud beauties, it was not to be easily won. The offshore reefs, dangerous teeth to rip the vitals from a ship, the forbidding aspect of the hills, the evil reports of the climate and the Indians, who were reputed to be bloodthirsty savages, all served to protect Maine. It was a land that had to be fought for; but it was worth the fighting.

This then is the geography of Maine, the sum of all the natural components that determined her history and, I think, the character of her people, down to the present day. Unless the geography is held clearly in mind, neither the history nor the people will make much sense.

When the white man first came to the shores of Maine, the land was inhabited by the Indians, of course. Everybody knows that. But there were men running the Maine woods and fishing the cold waters long before the Indians took the country for their own. Back in the dim dawn of Time, there were the Stone Age men, of whom little is known—but that little, as deduced from the artifacts occasionally uncovered at Caratunk and elsewhere, is good. Nobody knows where these people originated or what became of them or what they looked like; but the imperishable things that they made of stone tell that they had an eye for beauty. Their artifacts are as fine as any of the entire Stone Age.

They took pains with their work. Their flint spear and arrow heads were sharp and delicate, and their skinning knives keen-edged and tapered and hollow-ground to the thinnest possible edge. They killed the deer by throwing a weighted rawhide, like the bolas of South America, to entangle the legs of their quarry and bring it down; and they didn't use just any old stones of suitable size, shape, and weight for the ends of the rope. They shaped the weights into exquisite balance and proportion, which probably did make them easier to handle and more efficacious. But the three-petaled flowers that they engraved on the sides of the stones served no practical purpose, and must have been so carefully and elegantly done to satisfy some esthetic demand, the same demand that caused them to fashion for themselves necklaces of little blue stones, curved into slender crescents and pierced twice so that they could be threaded onto a thong. They must have been a rather charming people.

One other thing is known about them. They always put into the graves of their dead clay stained red with iron oxide. Nobody knows why. Perhaps they thought it would preserve the bodies, or perhaps it was used as decoration—in life as well as in death—or perhaps it had some religious significance, now long lost with their lost folkways and mode of life, and even their bones. There are never any bones in the graves. They long ago mouldered into dust, and all that's left is the red clay, either in lumps or spread over the bottoms of the graves. Its use must have been important to the Stone Age man, because it all came from the same place, so scientists say with assurance, a spot on the side of Mt. Katahdin, a great distance from some of the graves in which it has been found. Its presence bears mute witness to a long hard journey through difficult country. For whatever reason, the red clay must have seemed vital to the Stone Age man, that he would undertake a special trip to secure it.

Of the race which succeeded the lost Red Clay people we can say one thing with a fair degree of certainty: they appreciated high living. They were the ones responsible for the huge heaps of oyster shells found all along the coast, but especially on the tidal section of the Damariscotta River. In some places these shell piles rise twenty-five feet or more, and one is over seventeen hundred feet square. That's about forty-five million cubic feet of oyster shells in one pile alone, which represents a great many oysters consumed, to put it mildly.

In the vicinity of these shell banks there are frequently found articles lost by the participants in these colossal prehistoric clambakes, spoons and bits of broken pottery and primitive axes and knives. Somehow it makes the Oyster Shell men seem more real, that they could go to a picnic and break a dish or lose a spoon, even as you and I. The spoons are of copper and the pottery is finely worked, indicating a quite highly advanced culture. Sometimes, too, are found the bones of the picnickers; but whether they died of overeating or as the result of the kind of Donnybrook that occasionally occurs even on present-day picnics can't be determined at this late date. Some of the bones suggest that the Oyster Shell men occasionally stood over six feet tall. But that's about all we know concerning them. The bones crumble to dust when exposed to air, and all that is left of those ancient tribesmen is their strong teeth. The oysters, too, have almost vanished from Maine waters. Only a very few are now found.

We know quite a lot about the Indians who came after

these prehistoric races and inhabited Maine at the time of the arrival of the white man, although not as much as we should know. None of the explorers or settlers were interested enough in the aborigines to make a real study of them. To them, an Indian was an Indian, and who cared about minor distinctions anyhow? I suppose they're not to be blamed too much. They had enough on their minds, with discovering and establishing themselves in a new land, with keeping themselves alive, with worrying about claiming territory for their various monarchs, and with getting back home safely, to concern themselves with the taking of notes on the native population. But it's too bad, all the same.

We do know that there were two distinct races of Indians living in Maine then. There were the Mikmaks in eastern Maine and New Brunswick, a confederation of seven tribes. But the larger part of the state was occupied by the Abenakis (or Wabanakis), who called themselves the Dawn People. The Abenaki nation was composed of a great many tribes, although exactly how many or what each was called is not now known. They spoke a common basic language and could converse with each other, but each tribe had a characteristic dialect. Their difference in speech was comparable to the difference between the speech of a State of Mainer and a native of Georgia. They both speak English, but— Each Abenaki tribe had its own stamping ground, its own governmental, social and industrial structure, and its own style in clothes, weapons, houses, and canoes. The fact that they were all Abenakis didn't prevent them from carrying on guerilla warfare with each other, either, if sufficient provocation arose.

The Mikmaks were naturally aggressive and warlike, but fortunately for the whites, they were in the minority and confined to easternmost Maine. The majority of the Indians, the Abenakis, were basically a peace-loving people. Except for the Passamaquoddies and a few other coastal tribes, whose economy was based on fishing, the Maine Indians were farmers at heart. Of course, they hunted and fished, too, as farmers universally do; and they were extremely brave and resourceful fighters in defense of their homes or for what they considered a good cause, as men of spirit have always been everywhere. But their true interest lay in their little fields of beans and squash and corn and pumpkins, and in the gathering of wild grapes and berries and nuts and edible roots. They collected maple sap in the spring and made maple syrup and sugar, just as Maine farmers do today, and dug and ate dandelion greens and the young fern fronds now called "fiddleheads," as a blood tonic in the spring after the long winter without greens.

Because they were more or less tied to the fields which they had with great labor cleared and improved, their villages were permanent. Sometimes they went on the warpath or took a trip to the shore to fish or dig for clams and mussels, but they couldn't be gone very long. Their gardens needed constant attention, and there was a lot to do at home around the village. Their houses were built of timber and roofed with bark or thatch, and in winter they were banked with sod and leaves against the cold, as Maine farmhouses are today. Sometimes they built wigwams of light poles and birch bark or skins, but only as temporary summer quarters or when they were vacationing at the beach.

Their pottery was rather crude and rough, possibly because of lack of really fine clay; but they made wonderful baskets, the best of which were absolutely watertight. They could boil corn or lobsters in them by heating stones in a fire and dropping them into the water-filled baskets. They carried fire along with them, when they traveled, by enclosing a piece of smouldering punk between two large clam shells and encasing the whole thing in a cocoon of wet clay.

They kept dogs, not as draft animals or for hunting, but simply as pets and watch dogs. Anybody who has lived in a wild and lonely country knows how much company a dog can be, and apparently the Abenakis felt about their dogs as country people today feel about the big brute who warns them of strangers passing or comes to nudge with a cold nose to be scratched behind the ears. In an Abenaki grave uncovered a few years ago there were found the skeletons of a teen-age boy and his dog, curled up at his feet. The bond between a boy and his dog is no refinement of modern feeling, then, but goes back for centuries; and I find it moving to think of that Indian boy and dog, who so loved each other that they must take the last and longest journey together.

For hunting and in war, the Abenakis used short and powerful bows of rock maple, white ash, or ironwood, and arrows headed with stone or iron and tipped with feathers to hold them in straight flight. They also had spears and heavy clubs with natural knobs for heads, and tomahawks with stone or iron blades. They used the arrows and the spears for fishing, too, but they had in addition hooks and lines, nets, and weirs. In the working of their garden patches, they used hoes made of moose antlers or large clam shells, spades of wood or horn, and rakes made by shredding the ends of saplings into many parts, which were spread and held in place by root or bark fibers. Their rakes were very much like the bamboo rakes commonly used on lawns today.

All the tribes were very skillful at curing the hides of the animals they killed, especially the skins of the moose, the deer, and the caribou. Of this pliable leather they made clothing, robes, and moccasins, which they trimmed elaborately with dyed porcupine quills, colored moose hair, and, after they had established trade with the whites, with beadwork. But they had fabrics as well, woven from moose hair, cedar bark, milkweed down, and other natural fibers. They had mats and carpets woven of rushes, as well as fur rugs, on the floors of their homes. When the deep snows of winter covered the land, they walked on long snowshoes with bent wood frames and rawhide webbing. They lived comfortably and conveniently through a trait that seems to develop automatically in those who adopt Maine as their native land: an ingenious adaptability, a talent for making do with what is at hand.

Almost every primitive people has one source of a great many benefits upon which life depends. The Eskimo had the seal, the Laplander had the reindeer, and the South Sea Islander had the palm. The Maine Indians depended on the beautiful white birch. They made canoes of the bark, some small, some large enough for a party of two dozen or more. These were extremely seaworthy, so that the Indians took trips to islands far offshore in them. The famous Oldtown canoes of today are patterned exactly after them, and are considered the best-designed canoes in the world. Toboggans were made of wood laths and birch bark for hauling in winter, and birch bark formed boxes and bowls and household utensils.

Under the rough outer bark of the birch lies a tissue-thin layer of rosey-tan inner bark, and this the Indians used for paper. They had a written language of symbols, and they recorded and preserved treaties and other important matters on this bark. Bark scraps were used as tinder, and the wood of the birch was a common firewood, since even when green it kindles fairly easily, although it will not hold a fire as well as the harder, slower-burning maple, or form as good a bed of coals. Birch poles were used in the frames of houses and wigwams and for the handles of tools; and Indian children amused themselves by swinging the birches, as New England country boys and girls do today—by climbing to the slim top of a straight white tree and then, holding fast with the hands, launching out into the air to be set gently back on the ground by the graceful, pliant tree. The birch was most useful, as well as lovely.

There have been a great many misconceptions about the Maine Indians. They have been pictured as a horde of howling, vicious barbarians whose chief recreation was torture and slaughter. Actually there were never more than about three thousand Indians in all Maine, even in the most populous times, and these were concentrated on the coast and along the shores of the larger lakes and rivers. The forested and mountainous hinterland was almost unpopulated, because it offered no means of livelihood.

As for viciousness, the Abenakis never acted as aggressors in the battles with the whites. They were really a gentle, moral, hard-working, peace-loving people, until they were pressed too hard or taken advantage of too often. Then they lost their patience, or perhaps they realized that their way of life was at stake, and took retaliatory steps. War parties did swoop down on settlements and isolated cabins, burning, killing, scalping, and carrying away captives. I have no doubt that these war parties looked like hordes of screaming devils to the terrified victims, but there is no dependable record of any one of them having exceeded two hundred in number—which I'll grant is plenty, but not exactly countless. The warriors did not wear war bonnets or shave their heads, as is sometimes imagined. The Indians who did that were the tribes of the Great Plains and the New York Iroquois.

Another common error is the legend of Indian princesses and queens. I know that the idea of a beautiful Indian princess is very romantic, and that the story about Aaron Burr's affair with an Indian queen, Jacataqua, makes good reading. But in cold fact, there never was such a thing as an Indian royal family. The Indians everywhere in America practiced a form of true democracy. The chief was chosen for his abilities, held the office only as long as he was capable of discharging his duties, and did *not* pass it on to his son. Sometimes a village had two chiefs, a war chief and a peace chief, since the talents which distinguish a man in battle don't necessarily qualify him to administer village affairs wisely.

It's true that occasionally the chief's son did become chief in turn, but this was because of inherited traits of leadership and not by right of royal blood line. It's possible, of course, that the son of a chief was in an advantageous political position to take over the reins of government, and so had an edge on his rivals. But he didn't keep his job long unless he had what it took to make his claim stick.

Today Maine has between nine hundred and a thousand Indians, divided about equally between two tribes, the Passamaquoddies and the Penobscots, the only tribes left of the dozens that once inhabited the land. Most of them live on reservations, although some do not. The Passamaquoddies are found in eastern Maine, where the larger of their two reservations is at Pleasant Point near Eastport. The Penobscots live on Panawamske or Indian Island, a reservation on an island in the middle of the Penobscot River at Oldtown. They dress as we do and live in frame houses and drive modern cars, although they do retain their own language in addition to English, and sometimes hold pageants and celebrations in which they wear the tribal costume and perform the old ritual dances. But most of them no longer really understand the original significance of these rites.

The Indians are legally wards of the state and as such are untaxed; but they are not objects of charity. They take advantage of the tourist trade in summer—as who doesn't in a tourist country—by making and selling baskets, moccasins, and Indian curios and souvenirs. In winter they pursue the same occupations as their white neighbors, lumbering, trapping, carpentering, or whatever job offers itself. Many of them have distinguished themselves in our various recent white-man's wars by their courage and brilliant initiative under fire. They didn't change their nature when they changed their clothes.

The Penobscots have a representative in the Maine State Legislature, and they are the only Indian tribe in the entire United States to have the privilege of sending a member in equal standing to any state governing body.

The Indians, as well as the geography of the coast, had a part in shaping the history of Maine, and it's too bad that we didn't learn earlier to get along with them. A different relationship might have made unnecessary the writing of some fairly grim pages.

2 · Discovery and Colonization

PROBABLY the first Europeans to lay eyes on the coast of Maine were the Vikings under Leif Ericson; so technically they should be considered the discoverers of the country. They didn't do much about their discovery, and what we know of them there is mostly conjecture or the result of a few bits of circumstantial evidence. We know that in A.D. 1000 or thereabouts, the Norsemen did cruise along the New England coast as far south as Rhode Island. Nobody of their bold and adventurous temperament would simply sail past as spectacular and intriguing a shore as that of Maine as seen from the sea. They'd be compelled to investigate, and apparently investigate they did.

We know this because there are dug up from time to time in various localities bronze tools and weapons of Norse origin. They're buried deeply enough so that they must have been lost about a thousand years ago. Near Pemaquid, several feet down, is an unexplained fragment of paved road that may have been built by the Vikings and probably was; and on Monhegan and Outer Heron islands, as well as at Popham on the Kennebec, have been found mysterious cuneiform characters which a great many people think were made by the Norse, although no one to date has been able to decipher them, and they may be simply natural scouring and weathering of the rock ledges.

If the Norse actually established settlements, they must have been of a temporary nature, perhaps camps for the salting of fish and the drying of nets, or bases for use while ships were careened for repairs. At any rate, very little trace of them remains now, and nothing that can remotely be considered interesting ruins. The Vikings made no record of their discovery and passed down no written accounts of their voyages or descriptions of the new country. Their visits were primarily business trips for fish and particularly for shipbuilding lumber, which was in short supply at their nearest colonies on Greenland and Iceland.

In time they stopped coming, probably because the native Indians began to resent them and, having as good weapons and the advantage of familiar terrain, were able to repel them. The Norse were the first white men to view the territory, but as far as effect on Maine history is concerned, they might just as well have stayed at home.

It was almost five hundred years later, in 1498, six years after Columbus' voyage to the West Indies, that a European not only saw the rough rocks of the northern Atlantic coast of America, but described it in writing as well. The man was John Cabot, commanding the first English vessel to come to the western hemisphere, and we're not at all sure that even he really visited Maine. It's very likely that he went no farther south than New Brunswick on that trip—he made others later—before he turned home. England was not at that time interested in a forbidding, forest-covered territory that contained none of the more obvious forms of wealth, such as Inca gold or emerald mines, or offered no opportunity for easy colonization. But Cabot at least got it down onto paper that such a land existed.

The first European who unquestionably gazed upon the towering pines and granite ledges, the surf-smothered reefs and sheltered reaches of the Maine coast was a man with a very romantic name, Giovanni da Verrazano. He was an Italian from Genoa, but at the time, 1524, he happened to be in the employ of France. He coasted along among the islands, but he made no attempt to establish any colony. His importance lies only in his being the first one of whom we are really certain.

The next year, 1525, came Esteban Gómez, a Spaniard. Like most of the Spanish voyagers of the time, he was looking for gold and fabulous jewels; and since it was very soon clear to him that he was looking in the wrong place, he upped anchor and went away. He, however, unlike his predecessors, left his mark on the map. He named one island Campo Bello, or Beautiful Country, and we still use the name, although we make one word of it; and he named three famous bays, Bahia de Casco and Bahia de Saco (which mean "Bay of the Helmet or Skull" and "Bay of the Sack," respectively, and are known to us as Casco Bay and Saco Bay) and Bahia Profundo, which means "Deep Bay" and has been corrupted into Bay of Fundy, where the tides are the highest in the world.

Then in 1597, Simon Ferdinando, a Portuguese navigator in the service of England, was on the Maine coast briefly, but he did no more about colonizing it than any of the previous explorers had done. At that time, exploration was being carried on almost entirely for the purpose of locating spectacular treasure stores, or in an effort to find a northwest passage to the Orient. Visits to Maine were largely in the nature of accidents.

A hundred years after Cabot a second English ship, outfitted by Sir Humphrey Gilbert, came to anchor in Penobscot Bay. Sir Humphrey was an English navigator and friend of Queen Elizabeth, who had granted him a charter to colonize the New World, probably partly through friendship and partly in recognition of his services to the Crown against France and in Ireland. The captain of this 1598 ship, John Walker, went ashore and took formal possession of the land in England's name, thus establishing first claim to the territory. He thought he had rediscovered "Norumbega," which was the first of many names the country was to bear—Norumbega, Sagadahoc,

New France, New England, Nova Scotia, Lygonia, Acadia, Laconia, Bay Colony, North Virginia, New Somersetshire, the County of Cornwall of the Duke's Province, and some others, until it finally became the State of Maine.

Most of the names had a good reason for being and explain themselves, but no one knows exactly which of the early voyagers is responsible for Norumbega and for the wildly fantastic tale that went with the name. First accounts of it appear as early as 1539, in *Rasmusio's Voyages,* but probably the author was writing from hearsay. We can only imagine how the story started. Very likely an early explorer stumbled onto one of the more elaborate Indian villages, perhaps along the Penobscot, where the houses were large and permanent and the Indians clad in fine skins. Perhaps he was so surprised to see such a flourishing and orderly community in the middle of the wilderness that he described it later with a little more enthusiasm than it warranted. By the time the tale had gone through several tellings and arrived back in Europe, the Indian village had been transformed into a great city, with turreted castles and crystal towers, where the walls were overlaid with gold leaf and encrusted with gems, and the inhabitants used handfuls of pearls as small change and counted their fine jewels by the peck.

Of course, the whole thing was perfectly ridiculous to anyone with the slightest knowledge of the country; but the story received wide circulation and almost universal belief, so that a great deal of time and energy were wasted subsequently by explorers trying to re-locate the fabulous city of Norumbega.

Or perhaps such credulousness was not really as silly then as it sounds now. The European ear and mind were accustomed to hearing and believing reports brought back from Mexico and Peru, reports equally fantastic of gold and gems, but with this difference—that they were demonstrably true. If such things existed in one part of the New World, why not in another? Especially would they be believed by people half-convinced already because they wanted to believe. They weren't true, as we know; but they did have this one result, that the first formal name given the coast of Maine was Norumbega, the name of the mythical city.

To progress: Sir Humphrey Gilbert (Walker's backer) had a half brother, Sir Walter Raleigh, whom he infected with his interest in and enthusiasm for the new land. At some time earlier, King Edward IV had established an organization which he rather overelaborately named "The mysterie of merchant adventures for the discoverie of regions, dominions and islands and places unknown," a designation which covers a lot of territory and gave its charter holders considerable leeway. Later the name was boiled down to "The fellowship of English merchants for the discoverie of new trades," and it was under these grants that Gilbert and Raleigh operated.

In 1603, two of their ships, the *Speedwell* and the *Discoverer*, captained by Martin Pring and Edmund Jones, explored the coast and stopped off at Monhegan Island. where they picked up a little birch bark canoe and carried it back to England. That canoe seems a small thing to have greatly influenced the history of Maine; but it was something that could be touched and examined, and it was something the like of which the average Englishman had never seen. It appealed to the imagination, and it did more to arouse interest and curiosity in the new country than anything that had gone before. It may well have been the reason why Sir Ferdinando Gorges decided to devote himself and his fortune to Maine matters. Gorges brought a shrewd and vigorous mind to the problem of exploration and colonization. His decision to colonize Maine can truthfully be called the turning point in the early history of this territory.

Sir Ferdinando was a remarkable man. In spite of the Latin flavor of his name, he was a Somersetshire Englishman. He was a brave and fiery swordsman endowed with great qualities of leadership; and when he was only twenty, he was placed in full command of a regiment in Flanders.

He was also a polished and handsome young gentleman, and with this combination of virtues attracted the attention of Elizabeth. He was a great favorite of hers; and it was while he was adorning her court that he became an intimate friend and crony of Sir Humphrey Gilbert, Sir Walter Raleigh, Sir Francis Drake, and Sir John Hawkins. It was through association with these professional adventurers that Gorges first became interested in the New World.

At first his interest was probably mild; and, in any event, he had other things to occupy his attention. There was the repelling of the Spanish Armada, during which he was captured and imprisoned in Lille; and, after he was freed, there was the siege of Paris, when he was wounded; and the battle of Rouen, where he was knighted for gallantry by the Earl of Essex. And that's not all. Home from the wars, he became involved in politics to the extent that he almost sacrificed his neck. He was sentenced to be beheaded for some involved political misstep, and only pressure on the part of his powerful friends saved him. His was a very stormy and varied career, up until 1603, when Martin Pring and Edmund Jones and John Smith (of Pocahontas fame) came home from the Maine coast.

Gorges was, in spite of his romantic name and almost foolhardy courage in war and politics, a very hardheaded and practical businessman. It seems an unlikely combination of talents, but it existed nevertheless. He was not going into a business venture until he had thoroughly investigated its possibilities; and when his friends Raleigh and Gilbert tried to enlist his aid, he sought out Smith, Jones, and Pring—and if that isn't a combination of names completely lacking in glamor, I never heard one. But be that as it may, those gentlemen had explored the coast fairly thoroughly, made reasonably accurate maps, and kept detailed, factual, and exact accounts of what they'd seen and done. They were the first ones to bring back dependable reports of the Maine coast—reports as unadorned and simple as their names—and they and their little canoe were responsible for Sir Ferdinando's decision to participate in the colonization of Maine.

Gorges' friend Raleigh had by this time lost his head on the block, so Sir Ferdinando entered into partnership with the Earl of Southampton and the Earl of Arundel. They outfitted the ship *Archangel,* Captain George Weymouth, and sent it on a voyage of exploration. Weymouth was the one who planted those peas and barley that grew so fast, or so he said. But that's not all he did. He kidnaped five Indians at Allen's Island, near the present Port Clyde, after disarming their suspicions by gifts and kindnesses, and took them back to England. Their names, just for the record, were Amoret, Skidwares, Tasquantum, Mandeo, and Saffacomoit. I hold no brief for this act, since it was a deed of treachery and dishonor; but the results were better than they had any right to be.

Eventually some of the Indians were returned to their native land, and when the Pilgrims landed at Plymouth, you will remember, they were met by the Indian Samoset, who greeted them with the friendly phrase, "Welcome, Englishmen," and followed this up by various neighborly services that possibly made all the difference between their survival and nonsurvival. Well, Samoset was a friend of Squanto, a nickname for Weymouth's Tasquantum. After Tasquantum had been repatriated, he taught Samoset a little of the English he'd picked up on his travels, and also apparently gave a good report of his treatment while abroad, so that Samoset was, very fortunately for the Pilgrims, well disposed toward the white man.

But that's beside the present point. Three of the captives were presented by Weymouth to his sponsor, Sir Ferdinando, probably as slaves. But Gorges had more vision than his agent. He saw in the three Abenakis a great opportunity for advertising and, more important, an unequaled source of reliable information concerning Maine. To draw attention to his ventures overseas, he arranged to have his guests—for that is how he considered them—presented at Court, the first North American Indians to have that

honor. I can't imagine what they made of the whole pro-
ceeding, but they were used to their own solemn tribal
ceremonies, and acquitted themselves with credit. They
were entertained widely around London, and enjoyed
quite a vogue. Sir Ferdinando was a modern when it came
to advertising and publicity.

The other part of his plan required more time and a
great deal of patience. Before he could extract any great
amount of information from the Indians, he had to teach
them to speak English with reasonable fluency and accuracy; and this he did, or had done. At the same time, he
had to build up in them a complete trust and confidence
in himself and his motives, so that they would answer his
questions freely and fully. In this, too, he succeeded, so
that he now possessed what amounted to walking guide-
books to Norumbega; and he spent hours and hours picking the brains of his red visitors. In the end, what had been
a lively interest in the colonization of the New World
became an obsession that governed the rest of his life.

He had hard luck at first. In 1606 he sent out the
Richard of Plymouth, under Captain Henry Challons, to
establish a colony. Captain Challons decided that he didn't
know the way to Maine, so he'd better go to Virginia first
and then work up the coast. It was his misfortune that he
ran into a Spanish fleet near Porto Rico, where he had no
business being anyhow. His ship was seized, he and his crew
were captured, and the whole project was ruined. What annoyed Sir Ferdinando most was the fact that two of his
priceless Indians were lost in this affair. He could afford
another ship and crew and he could easily find a more satisfactory captain than the timid Challons; but he couldn't
replace the two Indians on whom he'd spent so much time
and trouble.

His next venture was the ill-fated, climate-testing Popham colony of 1607; and, as we know, that was a fiasco.
Shortly after that, Gorges' partner in this undertaking,
Lord Chief Justice John Popham, died, and their company, known as the Plymouth Company, failed. After

that King James forced Gorges to sign over the northern portion of his grants to Sir William Alexander, but even then Gorges did not give up his conviction that it was possible to develop Maine. Popular interest was now dead. Nobody any longer wanted to go to what was supposed to be an impossible country, and Gorges discovered that if he was going to proceed, he would have to do so alone.

He still thought that his Indians' testimony concerning the country was more dependable than the peevish tales of hardship brought back by the Popham colonists. So in 1616 he finally managed to scrape together enough of his own money to finance a small ship, and employed Captain Richard Vines to sail her. The crew consisted of sixteen men, almost all of them Gorges' personal servants, the best party he could muster in face of lack of funds and lack of interest.

Vines sailed to the mouth of the Saco River and proceeded upstream to what is now Biddeford Pool, where the party built some cabins and spent the winter. They had a very good and comfortable winter, too; so good that fourteen years later Richard Vines retired from the sea, went back to Biddeford Pool, and made his home there for the rest of his days. This little expedition settled forever the question of whether white men could endure the Maine climate, and marked the beginning of the colonization of Maine.

It also served to justify Gorges and to raise him rapidly in fame, fortune, and popularity. He was appointed viceroy of New England, with full legal, civil and ecclesiastical powers. He was, on paper at least, an absolute monarch, the king of New England. But he never took over his kingdom. One thing or another prevented it. First he thought that he'd be more effective working for his dream if he stayed in England for a while; so he sent in his own place William Gorges, a near relative, to act as his deputy while he expedited matters from overseas. By 1642, he'd established by remote control the thriving little town of Gorgeana, which is the York of today; and he

was directly responsible for the settling of Wells, Biddeford, Portland, and Brunswick, as well.

Then came the fall of Charles I. A dyed-in-the-wool
Royalist, Gorges, now an old man, took up arms for
Prince Rupert. Rupert failed, and Gorges was stripped
of his fortune and all his holdings, and imprisoned. He
died brokenhearted without ever seeing the country for
which he had done so much. His grave in England is
unmarked, and his name lives on only in an almost forgotten old fort in Portland Harbor—and in the title by
which he is generally known, The Father of Maine. If being a good parent means—as I think it does—working
tirelessly and selflessly to develop in a child the potentiali-
ties for greatness that possibly the parent alone senses or
suspects, then Gorges was indeed a good father to Maine
and deserves the title.

While all this was going on, there were other visitors
along the Maine coast. There were Gosnold in 1602 for
the English and Henry Hudson for the Dutch in 1609.
Neither stayed, but Hudson has the distinction of cutting
the first of the millions of mast pines that were to be
sacrificed to that purpose in generations to come. He cut
and stepped a mast for his famous *Half Moon*, somewhere
along Penobscot Bay.

Then in 1610 there was the English captain, Samuel
Argall, driven north by a storm, so that his first visit was
accidental. He was to come back later with rather dire
results; but the noteworthy thing about his initial voyage
is that during it he reported in his log the presence of the
Gulf Stream, the first report that we have of it. He said
that it was a strong current that bore the ship rapidly
along, even against a brisk headwind. How the others
missed such an obvious feature of the seascape I don't
know; but, if they noticed it, they kept the fact to themselves.

And starting in about 1614 and for decades after, Maine
waters were alive with fishing boats from other colonies

and from Europe. These men came to fish, not to colonize, and they established bases ashore only to dry their catches in the sun on the rocks or on pole racks, or to extract the valuable oil. Three trips a year was the usual schedule, but the business was so profitable that some owners kept fishing boats working along the coast the whole year round. It was not unusual to see forty or more of them in any of the sheltered coves or harbors during a storm. So the waters of Maine were not empty, although the land itself was very sparsely populated for quite a while.

While Gorges and other Englishmen were worrying about settling the southwest portion of Maine, the French were really working on the same idea in the northeast. Sooner or later as they both expanded their territories, they were bound to run into complications. The French claim, if we go by priority of residence, was the better, since in 1604 they established a colony on Dochet's Island in the St. Croix River. They were consequently the first and only Europeans on the continent north of Florida. But it's easy to see how confusion came about. No one knew who owned what. James I, for example, when he gave all of Nova Scotia and much of the country south to Sir William Alexander, either didn't know or didn't care that King Henry of France and Navarre had already issued a patent for the same territory to Pierre du Gast, the Sieur of Monts.

Pierre du Gast acted promptly. He gathered together a company of seventy men from all walks of life—noblemen, jailbirds, priests, soldiers, Huguenot preachers, and all-round adventurers—and set sail for his new holdings. They landed at Dochet's Island in the mouth of the St. Croix. In spite of the seeming incompatibility of the members of the party, they worked well together and built a very sturdy little settlement, complete with barracks, workshops, and houses, all enclosed by a stockade. Here in 1604 they conducted the first observance of Christmas as a religious holiday ever to take place in North America. The winter was very severe, however, and they suffered such hardship and so many of them died that in the spring they picked up and moved across the Bay of Fundy to what is now Port Royal. There's nothing left on Dochet's Island today except a lighthouse and a bronze plaque; and the island, although it lies on the international boundary, belongs to neither Canada nor the United States but is neutral territory, sacred to the memory of that first band of settlers.

Among du Gast's company was Samuel de Champlain, probably the most important and widest-ranging explorer in the history of North America. With his later, western expeditions we are not concerned. What concerns us is the fact that, using Dochet's as a base, he explored thoroughly the entire coast of Maine, poking into every little inlet and investigating every island, making the first complete and reliable maps and reports, claiming it all in the name of France, scotching forever the rumor about the glittering Norumbega, and erecting a cross at the Kennebec to mark the site of a proposed mission and monastery.

It may have been this cross for which the Jesuit Fathers Biard and Massé were looking when they ran into the fog that landed them on Mt. Desert Island in 1613. These Fathers were not of the original Dochet's Island group, but had been sent out later by a very pious Frenchwoman of considerable means, the Marquise de Guercheville, and some of her devout friends at Court, including Queen Marie de Medicis. The original idea was that they should minister to the spiritual needs of the Du Gast company; but that hard-living, hard-boiled crew didn't welcome the notion, and told the missionaries as much, suggesting that they go on back home.

The Jesuits decided that since the Marquise was undergoing considerable expense in the interests of saving souls, they should justify her efforts. There would be, they thought, plenty of heresy to correct among the native Indians down along the coast; so they set sail to the southwest. As we know, they became lost in the fog, found themselves off Mt. Desert, and there established their little

Mission of St. Sauveur, the first mission and monastery in the New World east of California. They were really good, simple, devout men. They established friendly terms with the Indians and for a time lived a life of peace, usefulness, work, and prayer—the kind of a life they visualized as being proper to men of their calling.

Meanwhile, however, the Samuel Argall who discovered the Gulf Stream was commissioned admiral of Virginia, with instructions to go back to Maine on an exploring trip and to prevent, if necessity arose, the French from encroaching on the property of the Virginia Company, which at that time claimed everything up to the banks of the St. Croix. Argall had been that way two years before and seen no signs of any French, so he didn't anticipate trouble. He looked on the whole jaunt as primarily a fishing trip. He was very much surprised indeed to sight the new little colony on Mt. Desert, which had been in existence only a few weeks. Promptly abandoning his fishing, he went ashore. His orders were to prevent French colonization, and he went about the assignment zealously. First, he burned the buildings of the mission to the ground. Then he set fifteen members of the colony adrift in small boats, very probably to perish. Fortunately for them, they were picked up by a French ship in the Bay of Fundy and returned safely home. The remaining members were taken to Jamestown and eventually to England. Father Baird returned to the University of Lyon, and the others were repatriated. Argall had effectively carried out his orders.

This was the first clash in the long struggle between France and England for predominance in the Western Hemisphere, although nothing much came of it at the time. The two countries were technically at peace with each other, so they contented themselves with an exchange of tart notes, at the conclusion of which England returned her ship *Jonas* to the Marquise de Guercheville, but refused to make any recompense for loss of life or destruction of property.

It was inevitable, of course, that a state of war should come into existence between the French and English in the New World. Not only were they traditional enemies from way back, but now they had a real bone of contention, vast and potentially valuable territories. And perhaps more important than that was their religious difference. The Puritans regarded Catholicism with positive horror, and felt—probably sincerely—that all Frenchmen were the Devil's advocates. They were unable to appreciate the good work the Catholic missionaries were doing among the Indians, not only on a spiritual level but on a material one as well. Their Puritan bias was fanatical; and, as is common in any war with religious undertones, this war was often conducted savagely and viciously. The poor Indians were caught in the middle. Some fought on one side and some on the other, depending on who got to them first; and some changed sides when it became politic to do so, or when they'd been disillusioned by their original allies.

But long before the Indian wars started in earnest, the fur trade had begun to boom. As early as 1615, Sir Richard Hawkins, son of Sir John, visited Maine and picked up a cargo of furs which he sold at a handsome profit in European markets. This gave impetus to the trade, which went on in a desultory manner for a few years, with the masters of ships simply collecting any furs the Indians wanted to bring down to the anchorage and sell. It was a rather haphazard arrangement, but it was good enough for men whose primary interest was exploration rather than trade. In 1628, however, fur entered a new phase and became Big Business.

Let me explain the circumstances of the transition. So much attention has been given to the ethical and spiritual aspects of the Pilgrims' expedition to Plymouth, and to the romance of their New World struggles, that the crass question of how the whole project was financed has been rather neglected. It wasn't easy. The Pilgrims managed to scrape up enough money for stores and supplies, which had to be paid for in cash. Merchants were understandably dubious about extending credit to customers who were going off out of reach to the other side of the ocean, where there were no courts or other legal means of collecting debts. This outfitting took all the money the party had, not a very serious matter once they'd arrived at their destination, since money was of no value in the New World anyhow.

But they did have to get there in some way. Fortunately for them, the shipowners didn't take such a rigid view of cash-on-the-barrelhead. They were going to get their ship back anyway, barring Acts of God, and they were agreeable to the idea of payment for its use on the installment plan. This was very likely the first example of the modern innovation advertised by various travel agencies, whereby you take your vacation now and pay for it next winter. However—

Of course, there wasn't any money in circulation in the New World then or for years to come, but the necessity of paying off still remained, and what to do! The Pilgrim Fathers decided that furs were the answer and that, since the fur-bearing animals of eastern Massachusetts were scarce and not particularly valuable, they'd better branch out to a more rewarding territory. So in 1628 they established the fur-trading and trapping post of New Plymouth on the Kennebec, at what is now Augusta; and the following year they set up another at Bagaduce, now Castine, on Penobscot Bay; and later still, another at Machias. These were successful from the start, and within ten years' time all the payments for the *Mayflower* had been met and the Pilgrims had a solid backlog of cash for emergencies.

The Castine and Machias posts, however, were within territory recognized as French. In establishing them, the Pilgrims were asking for trouble, and they got it. The French were highly annoyed and sent out two expeditions, one under LaTour, who took possession of Castine, and one under D'Aulney, who destroyed the Machias post almost before it was well under way. Machias was of no use to the French, so they abandoned it. It was left to go back to the forest, until years later, in the early 1700's, the notorious Bellamy took it over with the idea of setting up a pirate stronghold and communistic state there, a fascinating affair that we'll go into later. Castine was something else again. It was worth bothering with, so the French built it up into a strong fort and village, which they named Fort Pentagoet.

The Pilgrims weren't very happy about this, but there wasn't much they could do, especially since those Englishmen who were settling more and more thickly west of the Penobscot and from whom the Pilgrims thought they ought to receive aid in a punitive expedition against the French refused to cooperate. They were peacefully minding their own business and didn't propose to stir up a French hornets' nest in their immediate vicinity. What's more, they found it convenient and profitable to trade with the Castine French, and they had no desire to alter the *status quo*. So the Pilgrims retired, disgruntled, from the scene.

Castine—or Pentagoet—remained in French hands until 1654, when Oliver Cromwell heard about their occupation and ordered the British to retake the town. They did so, but they allowed the French inhabitants to remain and conduct business as usual. Then in 1667, thirteen years later, the French and English ended, temporarily at least, a long period of squabbling and intermittent fighting by signing a treaty, under the terms of which all the territory east of the Penobscot belonged to the French, and that west to the British. This gave Castine back to the French, who, now that the shoe was on the other foot, allowed the British citizens to remain in residence and in business.

For a short time things remained fairly peaceful, and the pace of development quickened. The first land was *bought* from the Indians at Pemaquid. Heretofore it had simply been taken. But now a John Brown paid the equivalent of fifty beaver skins in firearms, powder, axes, and trinkets to Samoset for land about five townships in extent and, what's more, recorded the deed of sale at Monhegan, the first deed ever made in New England. York became the first incorporated city in North America, and the first court in New England was held at Saco. Scarboro was settled, and the first Quakers came to Maine and colonized at Piscataqua.

Everywhere little towns were springing up, and the land was being cleared for farms. While many of the English settlers immigrated from the old country, a surprising number of them moved in from Massachusetts and New Hampshire, attracted from the places of their original selection by Maine's abundant promise. The territory west of the Penobscot was thick with English settlers—or comparatively thick, at any rate.

To the east the French were equally busy, building villages and trading posts and entrenching themselves firmly on their holdings, as the English were on theirs. The French, however, emphasized one factor that the English neglected until rather late in the day—the religious factor. Many of the English had come to the New World to escape religious persecution at home, and they organized their Massachusetts colonies especially on a strict religious basis, sometimes persecuting those whose views differed from their own as relentlessly as ever they themselves had been persecuted.

But strangely, when they moved to Maine, they seemed to lose some of their zeal. Or perhaps those who went Down-East were the ones with the less-strong convictions. At any rate, while they often took ministers with them and observed the Sabbath and other doctrinal strictures laid upon them, they made little attempt for a long time to convert the Indians.

The French on the contrary were great missionaries. They established missions for the saving of Indians souls wherever they went, and in addition sent missionaries out into the wilderness to bring the Word to the far-flung tribes. Their motive, I believe, was mainly altruistic; they truly wanted to share the benefits of Christianity. So as early as 1647, the Jesuit Father Gabriel Druilletes—who was the first white man to view closely Katahdin—erected a mission at Norridgewock on the Kennebec.

He was succeeded by Father Sebastien Râle, a man whose far-reaching influence among the redmen cannot be over-estimated. Râle was fond of the Indians and deeply concerned with their welfare. He lived among them like one of themselves. He really wanted to understand his red brothers and worked continuously on a book about Indian culture and folkways, probably the only attempt made at the time along those lines. He also assembled a dictionary of the Abenaki language, and some of the prayers he wrote in that tongue are still being used today by the Indians. And he took up cudgels for the redmen when he thought they were being cheated or abused by either French or English settlers, and won their genuine love and respect. He was just one of many missionaries working equally selflessly among the tribes, but he was the outstanding example of his kind. Eventually he was killed in an English-inspired attack on his mission.

But the killing of Râle and the destruction of his mission could not wipe out the work he had done. The teaching and example of the French missionaries had been too good for that. Not only had the Indians embraced the religion of the French, but in the process they had developed a friendship. When the showdown came, the majority of the Indians allied themselves with the men who had treated them with sympathy and understanding.

3 · The French and Indian Wars

WHEN as a child in grade school I was forcibly subjected to the study of American history, I never could make head nor tail of the French and Indian Wars. There seemed to be so many of them, and I never could remember which came first, Queen Anne's War, or the Seven Years' War, or King William's War. Where the various treaties fitted in—the Peace of Aix-la-Chapelle, and the Peace of Utrecht, and the Treaty of Breda—was beyond me. I didn't even know where those places were and cared less; and, to tell the truth, I wasn't sure what the fighting was all about in the first place. So I just gave up and memorized without comprehension a list of names and dates, since the teacher told us they were important and made us positive he would give us a written test covering them.

Actually these wars are not difficult at all to understand, if you consider them as one eighty-five-year-long period of fighting, broken by intervals of uneasy truce, rather than as a series of individual conflicts. This period started in about 1675 and ended with the Peace of Paris in 1763, or twelve years before the Revolution. Those are the only dates and names that it's really necessary to remember. As for causes, these wars were just a side issue to the European struggle between England, France, and Spain for colonial and maritime supremacy. To European eyes, they were probably incidental and insignificant.

Those actually involved undoubtedly took a different view of their importance; and everyone living in what is now New England and Nova Scotia and west to the Great Lakes and headwaters of the Mississippi was either involved or in constant danger of being involved. To them the question of whether they would live to see the morning light was of understandable interest and concern; and, in spite of the contemporary European evaluation of the altercations between a handful of settlers and a pack of barbarians, in the end they affected tremendously the history of our country and consequently of the world.

In the sense of organized armies marching onto battlefields and of well-planned military campaigns, there really was no war at all. With a few exceptions, the whole thing consisted almost entirely of a series of Indian raids upon settlements and isolated outposts, and extended as far west as there were any pioneers. We are interested in the affair, however, only as it affected the coast of Maine. It was bad enough there, with plenty of burning of property, killing and scalping of individuals on both sides, and carrying off of prisoners into captivity.

Nevertheless it must be said that the Indian Wars in Maine were carried on somewhat more humanely than they were farther west. This is partly due to the fact that most Indian raids were accompanied by and in a measure controlled by French officers, who were civilized men, and partly to the fact that before the wars ever started, most of the Abenakis had become Christianized by the Catholic missionaries, with a consequent modification of their savage impulses.

The role of the missionaries cannot be overemphasized. There existed in France a close union between church and state that was absent between the English Crown and the Puritans. The Jesuits therefore had a political as well as a religious function and served not only as missionaries but also as agents of their King. Having won through their selflessness, the trust and friendship of the Indians, they were able to manage the tribes and enlist their services to the interest of France. I am not implying that the whole missionary movement was deliberately planned with the idea of making tools of the Indians, because this was by no means the case. But the priests were always in close touch with their government, and naturally they used their enormous influence for, rather than against, their temporal lords.

The reason why, after three quarters of a century marked by little violence between the French and English, hostilities should break out actively is very simple. They began to get in each others' way. Up to this time there had been a certain amount of fighting, but it was mostly organized expeditions by sea to prevent settlement by one on territory claimed by the other, such as the destruction of the mission at Mt. Desert or the taking of Pentagoet. These were purely local operations, carried out without appreciable help from the Indians, and without affecting directly the large body of scattered settlers, to whom it made no difference whatsoever whether a point they'd never see was in French or in English hands.

Now, however, the Indians were entered in the lists, and war broke out all over the place. In 1675, Saco was raided by the French and Indians and fifty-four prisoners were carried away. The next year Casco, Pemaquid, Arrowsic, Cape Neddick and Black Point were all burned and their populations either killed or abducted. No one was safe anywhere.

There is no object in describing in detail every one of these raids, since they all fall into the same pattern. When the danger was recognized as being acute, measures were taken to provide for defense in case of attack. Instead of making each house into a small fort to be defended by the few people who lived there, the usual procedure was to select one or two houses of a settlement as strongholds. These houses were chosen because of central position, size, or natural advantages such as elevation or a good water supply. Whenever an alarm was given or there was reason to be suspicious of an impending attack, everyone would gather at the fortified house and fight off the invaders as a group.

The benefits of this plan are obvious, but it didn't always work. The dwellings were strung out over such a large area that often it was impossible for everyone to be warned in time to seek sanctuary. Frequently the raids came as a complete surprise and found men at work in fields so far from the sheltering walls that retreat to them was impossible. On the really isolated farms, where there were no neighbors within a day's journey, the families had to do the best they could alone. Sometimes they were able to save themselves, but often they could not.

The means taken to fortify any point were simple, but they were reasonably effective against the simple type of assault that could be expected. The upper stories of structures were built to overhang the lower, so that fire could be directed down onto those of the enemy who came in to close quarters. Loopholes were pierced in walls to cover all approaches. Roofs were frequently sodded to prevent their kindling when arrows tipped with fire were directed onto them. And the whole installation was surrounded by a high stockade of logs, with a barred gate, which served the double purpose of slowing down an attack and providing a corral for livestock—if there was time to round up the animals and herd them in before the Indians struck.

Very often there was no time at all, and then the cattle were slaughtered or driven off, a very serious loss to any farmer who managed to survive the attack. In the French accounts of these raids there are references to the capture and destruction of "forts" where no forts existed to the English knowledge. The confusion is easy to explain. A fortified private dwelling looked like a small fort and was so reported by the French officer in charge of the expedition.

The success of the Indian raids depended upon one or both of two elements: surprise or what was considered treachery, although possibly that's a hard word for what might be more politely termed strategy. It all depends on your point of view.

For example, there were instances when one or two Indian squaws, claiming to be lost or otherwise in distress, approached English dwellings and asked for shelter and succor, which they received. Then in the middle of the night when their hosts were sound asleep the squaws would get up, open the door, unbar the gate, and let in their companions, who made short work of the house-holders.

Or two or three Indians, making a great demonstration of being unarmed, would approach a stockade and signal that they would like to have a talk with a committee of the inhabitants. Out would go two or three of the men of the place, to be surrounded and killed by warriors who sprang out from bushes or up from behind logs.

In his history of the times Francis Parkman refers to the Maine coast as "this unhappy frontier"; and, I suppose to those who were aware of the precariousness of their lives on this frontier, it always seemed better to grasp any feeble chance of maintaining peaceful relationships than to act as aggressors and possibly precipitate a crisis. That's the only way I can account for the success of some of these fairly transparent ruses.

The classic attack, however, was the surprise attack. The Indians were experts at this. As early as 1675, the Christian Abenakis were encouraged by the French to migrate to Canada and make their homes at various missions around Quebec and at the falls of the Chaudiere River. After that they and their tomahawks were always easily available when French policy required a raid on the English settlements. A war party would be raised and start down through the dense forests, across streams and mountains, to the thinly populated coast. To all purposes, they were intangible and invisible. Even if anyone had been living in that wilderness, the party's progress would have gone unremarked. The Indians could filter through the woods as silently as shadows, could live off the country, could go for long periods with no fire to warm them; could crouch still as stones and patient as trees when occasion demanded. They could drift to within rods of a settlement with no one, not even the dogs, the wiser. They could make themselves part of the earth they embraced while white men walked unheeding within speaking distance of them. They were a formidable foe.

Once arrived at their destination, they lay in the woods until the time was ripe for attack. Days of waiting meant nothing to them. Sometimes these attacks came at night, sometimes in broad daylight. The Indians seldom attacked in force, but split their number into small groups which attacked at several points simultaneously. Men working in fields alone or in pairs would be surrounded and killed, while the houses with their garrisons of women would be rushed and captured. Individuals occasionally escaped by hiding in corn fields or even in such unlikely places as under beds or in ovens; but more often the men were killed and scalped and the women and children borne off to Canada into captivity.

Both the French and the English paid a bounty for scalps, and the French paid additional sums for captives. That is why so many of the settlers lived to make the terrible trek to Canada. The endurance of some of the women and very young children as they made the long journey through dreadful country is unbelievable. That they survived is a testimonial to the ruggedness of the pioneer stock and to the treatment they received in the hands of their captors.

I don't mean that the Indians babied them along, or anything of the sort. They were expected to be able to keep up with the party, and if they couldn't, it was too bad for them. A blow with a tomahawk ended their troubles once and for all. This summary treatment was actually a form of humaneness, however, since the alternative would have been a slow and agonized death from exposure and starvation in the wilderness. But it was to the Indian interest to keep the captives alive and in reasonably good condition, and to that end a certain amount of rough consideration was shown.

The Abenakis as a rule were fond of children and good to them, and there is one case, perhaps exceptional, where a brave carried a small baby for days, rather than dispatch it by knocking its head against a tree. Unlike some of the western tribes, moreover, these Indians were not ordinarily given to torturing their victims just for sport. Instances of torture arose from what they considered provocation. They were almost never guilty of raping white captives, either. To see the men of your family killed and to be carried away from your home into a strange land cannot by any stretch of the imagination be considered anything but a horrible and shocking experience. But worse things could have happened to the Maine coast women and children who were captured by the Abenakis.

Once in Canada, the captives were in most cases handed over to the French, although sometimes a child was kept by the Indians and brought up as one of them. Some of the women were placed in French homes as servants, and some of the girls were entered in convents. There was always the hope and strong possibility that they would be ransomed and could return home.

But when the time came some of them had adapted themselves so well that they didn't want to go back. Occasionally a girl married a Frenchman or, brought up as a Catholic, became a Sister. Most of them, of course, were glad to go back to their own people; but one woman tried it and found life so bleak among those with whom she had no longer much in common that homesickness drove her back to Canada, where she spent the rest of her days— happily, we trust.

This is the background of the whole eighty-five years of the French and Indian Wars. It was the kind of thing that went on almost continually and few settlements escaped. Theoretically, all these people were entitled to protection by England, since they were all subjects of the Crown. But England was engaged in wars at home which absorbed her time, energies, and money; and it would have been impossible in any case to provide adequate military forces to insure the safety of every little shack along the frontier. Sir Edmund Andros, while he was governor of Massachusetts, did place garrisons of soldiers along the Saco and Kennebec rivers and at Casco Bay and Pemaquid. As long as these troops were in residence, there was some relief from the raids. However, when the people of Boston rose against Andros and placed him in custody, chiefly because they disliked him so much, the garrisons were withdrawn, and the Indians returned with redoubled zeal.

At this time, of course, Maine existed only as a part of Massachusetts, and all official action concerning her welfare originated in Boston. Boston was not pleased by the way things were going Down-East. What had been a very thriving and profitable trade was being ruined by French cruisers based at Port Royal in Nova Scotia, and Port Royal was, moreover, suspected of outfitting and paying Indian raiders to harass the coastal settlements, with sad results to the fur trade. Port Royal was, in fact, a very sore spot, the only cure for which would be its capture and decommissioning. The very man for the deed was at hand, Sir William Phipps, the high sheriff of Massachusetts.

Sir William Phipps was a knight of the King, it's true; but he was born plain Willie Phipps of Nauseag (now Woolwich), Maine. He was the youngest of twenty-six children (by the same mother, what's more) of a gunsmith of that place. His twenty-one brothers and four sisters were raised to clear the land, tend the farm, cut lumber, and in general conform to their time and place; but that wasn't good enough for the baby, William. I imagine that his poor mother was too busy and too tired to put the zest into his training that she'd applied to the others. At any rate, he was born ambitious and he grew up undisciplined, full of temper, afraid of nothing, and withal a tough, self-reliant customer. Anyone who thought he was going to settle down to become another salt-water farmer was mistaken.

At the age of eighteen he took matters into his own hands, paddled a canoe across the river to Arrowsic, and apprenticed himself for four years to a shipwright. During those four years, he heard a lot of sailors' yarns, and he became fired with a desire to see foreign lands and participate in great adventures. In this he was no different from many boys of his or any other day, but he did more about realizing his dreams than most.

At the end of his apprenticeship, he worked his way to Boston and got a job as a ship carpenter. Boston opened his eyes. With remarkable detachment and sense for a youth of his background and experience, he saw himself correctly as an ignorant lout and made up his mind to teach himself to read and write. In a fairly short time he was more literate than most presumably educated men of the period. Knowledge in this case did not bring humility. If anything, he became cockier than ever and announced that he intended to captain a ship of the King and own a big brick house in Boston.

How he met the beautiful daughter of Captain Roger Spencer I don't know. I don't suppose the problem offered too many difficulties for a good-looking, upstanding young man of his self-esteem. He not only met, but married, her. And now that he had influential seafaring connections, he managed to secure a contract to build a ship. He established a shipyard on the Sheepscot River, near his birthplace, and built his vessel. Just as he was about to get her under way for delivery, an Indian raiding party descended on the neighborhood. Phipps piled all the terrified inhabitants, including his widowed mother and his brothers and sisters, aboard ship and sailed them safely out of reach to Boston. This made him a hero and, while the exploit brought him no material reward, it did create for him a reputation for resourcefulness and courage and paved the way for a berth as captain of a ship engaged in the West Indies trade.

Although his experience as a mariner was negligible, if not nonexistent, Phipps made a very good captain, decisive and hard fisted. He was still obsessed by the idea of fame and fortune; and engaging in trade was, in his opinion, too long and slow a means to the King's ship and the brick house. In the West Indies he was constantly hearing tales of lost Spanish treasure galleons, so he decided to recover some of this sunken wealth himself. It was a project much better suited to his temperament than tamely sailing cargoes of lumber and molasses up and down the Atlantic. He financed the first expedition himself and actually did locate a sunken ship, salvaging enough gold to give him a talking point.

Then he went to England to try to argue King Charles II into going into partnership with him. Now it would occur to most obscure backwoodsmen that possibly the King didn't grant a hearing to just anybody who wanted to see him, especially if his business was of such an impractical and chancey-sounding nature as treasure-seeking. Phipps's view was that if Phipps wanted to talk to the King, the King had no choice in the matter. And Phipps's view was, oddly enough, the correct view. It took him a year to secure an audience; but, once he got it, he made up for lost time and came out of the interview with half his old boast come true. He was captain of the King's ship *Rose,* of eighteen guns and a crew of ninety-five, assigned to the recovery of Spanish gold.

The story of his adventure while treasure-seeking is fascinating, but it has no place here. It's enough to say that after many setbacks, a few mutinies, and not a little assorted skullduggery all around, he arrived back in England with over two million dollars' worth of gold, silver, and gems in his hold. He was given a share of the money, a gold chain and medal for himself, and a gold cup worth five thousand dollars for his wife; and he was knighted by the King and appointed high sheriff of Massachusetts. He returned to Boston after an absence of about five years and immediately set about building that brick house, at the corner of Salem and Charter Streets. And that's how he happened to be on hand and in a position to command the proposed attack on Port Royal.

In March of 1690 he set sail with seven ships and seven hundred men, and within three months he was back in Boston with Port Royal under his belt, so to speak. The capture had been almost ludicrously easy. The Port was garrisoned by only seventy soldiers, and Governor Meneval, seeing that resistance would be useless and stupid, surrendered without the firing of a shot. The inhabitants were promised security of life and property if they would swear allegiance to the British Crown, which they readily did.

Phipps appointed a president and six councillors from among the residents to control the town until they received word from Boston as to what their future condition would be. After that he dispatched Captain Alden to reduce any other French settlements he might find along the Bay of Fundy, and then went home.

Phipps took with him not only Governor Meneval and his garrison as prisoners, but also the bulk of Meneval's personal property, which the governor had entrusted to him for safekeeping during the voyage, and which he refused to return. This has nothing to do with the outcome of the French and Indian Wars, but it's a matter that puzzles me. Why in the world did Phipps want, among other things, four pairs of silk garters and four nightcaps trimmed with lace? He doesn't seem the type; or, if he had a hidden, softer side that craved these fripperies, why didn't he buy himself some, instead of holding out on poor Meneval? He could have well afforded them.

In any event Port Royal and most of Acadia—Nova Scotia and eastern Maine—was now technically in English hands, but that didn't mean much. Massachusetts had neither the men nor the money to secure her easy conquest, and England either couldn't or wouldn't send aid, then or a little later, when Boston decided to follow up the capture of Port Royal by taking the French stronghold of Quebec. Phipps was in charge of that expedition, too, and it was a dismal failure. He didn't have a large enough force for the job, and he waited so long in hopes of English help before setting out that the best of the season was over before he even got started. The whole thing was a mess.

But something came out of it that was to have an effect on the future. The colonists began to develop an attitude toward the Crown that was very different from their old filial dependence. They began to feel that if England couldn't show a little more interest in their problems, all right for England. They could and would handle their difficulties by themselves. This attitude was not as yet well defined, but the seed was planted and in time it would bear fruit.

As a reward for his efforts Phipps was made the royal governor of Massachusetts, which of course included Maine, and he succeeded in persuading the Penobscot Indians to sign over their land on both sides of the river to the white men. This was a truly remarkable achievement, because the chief of the Penobscots was the father-in-law of the Frenchman Baron de St. Castin, a man practically idolized by the Indians. But when Phipps was a little boy at Woolwich, he used to play with the Indian lads. They knew him, liked him, and what's more important, trusted him. It was a form of old-school-tie camaraderie. So the Abenakis signed the treaty and kept its terms until Phipps's death. He is buried in London, a far cry from the log cabin on the Maine coast, where he had been just the last and most ornery of the twenty-six Phipps kids.

The fact that they were both trusted friends of the Indians, that they lived at the same time, and that they had a great deal to do with the history of the Maine coast are about the only points in common between William Phipps and Jean Vincent de l'Abadie, Baron de St. Castin. Just look at the contrast between their names, the one so plain and forthright, the other ornate and poetic. Their characters were as diverse. Both were men of boldness; but, where Phipps was blunt and blustering and ambitious, St. Castin was polished and subtle and facile. Let me tell you about him.

He was a Basque, born on the slopes of the Pyrenees, where his noble family held vast estates from which they drew a princely annual income. No gunsmith's youngest son, he, who had to work his way to the top. He started at the top. Military service began early for French boys; and, when St. Castin was fifteen years old, he came to Canada as an ensign in the regiment of Carignan-Salieres, which had been assigned overseas. It was only by the accident of duty that he left Europe at all; but when, five or six years later, the regiment was disbanded and he was free to return home, he chose to stay in Canada. He liked the country and he liked the life.

During his tour of duty, he had become passionately interested in and sympathetic to the Indians, learning their language and living their life whenever possible. The Indians loved him and made him a chief, and some of them even regarded him as a minor god. He went into the fur trade with them, making a fortune of over three hundred thousand gold crowns, which he didn't need, since he was already a wealthy young man. The bulk of this money came from trade with the New Englanders, whom he cordially hated, but not too much to take their hard cash.

His main trading post was at the old fort of Pentagoet, later called in his honor Castine, although he didn't stay there all the time. He roamed around among the tribes, having a good time for himself. In fact, he perhaps had too good a time, since one priest reported of him that he "has need of spiritual aid to sustain him in the paths of virtue"; and on another occasion St. Castin complained to the governor of Canada that Perrot, the governor of Montreal, "kept me under arrest from the twenty-first of April to the ninth of June, on pretence of a little weakness I had for some women." And Perrot's successor,

Meneval, was instructed to see to it that St. Castin "abandon his life among the Indians" and behave himself in a manner "more becoming to a gentleman."

Meneval had his hands full with that assignment, but he was at least partially successful. St. Castin continued to live among the Indians, but his private life quieted down considerably after he was legally married by the Jesuit Father in charge of the little mission church on Panamawamske Island in the Penobscot River (now the Old Town Indian Reservation) to what the romanticists would call an Indian princess. The girl was the daughter of Madockawando, the powerful chief of the Penobscots; and, by marrying her, St. Castin acquired some useful family connections and the solid backing of that and allied tribes.

St. Castin's trading post at Pentagoet stood on very debatable territory. It had been occupied alternately by the English and the French and at this time was admittedly a part of the British royal domain. St. Castin really had no business being there at all. Sir Edmund Andros didn't think so, either, so he went in his frigate *Rose* and plundered the place. St. Castin escaped into the woods, and Andros sent him a message that if he wanted his property, he could come to Pemaquid and get it.

St. Castin was furious. The next year he went to Pemaquid with a band of his Indians, who hadn't been included in the invitation, and destroyed the town, along with several others. He'd always hated the English, and now his hatred was consuming. In fact, he became a worse menace than the Indians he controlled, since he was the inspiration and leader of a large part of their raids. For more than twenty years he directed his warriors against the English settlements, until his name was one used to frighten children into good behavior. Before he was through, even Portland, then called Falmouth, was burned to the ground and a hundred of the inhabitants carried away.

But twenty years is a long time to carry on an active, one-man war, and St. Castin was getting no younger. He was tired, which is not surprising, considering his age and the strenuous life he'd always lived. One of the several temporary truces was in effect in 1725, and St. Castin urged his only legitimate son, as grandson of an Abenaki chief, to use his great influence toward a lasting peace. The young man, who inherited his father's courage and brilliance as well as the outstanding qualities of his mother's race, went about among the tribes trying to persuade them to lay down their arms. The British mistook his purpose and captured him, sending him in chains to Boston, where he was kept prisoner for seven months.

At this the entire Abenaki nation, which worshiped the whole St. Castin family, was so incensed that they planned a concerted mass attack on the English everywhere, vowing that they'd never stop fighting until every Englishman or every Indian was dead. The war they planned was going to include every form of torture and outrage that they could invent and would have made those that went before seem like a child's game.

Luckily, young St. Castin, who seems to have been more reasonable and diplomatic than his father, succeeded in convincing the authorities of Boston that his intentions in addressing his tribes had been peaceable, so they let him go. He returned to the Abenakis and managed to calm them down. A period of peace followed which lasted for about twenty years, a remarkably long time under the inflammatory circumstances.

When these two decades were over, the elder St. Castin was dead, as was his wife. Their daughters were all well married to Frenchmen. The young St. Castin, the Abenaki chief, was also heir to the vast estates of his father's family in the Pyrenees and to a French title. So he sailed off to France to enter into his inheritance, and I can't find out any more about him. He apparently didn't come back to the Maine coast again. I can't help wondering, though, how he fared in Europe. He certainly must have encountered some things that surprised him in the Court circles of the day.

The peace was shattered, not by any local event, but by the outbreak of the War of the Austrian Succession (1740) in Europe. This war was about as far removed geographically and politically from the colonists as it could possibly have been; but nevertheless, they immediately became involved. Means of communication were decidedly erratic at the time, and Duquesnel, the French governor of Louisbourg on Cape Breton Island at the mouth of the St. Lawrence River, heard about the resumption of hostilties weeks before the news reached Boston. He thought this was a fine opportunity to steal a march on the British, who were then in possession of most of Acadia. He captured and burned a small English fishing village called Canseau, which was nearby. This wasn't much of a victory, since there were only a few fishermen there at the time and they offered no resistance.

But it so went to Duquesnel's head that he decided to go on and take the British stronghold of Annapolis (the old Port Royal under a new English name) in Nova Scotia, a move that he considered might well give him control of the whole of Acadia. And so it might have, if he'd been successful. His failure was his own fault. The British were unsuspecting, since they didn't know that a state of war existed. Moreover, as they hadn't been bothered for twenty years, they'd allowed their fortifications to fall into such disrepair that cows in neighboring fields could walk right over the walls into the town. But Duquesnel fooled around for three weeks, for no reason that's apparent to this nonmilitary mind, and at the end of that time some English ships came into the harbor by chance and scared him away.

This campaign in itself accomplished little or nothing, but it succeeded in irritating the English settlers. It's very possible that they'd have been perfectly satisfied to leave the war on the other side of the Atlantic, if Duquesnel's misguided zeal hadn't roused them. For twenty years everybody had been minding his own business and getting along very well, and there was no reason why this happy state couldn't have continued. However, Duquesnel had upset the apple cart, and now nothing would do but retaliatory measures. The most telling retort they could make, the colonists concluded, would be to capture Louisbourg.

This was a perfectly crazy idea. Louisbourg was the strongest fortress, French, English, or Spanish, in the Western Hemisphere. It was the only French naval station in North America, and the French esteemed it accordingly. They'd spent a quarter of a century and thirty million livres to make it impregnable, because it was of enormous value to them. It commanded the only good entrance to Canada, controlled the valuable fisheries off-coast, and served as base for a large fleet of privateers, which preyed on shipping to the benefit of the French exchequer. The French had no intention of allowing anybody to take over Louisbourg.

The man who suggested this harebrained scheme and bedeviled those in authority into accepting it against their better judgment was a Maine coast fisherman, William Vaughan of Damariscotta and Matinicus Island. He'd had a little trouble with the Louisbourg French over his fishing fleet, and he wanted the nuisance abated. He buttonholed the governor of Massachusetts, William Shirley, and persuaded him to lay the matter before the Assembly. The plan was turned down several times as impossible, but Vaughan was persistent and evidently glib.

He said the winter snow was so deep in Louisbourg that any assailants could walk right over the walls on the drifts. (Of course, they wouldn't plan to go in the winter in any case, but he disregarded that fact.) Cape Breton is notorious for terrible storms, high surf, and dense fogs, but Vaughan announced confidently that such things needn't bother their expedition at all. Moreover, he claimed that he had personal knowledge that provisions at the fortress were in very short supply, and that the garrison was on the verge of mutiny.

In the end, he managed to fast-talk the Assembly into adopting the plan, although his one vote majority is said to have come about because a member fell down and broke his leg as he was rushing to the meeting to vote against any such nonsense.

The whole project has a slightly musicomedy air, an out-of-this-world touch of irresponsibility, a zany lack of realism. The colonists hoped that the Crown would help them to the extent of a few regiments of soldiers and some battleships. When this help was not forthcoming, they decided to proceed alone. They had no army, no navy, and no heavy armament worth mentioning. This didn't seem to worry them at all. They could raise what would pass for an army. Every able-bodied man in the colonies owned and could shoot a gun, and most of them had had some experience, although not recently, in Indian fighting. So a call for volunteers went out. Although Maine's whole population was only one-fourteenth that of the entire Bay Colony, she furnished a third of the Massachusetts quota, or over a thousand men. This amounted to half the adult male population of the Maine coast, and that's one of the reasons why I'm considering the siege of Louisbourg as a part of Maine coast history, aside from its conception by a Maine man.

As for a navy, there were plenty of boats of all types and sizes along the coast, and about ninety of these were gathered together and fitted with guns. It was said afterward with good reason that one heavy French ship-of-war could have made short work of this hay-wire flotilla; but there just happened not to be any French warships on the scene. As for cannon to bring to bear on the stout walls of Louisbourg, it would have been impossible to take that kind of artillery with them even if they'd owned any so the colonists decided not to fret. They'd just capture what they needed from the French and turn the guns against their lawful owners. What the French were supposed to be doing while this took place I wouldn't know. The French garrison at Louisbourg was a force of trained and disciplined soldiers, not likely under ordinary circumstances to run screaming from their posts the minute some farmer with a musket said "Boo!" to them.

All these lacks were serious enough, the Lord knows, but the most serious of all was the lack of officers. Since the colonies had no standing army, they had no trained military leaders. The men who composed this scratch army wouldn't have obeyed them, anyhow. They were individualists, not used to taking orders from anyone and not inclined to start doing so now. Since someone obviously had to be in charge, Shirley appointed William Pepperell, a merchant of Kittery, Maine. He'd had no military training, but he was an able man and, what's more important, a popular one. Popularity was absolutely essential. All the men were volunteers, and if they didn't like the boss, they were perfectly capable of washing their hands of the whole thing and going home in a huff. The expedition was scoffed at by a man of the time. He said it had a fisherman as a contriver, a storekeeper as a general, and farmers, fishermen, and mechanics as soldiers; and that description isn't far from the truth.

Why did the colonists ever subscribe to such an idiotic scheme? It seems completely incompatible with the common conception of the New England Yankee character, which is supposed to be shrewd, reserved, cautious, and coldly canny. Undoubtedly it does contain those elements; but there is one quality of New Englanders that is seldom taken into account by those who do not know them well. They are capable of a great, contagious, almost naive enthusiasm for the most unlikely causes, the more unlikely the better. There seems to be no rule governing this enthusiasm. It simply breaks out in unexpected places and tight-lipped men become starry-eyed boys. It has been demonstrated time and again, as we will show. It's a mass throwing of bonnets over mills.

Such a wave of feckless enthusiasm now swept the entire

frontier for the forlorn and farcical hope of reducing Louisbourg, the Gibraltar of the West, as it was called. So on the fourth of March, 1745, with very little knowledge of where they were going or what they were going to do when they got there, the members of the expedition set sail for Cape Breton.

The angels have a soft spot for fools. The English Commodore Warren, who was in American waters with a small squadron, heard about the venture and decided to go to its aid. He hadn't been ordered to do so, but he hadn't received orders not to do so, either. Therefore he considered that he had a right to use his own judgment. He followed the heterogenous Yankee fleet up the coast and established a blockade of Louisbourg that was of enormous value. Then the weather, against all probability, held beautiful and bright. That coast at this time of year is almost always swept by furious storms, smothered with tremendous surf, and blanketed in impenetrable fog; but not this year. The land forces were able to disembark behind the city with no trouble and set up camp.

Across the harbor from the fortress proper there was a collection of storehouses containing much of the French reserve of food and munitions. William Vaughan sneaked around behind the low hills with a small party of men and burned these sheds to the ground, a very great loss to the French. As he was returning to the base the next morning, someone noticed that there was no smoke coming out of the chimneys of the Grand Battery, an installation that was supposed to defend the entrance to the harbor from the side opposite Louisbourg. Vaughan and thirteen men went down and took possession. There simply wasn't anybody there. It turned out that the garrison in residence had heard Vaughan and his party walking around in the night, and had fled across the harbor in rowboats. There's no explaining this senseless panic on the part of seasoned soldiers. We'll just have to accept it as a fact.

The Grand Battery contained thirty cannon. A few of them had been spiked by the defaulting garrison, but the advantage of a motley crew for an army is that it is bound to contain good mechanics and gunsmiths. They soon had the cannon back in commission and trained on the town. The expedition's wishful thinking on the subject of heavy arms was vindicated against all likelihood.

In order to make the fire really effective against the citadel, however, it was necessary to bring the guns up nearer. Louisbourg was protected on three sides by the sea, and on the fourth by a dreadful marsh, hip deep with mire and ice water. It would be impossible to drag cannon through that; or so everyone with sense conceded. The New Englanders had no sense. They built sixteen-foot sledges and placed the cannon on them. The horses and oxen they had commandeered from the surrounding countryside foundered in the swamp, so they turned them loose and stepped into the harness themselves, two hundred men to a sledge.

It was a terrible and inhuman undertaking, one to dismay the stoutest heart. Progress was measured by inches, and the route had to be changed constantly when the mud became so churned and liquified by the tramping of all those feet that the cannon were in danger of sinking out of sight. The men were exposed to fire from the fort and could work only at night or in occasional fog. It was cold, and permanently drenched clothing fostered an epidemic of what would now be called influenza. Many died of disease or wounds, and more lived the rest of their lives with impaired health. Still they labored on, their thin clothes in tatters, the shoes rotted off their feet. They'd come to capture Louisbourg, and no swamp was going to stop them. They man-handled the guns into position and opened fire on the town.

Very few of them had had any experience with cannon before, and some of the guns were blown up before the colonists learned how to load them. At first their aim was very bad indeed, but they kept practicing until their fire was deadly accurate. It damaged every building in the town and wore on the nerves of the inhabitants, who were already shaken by the conviction that they were dealing with madmen, a conclusion they'd reached after witnessing from the walls the business in the swamp. They believed, however, that if they could hold out long enough, aid would come from France, so they beat off various sorties for almost two months.

Then the great French ship-of-war, the *Vigilant,* carrying sixty-four guns and five hundred and sixty men, came sailing majestically in on a fair wind. Warren's squadron was off below the horizon on some sort of errand, and the *Vigilant* had a clear course into harbor. But apparently just for the fun of it she stopped to chase a little colonial privateer that was sailing along the shore. The little boat maneuvered out to sea, followed irresponsibly by the *Vigilant,* whose captain may not have appreciated the danger of his position. At any rate, Warren's squadron came slatting up out of the blue and, after a five hours' running fight, captured what amounted to Louisbourg's hope of deliverance.

This disaster completely discouraged the French, who were running short of both ammunition and food, and it encouraged the besiegers to make great preparations for a combined mass attack by land and sea. The French saw the writing on the wall and surrendered in mid-June. So the crazy scheme to capture the strongest fortress in the western world came to an unwarrantedly successful end.

Or was the success unwarranted? Not entirely. Basically the plan was unsound, depending far too much on luck and never from the beginning backed by sufficient power. But the weaknesses were more than made up for by the courage, endurance, and brilliant initiative of the attacking forces. They fought under great disadvantage, but they refused to recognize the impossible, and they took immediate advantage of every factor in their favor. Where a well-found, well-officered, well-disciplined army, fighting under the then accepted rules of warfare, probably would

have failed, they were either too ignorant or too enthusiastic to know when they were licked. So in the end
they achieved the impossible.

England was flabbergasted and a little worried. Naturally she was glad to have Louisbourg taken; but at the
same time, she was a little dismayed to discover that her
supposedly dependent colonies were stronger and more
aggressive than she had thought. It boded ill for the future.
William Pepperell was made a baronet, and Massachusetts
was refunded her expenditures in this campaign to the
tune of 217 chests of Spanish dollars and one hundred
barrels of copper coins. This was supposed to make everyone feel good about the whole affair.

In 1748, however, only three years after a thousand New
England men had died and been buried under the walls
of Louisbourg like "rotten sheep," Louisbourg was given
back to the French by the treaty of Aix-la-Chapelle. The
colonists were extremely bitter, feeling with some justifi-
cation that their efforts were unappreciated and that their
interests—which certainly weren't helped by French control
from Louisbourg of the shipping and fisheries—were being
disregarded. What was the use? they wondered; and they
were never to recover from their discontent.

Border warfare continued along the Maine coast for
another fifteen years. Possibly the settlers and the Indians
had become too accustomed to shooting on sight to stop
now. The British doubled and then trebled the bounty
on scalps, in order to teach the Indians a lesson. It didn't
work, naturally. Since scalp money was comparatively easy
money, settlers kept on killing Indians and Indians kept
on taking revenge. Moreover, the numbers of the Indians,
which hadn't been very great to start with, were reduced
now by warfare and especially by the various epidemics
that had swept through the tribes ever since their first
contact with the white men. The Indians saw clearly that
they were fighting for their very existence, a circumstance
which lent them the ferocity of desperation.

Finally in 1759 the British captured Quebec, resulting in the surrender of all of Canada; and, with the Peace of Paris in 1763, the Indian Wars in Maine ended. Maine coastmen drew a long breath and set about developing their domain.

4 · The Wars with the English

LET'S take a look at Maine, now that the menace of the Indian raids was removed and the danger of French occupation existed no longer. Maine never was, and isn't to this day, a land of easy living. The soil was stubborn, the waters bold, and the climate rigorous. But now that they could put their undivided attention on the problem, with no need to keep one eye over a shoulder and one hand on a gun, there were plenty of the hardy willing to gamble on the results of their own labor in this rugged territory. After the Peace of Paris, definite efforts were made by the land proprietors to attract settlers not only from other colonies but from Great Britian and Germany as well; and these efforts were so successful that in 1764 the population stood at 24,000. When you consider that in 1691 there were only four towns left inhabited as a result of the Indian attacks—Wells, Kittery, York and Appledore—you can measure that success. By 1779, there were forty towns in the province, Pittston being the last to be incorporated. Almost all this population was concentrated on the coast, for several reasons.

In the first place, there were no roads in the interior. Travel and transportation was almost entirely by water, the sea and river mouths serving as highways. In addition, the most obvious and profitable early industries were either directly connected with the sea or indirectly dependent upon it. An exception was the fur trade; but even there, the furs had to be exported in ships, so the posts were on the ocean or the large navigable rivers.

Farming at that time was negligible. There were small farms all along the coast, of course, but their produce was chiefly for home consumption. The first and for a long time the only exportable crop was corn, which had also been the staple of the Indians. This grain was easy to raise and easy to store. As early as 1635 there were water-powered mills along the the Piscataqua, where the corn was ground into meal for shipping away. There was plenty of game in the forests that came down to the back doors of the farmhouses, and plenty of fish in the sea that lapped the front doorsteps, so it wasn't necessary to raise cattle for beef. Each farm had only enough cows to supply its own butter, milk, and cheese, and enough pigs to vary the monotony of an all-vension-and-fish diet. Every farmer was also a hunter and fisherman, and usually two or three other things as well.

The fisheries were the first industry of the Maine coast, and the longest lasting. They started before the land was settled at all—in fact, as far back as the Vikings—and they're still going strong today, with much of the economy of the state depending, as it always has, upon them. At the time of which we are speaking, the fisheries were known as the New England Silver Mine, and trade with the West Indies was based upon them. In exchange for the dried fish, the ships came back loaded with sugar, molasses, rum, tobacco, spices, and some hard cash, as well as dresses, yard goods, and finery to please the women.

There were several types and grades of fish. Some of it, called cor-fish (or corned fish), was packed whole in barrels of brine; but most of it was salted and dried. The best consisted of whole, full-grown fish, so perfectly dried that it displayed no blemish and the flesh was almost translucent. The fish that had been salt-burned or spotted in the drying, or that was not as large and firm and fully fleshed, was called refuse fish. It was perfectly good to eat and in no way spoiled, but it sold at perhaps half the price of the other and was bought in great quantities in the West Indies as food for the slaves.

The fish for the epicure, though, was the dun-fish or dark fish, which brought about three times as much as any of the other kinds. Only pollock caught in the summer season was used to make dun-fish. It was cured very carefully on the rocks, without much salt, and then piled in a dark place and covered with salt marsh hay. This darkened the color and was supposed to give the fish an unusual and subtle flavor. The first of the Pepperell family —Sir William Pepperell's father—laid the foundations of one of the earliest fortunes in America by specializing in the dun-fish, at the Isles of Shoals, and he traded his dark pollock not only in the Indies, but in England and in Spain, Portugal, and other Catholic countries as well.

You can't go into the fish business on a commercial scale unless you have one or more ships; so naturally the shipbuilding industry flourished all along the coast. In fact, the English shipwrights at one time appealed to the crown to devise some scheme to restrict the number of ships built in Maine, since their own profits were suffering serious inroads as a result of the overseas competition.

Conditions in Maine were ideal. There was plenty of excellent timber growing right to the water's edge, countless suitable natural sites for the building and launching of large vessels, and an endless supply of cheap labor. Everyone, at one time or another, built a boat of some sort, and it was standard procedure for a farmer to lay ways in his barnyard, cut timbers from his own woodlot, and set his several sons to shipbuilding in the slack spells between planting and haying or haying and harvest.

When the craft was done, it would be launched and anchored in the cove in front of the house and, manned by the boys of the family, engaged in coastal trade of their own produce. This kind of family enterprise was a natural outgrowth of having the sea for a front dooryard, and most farmers depended equally upon their fields and the in-

Ancient, weather-beaten hulks wallow in the water at Wiscasset.

come from the family schooner to make ends meet. It was as normal for a farmer to be a shipowner then as it is for him to own a pick-up truck now.

The first ship built in Maine—or in the New World— was the *Virginia* of the Popham colony, in 1607. She was of about thirty tons, not a very large vessel, but she long outlasted the colony, which gave up in about a year or less. She made voyages up and down the coast collecting furs and delivering salt cod and sassafras root; then for about twenty years she was on the tobacco run between Virginia and England; and finally she was wrecked off the Irish coast. She established a good tradition for seaworthiness and usefulness which Maine ships have always maintained. Some people have a feeling for ships, and some have not. If you have, you can't help developing a sneaking fondness for the sturdy little *Virginia*.

Originally the building of a ship was an individual enterprise, but it wasn't long before contract building came into existence, and large shipyards were established in such places as Portsmouth, Bath, Boothbay and Wiscasset. Many of them exist to this day, although the shipbuilding industry has changed a great deal from what it was before the Revolution.

Closely allied to the building of ships was the cutting of lumber. Great quantities went into the wooden hulls and tall masts, and when the supplies near the coast were depleted, crews of the famous Maine lumberjacks penetrated the interior by way of the great rivers and cut the timber along their banks, driving the logs down to the sea on the spring freshets. Not all the lumber was for local consumption. Much of it was exported to England as boards, as pipestaves for the making of wine barrels, as shingles and siding, and especially as masts. As we know, the King claimed ownership of all mast pines over twenty-four inches in diameter a foot from the ground, and these were supposed to be cut only for his use. Special ships were designed and built for their transportation to England, and great care was taken in their felling, to prevent their being broken or warped. A great swath was swamped through the forest in the planned line of fall, all minor growth being cleared away; and a soft bed of branches, saplings, and snow was constructed to cushion the shock.

Once down and limbed out, the masts were "baulked" or dragged to the nearest watercourse by oxen—sometimes as many as forty being required—and floated down to their destination, where they were hand-hewn "sixteen sides" and loaded onto ships. The peculiar shape of the town square in Freeport is said to have been dictated by the need for room to turn the great sticks at this point of their progress from lumberyard to harbor. Each mast was worth about five hundred dollars, so the care taken not to injure one is understandable.

Injured they were, though, and deliberately. The colonists didn't relish having their best timber appropriated. Their contention was that if a tree stood on land legally granted to a man, it was his tree to dispose of as he pleased. The colonists felt very strongly on this point if the tree happened to be in their way when they wanted to clear a tract for planting, or if they needed the lumber themselves. So if they dared, they cut the tree anyhow. If this seemed too risky a business, they started brush fires to ruin it for mast purposes, although usually they could salvage enough lumber for clapboards and rafters for their barns.

Sometimes too they cleared away all the smaller growth from around the foot of the tall white pine bearing the Broad Arrow of the King. The soil of Maine is a thin cover over solid rock, so that the roots of trees are wide-reaching, but of shallow depth. The trees depend on each other's protection to keep themselves upright. When exposed to the full force of the wind, they are uprooted and come crashing down. Then they were no good for masts, having suffered weakening strains, but there was nothing wrong with them for other uses. They were quickly sawed into boards and trimmed to less than the damning twenty-four-inch width.

The British Navy Board repeatedly complained, too, about the makers of clapboards and shingles, who could use in their business only perfectly straight-grained wood that would split well. They would chop into a standing pine to test the grain; and, if it was not suitable, simply move on to another tree, leaving the first to die. According to modern standards of conservation and quite aside from the need for masts, this really was a wasteful and deplorable practice.

All the early industries of Maine were closely connected and interdependent. The fisheries supported and leaned on the shipbuilders, who in turn supported and leaned on the lumbering operations, and the farmers were involved in all three activities. Almost as old an industry as lumbering was the lime-burning business, which was no more independent than any of the others. In 1733, in the middle of the French and Indian Wars, William McIntyre built the first lime kiln near where the state prison now stands in Thomaston, and as conditions calmed down after the Peace of Paris, the industry flourished. It was centered in the Thomaston-Rockland-Camden area, where there were enormous deposits of good limestone. Thirty cords of wood were required to fire one kiln, so firewood was in great demand. A countless fleet of little boats called kiln-wooders came into being to bring fuel to the kilns, and an army of men was employed to sail the boats and cut cordwood. In addition, the slabs and edgings from saw mills were burned, and the collecting and shipping of these "skoots" became a separate business. The kiln-wooders were not very sound boats. They didn't have to be. Their buoyant cargo would keep them afloat if necessary, and in any case they never ventured far from shore. They were cheap, slapped-together things, often with decks so high-piled with skoots and cordwood that they looked like floating woodpiles, and the helmsman couldn't see over the load to steer. In choosing his course he had to depend on the shouted instructions of a man perched on top of the heap.

The ships that took the lime to market were something else again. They had to be absolutely tight, since the lime, if it got wet, generated enough heat to start a fire which it was impossible to control by water. These lime schooners had double bottoms to keep the cargo out of the bilge, and double decks to prevent leakage from above. The captain prowled around sniffing constantly for the odor of slaked lime. If he detected it, the entire crew got busy sealing every crack of the ship, including the hatches, in hopes that lack of oxygen would discourage fire, while the captain headed his craft at full speed for the nearest harbor. There he anchored at some distance from other shipping, and all hands stripped the ship of everything that wasn't nailed down and some things that were.

Then they simply sat it out on shore, waiting to see whether or not the entire ship was going to burst suddenly into flame. Sometimes she did, and sometimes she didn't. You couldn't tell for sure in much less than two or three months. If she did, the only course was either to let her burn or to cut a hole in her bottom and sink her in a shallow spot. The fire would thus be put out, but usually the cargo swelled and burst all seams beyond repair. Hauling lime was certainly a risky business.

The only other way by which a man could earn a living on the Maine coast of those days was by engaging in trade. The merchants exchanged the local products of fish, corn, lime, lumber, and furs for those necessities and luxuries that couldn't be grown or manufactured in Maine. This seems a rather short list of commodities to offer, but it was enough to keep everyone busy and reasonably prosperous, and to make a few rich by the standards of the day.

Actually there was one other item of trade that enjoyed a brief, brisk, and to my mind rather gruesome period of activity. Scalps taken from the French or the Indians sold in England for from five to a hundred pounds and enjoyed a consequent boom as articles of commerce. I have no idea what determined the value of a scalp, or whether they were used in the manufacture of such things as wigs

Once a familiar sight, logs float past Whiting, destined for a sawmill on the shore. Log drives are now banned by law on account of their contribution to pollution.

or haircloth, or were bought solely as souvenirs. I don't know whether a blonde, curly scalp was worth more than a scalp of straight black hair, or whether the price depended on the notoriety or social status of the original owner; and to tell the truth, I think the whole subject is revolting, so let's not speculate any further.

At this time the western boundary of Maine had been established as the mouth of the Piscataqua River (between Kittery, Maine, and Portsmouth, New Hampshire), the middle of the Salmon Falls River to its headwaters, and thence north-two-degrees-west for 120 miles; which is about where it lies now. The eastern boundary was a bit indefinite. The French had claimed everything east of the Penobscot, but now of course all that land as well as Canada belonged to the British; so it didn't make too much difference where Maine ended in that direction. People were too busy scratching a living to worry unduly about the eastern limits of their province. The political situation didn't bother them much, either. They were subjects of Great Britain under the immediate jurisdiction of Massachusetts, who appointed a president for them, the first one being Thomas Danforth. Since no very vital issues were at stake during this brief period, very few cluttered their minds with politics.

The first sign of discontent with the *status quo* occurred in 1765, with a mob in Falmouth (now Portland) seized and destroyed some tax stamps. No more came of this until 1774, when the towns of Saco, Falmouth, and Machias protested against paying the tax Parliament had imposed on them. A convention was called at Falmouth, and the delegates resolved that they couldn't be taxed without their own consent, and labeled the tax "a dark design framed to abridge their English liberties." The colonies had been disgruntled ever since the British gave Louisbourg back to France, and now that they put their minds to it, they could think of a lot of grievances they'd suffered and had no intention of continuing to suffer. They considered themselves quite capable of conducting their own affairs and they wanted to do so with no inter-ference or hindrance from the English, who, they felt, merely used them without benefiting them in any way.

During the Revolution which followed this widespread discontent, Maine suffered more and played a more im-portant part than is commonly credited. Larger, more widely publicized campaigns conducted elsewhere have distracted attention from Maine's role, but the role was significant nevertheless. Even before the Declaration of Independence, Maine had fought on land and sea. Arnold's famous expedition against Quebec in 1775 was assembled and outfitted along the Kennebec, a large number of Maine men were enrolled in his company, and Maine guides saw him through the wilderness. In the same year, the first naval battle of the Revolution was fought when the citizens of Machias, with no cannon and only a few small arms for which they had insufficient powder, attacked the British armed *Margaretta* with such persistence and ferocity that she was forced to surrender.

In 1775, too, a British fleet under Captain Mowatt attacked Falmouth without provocation (actually he'd had a hassle over the price of some masts with a local dealer) and burned the city to the ground, the second time the place had been completely destroyed by fire. The British went on to capture Castine and harass the coast both east and west, a coast inadequately fortified and almost literally unprotected against the enemy.

Maine's position was unenviable. Both sides enlisted the services of the Indians and paid good bounty for scalps, so the terrifying conditions of the French and Indian Wars came into existence again. Maine bore the brunt of this guerrilla warfare, since she was the buffer between Canada and the better fortified colonies to the south. Moreover, her manpower had been drained away to fight with the Continental Army on other fronts. (There were more than a thousand Maine men at Valley Forge alone.) Communication with headquarters in Boston was difficult and at times impossible, so the settlers seldom knew how the war was progressing, except that their own area was taking a terrible beating. The entire coast was constantly subjected to raids from British warships based on the Castine peninsula or in Canada, when most of the food and useful goods was seized for aid and comfort of the enemy. If the colonists of the Maine coast had given up and thrown in their lot with the British, it would have been neither surprising nor blameworthy.

But they were a tough, stubborn, independent lot. They'd lived through Indian wars before, and almost to a man had had experience in hand-to-hand battles with vicious pirates and savage cannibals at the far ends of the earth. So now they put up a resistance that was like a forest fire, breaking out in unexpected places when it was thought to be under control. No great campaigns were conducted on Maine soil, but the English didn't dare to withdraw and leave Maine alone to her own devices.

They couldn't afford to turn back the coast with its safe harbors, active shipyards, and ablebodied men to the service of the revolutionists. And even under the policing of the British navy and garrisons, ships were still built and launched. One was the *Ranger,* launched at Kittery in 1777, which under John Paul Jones carried the news of Burgoyne's surrender to Europe and received in Quiberon Bay in Brittany the first salute ever given by a foreign power to the American flag. Another was the *America,* a gift of the French government and the first line-of-battle ship ever to be constructed in this country. No wonder the British didn't feel like retiring to give these activities full rein. Although the fact has not been given due recognition by many historians, Maine may well have determined the outcome of the Revolution. Had the British been able to divert to other fronts the ships and troops necessary to keep Maine under even partial discipline, they might easily have succeeded in subjugating the rebellious colonies. So the British victories in Maine were very costly to them, and actually they gained the English nothing of any real value to their cause.

In 1779 Boston decided that the British occupation of Castine was a menace that should be eliminated. The English were building a strong fort there, called Fort George after the King, and they were raiding and plundering the entire coast. They'd developed an institution which is mentioned in almost every town history of the area, the "shaving-mill." No one really knows the origin of this name, although there are various explanations which amount to guesses and don't explain it. The shaving-mills were nothing but small boats, sometimes schooners, often merely barges, which ranged up and down the coast collecting food, cattle, guns, ammunition, and anything else the British could use, without bothering to pay for it.

The British got all the blame for the depredations of the shaving-mills, although there is evidence that many were operated by colonial Tories or even by just plain businessmen whose interest in profit outweighed their patriotism. Be that as it may, an expedition of fifteen hundred men under General Lovell, with artillery commanded by Paul Revere, was sent out from Massachusetts to stop this activity. Their fleet consisted of twenty-four transports, nineteen heavily armed ships, and the frigate *Warren* of thirty-two guns. The naval arm of this powerful force was under the command of Captain Gurdon Saltonstall.

They shouldn't have had any trouble in reducing Castine. Fort George was still under construction, and the defenses were not yet in place. Moreover, there were only three British ships in the bay, which were immediately captured. The troops landed, occupied the heights, and were in a fine position to assault and take the town under covering fire from the fleet. But the American officers got to bickering among themselves; Lovell and Saltonstall couldn't agree about coordination of their attacks, and they stalled around for two weeks doing nothing, while the British worked like beavers strengthening their fort. Lovell's excuse was that he was waiting for reinforcements from Boston, although one can't quite understand why he needed them, since he already outnumbered the British garrison and should have had the situation well in hand.

The reinforcements didn't show up. Instead, five big British frigates sailed into the bay to the relief of the fort, and the entire colonial fleet went scurrying up the river like a bunch of terrified sheep. It was a disgraceful display of faintheartedness. Since there was no way out of the shoaling estuary, the force was in a trap. Instead of standing to fight, the ships were beached and all those aboard deserted them and fled in disorder into the woods. They did have the sense, for a wonder, to burn their boats behind them, so at least all that valuable shipping didn't fall into the hands of the enemy. The expedition made its way back to Boston as best it could overland and on foot. And that ended any attempt to retake Castine from the British, who continued in business as before.

Finally Cornwallis surrendered at Yorktown, and in 1783 the Treaty of Versailles gave the colonies their freedom and the right to call themselves the United States of America. Then the question of boundaries became important. The English were keeping the territory that they'd acquired from France at the close of the French and Indian Wars, and they contended that the area of the old French Acadia had always extended west to the Penobscot River, and therefore that should be the line between Maine and Nova Scotia. (This was a different tune from the one they had sung while France was in possession.) Rather surprisingly, the Americans were able to produce the original grant given by James I to Sir William Alexander in 1621, expressly stating that the western boundary of Nova Scotia was the St. Croix River. The British commissioners apparently decided it would be improper to dispute a ruling of one of their own monarchs, so the St. Croix has been the international boundary ever since.

The ownership of some of the Bay of Fundy islands, however, remained undetermined for a long time after and it wasn't until decades later, in 1842, that the matter was settled by the terms of the Webster-Ashburton Treaty.

The story is that the members of the British commission dined and wined Daniel Webster so lavishly that he, in a state of euphoria, agreed to a boundary line several miles west of what he'd originally had in mind. Consequently, Campobello and Grand Manan islands belong to Canada instead of to Maine. This isn't a matter over which I'm advocating going to war with England at this late date; but a quick glance at any map of the district will show you that these islands are much nearer to the Maine coast than they are to any point in Canada and they would seem to belong geographically and reasonably to Maine.

The thirty years after the Revolution ended saw great changes in Maine. For one thing, the Indians became official wards of the state, no longer possessing control over lands of their own. This put an end forever to any threat of Indian uprisings and opened the land to safe development. Immigration increased by leaps and bounds, so that in 1790 the population had quadrupled to over 96,000, and in 1810 it reached the figure of almost 229,000, a very rapid expansion. Massachusetts gave Maine, which she still owned, eight senatorial representatives, and after the adoption of the United States Constitution, Maine became a representative district of ninety-three towns and plantations.

For the first time, Maine began to entertain notions about breaking away from Massachusetts. Her problems were not those of Boston. Not only were her industries and way of life remote from the understanding of Massachusetts men, but her very soil was disconnected from Massachusetts soil. A strip of New Hampshire separated the two territories. Control from Boston was a cumbersome business and, according to Maine lights, an unintelligent one. Final severance was not to come for some time, but the idea was in the air, and in 1785 the *Falmouth Gazette,* the first newspaper in Maine, was established for the declared purpose of agitating for separation.

There were other signs of growth and development. In 1791, Portland Head Light, which is today the oldest lighthouse on the entire Atlantic seaboard, was built. Three years later, Bowdoin College received its charter from the Massachusetts General Court and opened officially in 1802. The first bank in Maine, the Portland Bank, was established in 1799, and in 1801 Maine's first free public library was founded at Castine. The first cotton and woolen mills in all of North America were built at Brunswick, and the first paper mill near Bangor. Maine was thriving and showed bright promise of continuing to thrive.

The Embargo Act of 1807, which forbade trade between the United States and any foreign country, rather dimmed this promise. Maine's shipping had grown tremendously, and a great network of trade routes spread out from the little safe harbors of the Down-East coast to cover the entire globe. Signing onto a ship was a part of the standard education of most Maine boys, and before he had need to use a razor, the average lad had visited the principal ports of the world, helped fight off pirates, been chased by privateers, and seen shipmates removed from his side by British press gangs.

Edward Preble of Falmouth was just such a boy. He ran away to sea from his father's farm at the age of sixteen, later served as a midshipman in the Massachusetts State Marine, was captured by the British during the Revolution, fought the Barbary pirates after his release, and eventually commanded the U.S.S. *Constitution*. He was to be known as the Father of the U.S. Navy, since so many officers later to distinguish themselves received their training under him. He was outstanding, but hundreds of other boys had just as exciting adventures while still in their teens. It's a wonder that any of them were content to come home and settle down; but many of them did. The voyages were simply a boot training for later life, when they became successful merchants who knew their business from the bottom up.

The old China trade was established during this period. Heretofore Americans had depended on the Dutch and

English East India companies for tea, silk, spices, and other Far East commodities. Now they sent their own ships into the Orient, taking out such humdrum cargoes as salt beef, salt cod, pickled Maine salmon, barrel staves, and oak timbers. The things they brought back sound wonderful, although I couldn't possibly identify half of them: Beerboom Gurrahs and fine and coarse Policates, for example, or Allabad blue and Chittabudy Baftas; and the more recognizable bandanna handkerchiefs, spices, tea and silks, of course. These voyages weren't easy. There were the usual perils of the sea, plus the danger of being cheated by the sharp traders with whom one did business on the other side of the world, plus the natural pitfalls waiting for a sailor in a foreign port at the end of a long and boring stretch at sea. Then there were always the pirates and the press gangs. A captain had to watch himself every minute.

He wasn't always safe even after he'd made the round trip and was back in his home port. A Captain William Sturgis had a very disillusioning experience. He was in command of the *Atahualpa,* owned by Theodore Lyman of Kennebunk and engaged in the China trade. Bound for Canton with a load of Mexican dollars, he was becalmed in Macao Roads. Sixteen pirate junks attacked him there, and Sturgis barely held them off with a few small cannon until a breeze came up and he was able to escape. When he arrived back home with ship and cargo safe and sound, the owner, Lyman, discovered that Sturgis had taken the cannon along without asking permission. And in spite of the fact that the guns had saved Lyman's ship and investment, Sturgis was forced to pay freight on them halfway around the world and back because they were his own idea and therefore his own personal property and responsibility.

In 1793 France declared war on England, and this increased the normal hazards of the American sailor's life. Both sides preyed on American shipping for the supplies and ships they so sorely needed, and in addition England began stopping American ships on the high seas and kidnapping sailors. She was fighting for her life, and her chief weapon was her navy, which desperately needed men. Her pretence was that those whom she removed from American vessels were lawful subjects of the Crown, but during the emergency she was not particularly fussy about credentials. American sailors took to carrying birth certificates and descriptions of their own appearance in writing, but in spite of this precaution many a Maine man found himself serving in the British navy during the French wars. It was this practice that finally impelled Jefferson to declare the embargo.

The immediate effect of this in Maine was to make sleepy little Eastport the busiest harbor in the United States. It was a very simple matter to transfer a cargo of vital materials from an American to an English bottom out in Passamaquoddy Bay or on the shores of Campobello or Grand Manan. In a single week, for example, thirty thousand barrels of flour from the south were landed at the warehouses and then, from lack of space, on the shores. And, although guards were placed all along the waterfront at intervals of two hundred feet or so, it all disappeared quickly and mysteriously. You see, flour was worth only four dollars a barrel on American soil, while two miles away it commanded a price of sixteen dollars plus a three dollar transportation fee. A swarm of boats of every type, from barges down to canoes, plied back and forth every night and all night, moving flour and every other kind of goods to the better market. The coast with its many small islands, hidden coves and sheltered back channels was a smuggler's Paradise, and it would have seemed like ingratitude to Providence not to take advantage of the fact.

At last the confiscation of American ships and cargoes and the impressment of American seamen reached such proportions that the United States felt obliged to declare war on Great Britain. The British saw the impossibility of strangling American commerce without first putting the lid on the shipbuilding activities along the Maine coast, so they came down from Canada and occupied the territory as far as the Penobscot, again capturing Castine and making it a port of entry. But at first they weren't much more successful in bottling up Maine than they had been during the Revolution. At the beginning of this War of 1812 the American Navy consisted of only six first-class frigates and six smaller ones, while the British had nearly a thousand ships-of-war. However, Congress started issuing letters of marque and reprisal to almost anyone who wanted one and who owned a boat bigger than a dory. These letters could almost be considered licenses to practice piracy, being virtual permits for the holder to seize any English ship that she ran across and felt big enough to capture and bring into port for the prize money.

Thus practically every American boat that could float augmented the regular Navy, and those persons who didn't already have a ship hastily went about building one. These American privateers prowled the four watery corners of the globe, and in the first seven months of the war they succeeded in capturing thirteen hundred prizes. So far from putting the Maine shipyards out of business, the British blockade only stimulated their efforts.

Hostility between the Americans and the English along the Maine coast was not always, at first, one hundred per cent wholehearted. When a shipment of English goods was destined for a Maine port, there was sometimes a gentleman's agreement that it should be allowed to pass unmolested by the English; and if there seemed to be any danger that it might not get through, occasionally the British even furnished a convoy to protect it from the zeal of any who might not be in the know. This was good for British trade, and in addition the British hoped that it would engender enough good will among the Down-Easters so that they would at least remain neutral, if not actually friendly to the English cause. This policy was in force at the time of the famous fight between the *Boxer* and the *Enterprise*.

The British *Boxer* was convoying the American *Margaretta* loaded with English wool from Halifax to Bath. In order to make the picture look good and to give the impression that he was really trying to capture the smuggler, the English Captain Blythe ordered a few rounds fired well over his suppose prey. The *Margaretta* escaped into the mouth of the Kennebec, as she was intended to do, and the British crew casually went ashore to pick blueberries. As it happened, some fishermen off Half Way Rock heard the sound of that unnecessary and superfluous firing and reported the matter to the American captain of the brig *Enterprise*, lying in Portland harbor.

Her captain, Burrows, was only twenty-eight years old, full of energy and ambition, and spoiling for a fight. He promptly upped-anchor and went boiling out to look for the *Boxer*, whose Captain Blythe was just a year older and just as cocky and full of spirit. They encountered off Monhegan Island and for an hour engaged in a red-hot battle, a fight which, according to many accounts, both the young captains seemed to regard as a great lark. But it was the last fun either of them ever had. They were both killed in the battle.

Their double funeral was probably the most impressive that Portland has ever seen. The two bodies were brought to the landing on two barges draped with black and rowed slowly and solemnly by muffled oars, while all the shipping in the harbor fell in behind in a great water-borne procession. Every bell in the city tolled, and the guns of the Artillery Company saluted at one minute intervals as the youthful captains were carried ashore. The entire population lined the sides of the route as the cortege proceeded up Fore Street and into Pleasant and High, with Burrows' coffin followed by the American sailors, and Blythe's by his own seamen. The bells tolled, the guns boomed, and everybody wept. The bodies were buried side by side in Portland's old Eastern Cemetery, and the stones marking the graves may be seen there to this day.

After that the war along the coast was pushed more

vigorously. Castine was made a British naval base, and all the nearby towns, including Bangor, were captured and annexed to the English domain. A really effective British blockade put an end to all coastal activity, and trade with Boston had to be carried on by the slow and tedious means of ox carts and horse-drawn wagons, creeping over roads that were little more than dirt lanes, sometimes muddy, sometimes deep in dust, sometimes drifted with snow, and always narrow and rough. This motley assemblage of vehicles was known variously as the Mud Clipper Fleet or the Horse Marines; and while the Maine Yankees could still laugh at their plight by making such feeble jokes about it, the fact remained that their economy was very seriously crippled. Everybody was relieved when the Treaty of Ghent in 1814 concluded hostilities.

The failure of Massachusetts to provide adequate protection for the Maine coast during "Mr. Madison's War," as the War of 1812 was commonly called, and the strong local feeling that Maine was being treated like a stepchild by her supposed government resulted in her secession from the commonwealth in 1816. For four years after that she existed in a very peculiar position, that of a small independent republic with her own government, her own constitution, and her own capital. This was not entirely from choice. True, she didn't want anything to do with Massachusetts; but she did attempt to join the Union as a separate state. Apparently Washington was no more enthusiastic about Maine than Maine was about Massachusetts.

Finally, in 1820, she was admitted as the twenty-third state of the Union. To this day she's so proud of her statehood that the hackles of every red-blooded native—who loathes being called a Mainiac—rise at the use of the abbreviation *Me.* as a commercial gimmick flaunted on bumper stickers and in promotion brochures: Explore Me, Dig Me, Sleep with Me, Meet Me in the Woods. Me indeed! This is the State of Maine, and we'll thank everybody to remember that.

5 · The State of Maine

ALMOST IMMEDIATELY upon reaching the eminence of statehood, the citizens of the ex-province of Maine began acting like State-of-Mainers. The first thing that they did was to elect their own governor, and they chose a man so completely typical of the time and place that he seems almost tailored to order, almost a blueprint of a Maine governor rather than an actual person. His name was William King.

William King was born in Scarboro; and, at the age of seven, when his father died, he went to work in a sawmill. Twelve years later, at nineteen, he was still working there and he didn't have a pair of shoes to his name. All he had was a yoke of steers that had somehow been salvaged from his father's estate. He apparently decided that there was no future for him in Scarboro and that he'd wasted enough time there already. So, barefoot, he drove his steers the forty miles along the coast to Bath and found the kind of work he best knew how to do in a sawmill in nearby Topsham. Here he got into his stride. He shortly owned half a saw, then a whole one, then the whole mill. Next he managed to acquire some timberland and a store, and six years after his shoeless arrival with his steers, he was building his own vessels and shipping his own cargoes. At this point Topsham became too small for him, so he moved to Bath.

The larger community was no more difficult a nut for him to crack than little Topsham had been. He opened a store and, because he was one of those Yankees that can't help making money, pretty soon he was buying up warehouses along the wharves, then the wharves themselves, then the ships that docked at the wharves. The fleet thus acquired didn't give him scope enough for his abilities, so he started to build more and more ships. They were outstandingly successful in their ventures. One, the *Reunion,* paid for itself on its first voyage, then it paid for itself again on its second voyage, and again on its third; and after that it, along with its sister ships, kept right on making money.

I'm not entirely sure how much of this success was due to perspicacity and how much to luck. King was a smart man, all right, but he was uneducated and in some respects ignorant. For example, he had the bright idea of importing raw cotton from the South to be processed in Maine mills; and his vessel, the *Androscoggin,* was the first Maine ship to engage in this trade, which flourished and continued to flourish for eighty years. But when the *Androscoggin's* captain Nathaniel Harding, receiving orders to go to New Orleans and pick up a load of cotton, asked where New Orleans was, all he got for an answer was the not too helpful information that King *thought* it was somewhere on the Gulf of Mexico. Luckily Harding managed to get hold of an old Spanish chart by which he was able to locate his destination. Or maybe it wasn't entirely luck at that. Possibly King's great talent and the secret of his success was his instinct for picking capable men and the rather uncommon gift of being able to delegate complete responsibility to them.

You'd have thought that he'd have had his hands full with all these interests; but no. He branched out all over the place. He bought large tracts of land and went into farming, raising enormous crops of potatoes, which he sent in his own bottoms to the West Indies. He planted hundreds of fruit trees and sold the produce abroad. He organized the first bank in Bath, an institution whose notes of various denominations bore pictures of the several classes of vessels then in use: schooners, topsail schooners, sloops, brigs, and other ships. He was a prime mover, too, in the founding of the first Maine marine insurance company. He represented Bath in the General Court, and became a major general of the army.

He also built himself a great house on a hill and furnished it with the best the world had to offer, brought home from far places in his own ships: fine linen and porcelain, exquisite objects of art, beautiful furniture, and priceless rugs. It was a house fit for the entertainment of royalty, and in it he entertained the American equivalent of an aristocracy, the political, intellectual and cultural leaders of the new country. He'd acquired his own polish, so that he was at home in this company. William King had come a long way from the barefoot sawmill-hand of Scarboro.

During all this time, he'd been working tirelessly and agitating persistently for the cause of independent statehood, so that, when it was achieved finally, he was the obvious man to be chosen first governor. He discharged his duties with his customary fire and efficiency. He was quite a person; but he wasn't unique. There were plenty like him along the coast in those days, who took the material they found at hand and made fine lives for themselves. There are still plenty like him there, some of whom have achieved fame and fortune, and some of whom have not, but are none the less remarkable men.

The election of King as governor and the moving of the capital in 1827 from Portland to Augusta, which was more centrally located and a more appropriate site generally, were sensible and reasonable things to do. In some other matters the eccentricity which I'll have to admit is sometimes evident in the behavior of the State-of-Mainer was discernible. Take as an example the matter of the consumption of alcohol. Everybody drank. Rum was the common beverage—a mainstay of trade and therefore cheap and always available—and polite society drank imported wines and fine whiskeys. In addition, exotic brews, distillations, and fermentations were brought from all over the world in the tall ships to tickle the Maine palate.

The first two buildings to be erected in any new community were the church and the tavern, which was operated by and patronized by the most highly respectable citizens. It was unthinkable that a ship could be built without the aid of practically enough rum to float her being consumed in the process. On cold mornings, as soon as the men came to work, each was issued his first ration to get him under way, a healthy slug consisting of a full tumbler of rum and two of water, if he wanted water. This was repeated at eleven in the morning, to help him over the pre-lunch slump, and again at the low hour of four in the afternoon. And that wasn't all. Frequent excuses were found for the imbibing of an extra potion. Any special event marking the progress of the ship's construction, such as the raising of a sternpost or the hanging of the anchor or the nailing down of the final plank of the deck, called for a celebration, and all hands were summoned to bend the festive elbow. Rum was considered necessary to the building of a ship, and to most other projects as well.

Nevertheless and in spite of this fact—or maybe because of it—the first total abstinence society in America and for all I know in the world was founded in Portland in 1815, and in 1834 a convention was held and the first state prohibition movement organized. The subscribers debated accomplishing their ends by the use of moral influence, but finally decided that legal action would probably be more effective. In 1846 they managed to get a law passed forbidding the manufacture and sale of spirits. As is usual in these cases, it didn't work very well, and in succeeding years many other laws were made and revoked and made all over again.

Sometimes they were lenient enough to permit the making of cider—hard cider got a large percentage of the farmers safely through haying or a difficult calving—and sometimes they were stringent almost to the point of prohibiting even thinking about a drink. Strict or not strict, from the time of the first law in 1846 until 1934, when Maine followed the example of the nation and repealed, there has always been some form of prohibition law on the Maine books; not that it affected the amount of alcohol consumed very appreciably, but only the means of procuring it, the price, and the conditions under which it had to be consumed. That's what I mean by Maine eccentricity: the imbalance of the hard, fact-facing, practical outer man and the inner idealist.

The new state's zeal for reform didn't stop with correcting the drinking habits of her citizenry. Next Freemasonry came under scrutiny, and there was such a vigorous anti-Masonic movement that the brotherhood temporarily disappeared in Maine. Then the matter of the laboring man's working day was considered. In the shipyards, the men worked from sunrise until sunset, which in summer meant that they were often on the job for sixteen hours.

I don't say positively that there is any connection between the withdrawal of the rum ration and the sudden desire to do less work, but it may be significant that as soon as tea and coffee pots replaced the old brown jug, agitation for a ten-hour day began. The yard owners were shocked almost, but not quite, speechless. One old owner retained his powers of articulation sufficiently to announce that he was in favor of the ten-hour day, if it meant what he trusted it meant: ten hours before dinner and ten hours after. The ten-hour, six-day week become a fact, however, in spite of horrified opposition.

But pretty soon antislavery sentiment took hold of the public mind, to the exclusion of other minor reforms. This was a little surprising, since Maine had had no actual experience with slavery. Even in colonial days, there were literally almost no slaves at all in Maine. The few Negroes within the province were paid servants or laborers. Moreover, the prosperity of the coastal towns depended to an extent on the cotton trade and would suffer considerably if anything happened to upset the Southern economy.

Naturally the coast opposed Abolition violently; but the interior areas—where few people had ever seen a free Negro, let alone a slave—wouldn't let well enough alone.

The result was that antislavery men of both political parties, the Whigs and the Democrats, withdrew and formed a party of their own, the Free-Soil Party. In the fracas that followed, all party lines disintegrated and, when the dust had settled, the Republican Party emerged triumphant. It has held a somewhat precarious edge ever since. Its first candidate for governor, Hannibal Hamlin, went on from Augusta to serve in the United States Senate, and thence to the vice-presidency of the United States, a position he held under Lincoln during the Civil War.

In the period between Maine's achieving statehood and the outbreak of the Civil War, shipbuilding and shipping reached its peak. For a time there, shipbuilding pretty nearly *was* Maine. She built now not only for herself, but for most of the eastern seaboard as well, and for owners overseas. Conditions elsewhere had changed so, with the easily available timber having been cut off and cheap labor nonexistent, that a Maine yard could build a ship fifteen dollars a ton cheaper than anyone else could. Consequently the industry boomed. Even the tiniest town along the coast had its shipyard, and Maine produced well over a third of all the ships built in the entire United States. In one year alone; 215,904 tons were launched, and at one time there were 1990 vessels registered just in the little district of Machias; and this didn't include those that had been delivered to owners in other states, sailing under carpenters' certificates until they could be registered in their home ports. Maine led the world in the building of ships.

And what ships they were! Books which read like poetry have been written about them, and I wish I had the time and the space and the knowledge to do them justice. But I haven't; nor the ability. This was the era of the tall square-rigger, cloudlike under her acres of canvas and recognizable on any horizon of the globe as being of

Maine origin; and of the clipper ships, the lean race horses of the sea. They have been called the most beautiful objects ever made by American craftsmen. They had lovely names: the *Flying Dragon,* which held the record of ninety-seven days from Bath around the Horn to San Francisco, the famous *Red Gauntlet,* the *White Falcon,* and the great four-masted *Dirigo,* the first steel sailing ship to be built in America.

Following the clippers came the Down-Easters, designed and built by the master craftsmen of the Maine coast. Most authorities agree that in them the art of shipbuilding reached its peak and that they were the highest development of the sailing vessel. They combined the speed of the clipper with greater maneuverability and cargo capacity, and lower operating cost; and in doing so they did not sacrifice the clean-cut beauty of line that made the clippers legendary. One of them, the *Wandering Jew* out of Rockport, established a record of thirty-three days from San Francisco to Hong Kong that has never been beaten. These ships were unique to the Maine coast yards, and they commanded respect and awed admiration on every sea lane and in every port in the world.

It would be impossible to list every innovation for which Maine yards were responsible, or to discuss every class of vessel built there. But we must mention the vessel known as the great schooner, which has been called "the most weatherly and economical sailing vessel in the world." These great schooners were fore-and-aft-rigged ships like ordinary schooners, except that they carried four or six or eight or more masts. They were developed to meet foreign competition, which was cutting in on the profits of long voyages. The great schooners engaged chiefly in coastal trade, and could carry large-bulk cargoes like ice, lumber, granite, and lime, and still show a profit. Because they frequently found themselves obliged to unload in ports of shallow depth, centerboard and keel models were developed. They were not as exciting as the clippers and

Down-Easters, but they served their owners well and were perhaps the backbone of the Maine shipping industry.

All this running back and forth between the ends of the earth had its effect on the way of life of the Maine coast people. From being provincial in experience and outlook, they became possibly the most cosmopolitan group in the world. With the growth of the great fleet of Down-Easters, it became the rule rather than the exception for a captain's wife and family to accompany him on his voyages. The whole family would embark as a matter of course to be gone from home for a year or two, during which they would live aboard ship and visit every principal port of the world, as well as many little-known coasts and islands.

Their quarters were comfortable and even luxurious and beautiful, paneled in mahogany, satinwood, or bird's-eye maple, or painted white and embellished with carving and gold leaf. There were fine carpets on the cabin floors and comfortable and graceful furniture, often upholstered in damask or brocaded satin. Sometimes a musically inclined wife took her piano with her and taught her little daughters to play it.

Lessons went on as regularly as though the children were still at home in Bath or Rockland or Machias. The home-town teacher outlined the work to be covered during the period of absence and furnished the necessary books; and the parents of the child saw to it that the assignments were done. One girl, Joanna Colcord, mailed her completed high-school examination papers from Hong Kong, and received her diploma when her father's ship arrived home in Searsport six months later.

It was a highly modern type of education that these children received, of the sort widely publicized in a much later day. Geography was a thing of experience rather than of reading and memorizing. No girl who had accompanied her mother on a shopping trip for fresh vegetables or dress goods in a port of Siam or China or Spain was likely to forget the customs, products, and climate of those countries. No boy who had helped his father find the ship's position at sea or laid off on the chart the day's run was apt to consider mathematics a useless and impractical mystery. History was something these children frequently saw happening, and often their families entertained aboard men whom they were to learn in later years had been world figures.

It's no wonder that they commonly abandoned the usual counting-out rhymes in their games—the staid "Eenie, meenie, minie, mos"—and made up their own much more interesting jingles, using words like Pernambuco, Ilo-Ilo, Madagascar, and Barcelona. They had a marvelous time, and it wasn't as though they were really far way from contact with home. In the harbor of Calcutta or Honolulu they were always running into next-door Maine-coast neighbors. The ports of the world were their back yard and the whole globe their familiar neighborhood.

They brought home from these long voyages not only the things in their heads and hearts—the knowledge and the attitudes that would last them all their lives—but material objects as well, things that survive to this day. The mansions that the captains built in their home ports from the profits of their ventures were crammed with lovely things from everywhere—exquisite china and silks, lacquered chests and furniture, figures of ivory and jade, and priceless rugs and tapestries, as well as more trivial and homely things—a pretty shell picked up by a child on some beach at the Antipodes, or a paper and bamboo fan bought in a teeming bazaar by a woman who found the heat too oppressive.

Even the names many of these people bore, some of which have been handed down to their descendants to this day, came from far lands. I know a woman who was named for her grandmother, Ceylon, who was named for the place of her birth. There were Persias, too, and Indias and Mindoros and even an Oceanica.

Many men and women who died just a short time ago could give the place of their birth only as a latitude and longitude on the high seas. Pregnancy didn't keep many wives safe at home. As the time of delivery approached, a midwife was taken on at a port of call; or the father, who as captain had some medical knowledge, officiated. Infant mortality under these conditions was surprisingly low—lower, in fact, than it was ashore, either because the middle of the ocean is a relatively antiseptic spot, or because the general health and vitality of women who took long voyages was better than that of those who stayed at home doing their housework. It was a period that reached its peak in the decade before the Civil War; but it's impossible to set a limit to its influence on Maine thought and character.

The decline of Maine shipping started before the Civil War. In 1857 the whole country was subjected to a severe depression, which amounted to a disaster to the shipping interests. Once proud vessels rotted at their anchorages, and trade was at a standstill. The Civil War completed what was already begun. The South recognized, of course—just as the British had done in the War of 1812 —that, if she hoped for success, she'd have to make active war on the trade-carrying ships of the North, which meant chiefly those of Maine.

This was a sad business all around. Because of their means of livelihood, the people of the Maine coast had many ties with the people of the South. It wasn't only a matter of business, either. Bonds of friendship and affection had been formed in the half century of the cotton trade, so that there was a great deal of truth in the remark that Bath and New Orleans were closer neighbors than Richmond and Washington. Families had intermarried, and many a Southerner owned substantial shares in a Down-East vessel. It was impossible to terminate this complicated relationship suddenly, without bitterness and grief arising from conflicting loyalties. Although Maine was geographically the state furthest removed from the battlelines, she was emotionally and economically very deeply involved.

Four days after the firing on Fort Sumter, President

Jefferson Davis of the Confederacy started issuing letters of marque and reprisal. All Southern shipping immediately armed and went into the privateering business. For nearly six months, Maine vessels paid a terrific toll, caught off base as they were, unarmed and in many cases unsuspecting. Scores of ships from Machias and Rockland and Bath fell into Confederate hands, with their crews and cargoes. In a brief ten days, for example, the Confederate privateer *Calhoun* alone captured Maine ships to the value of $150,000. Later this privately owned fleet was augmented by a regular Southern navy, consisting largely of ships built and bought in England; and then the depredations on Maine shipping increased. There's no way of estimating accurately how many hundreds of beautiful Maine ships were captured and burned, or how great the loss sustained.

Portland has the distinction of having actually been raided by Southern forces, remote as she was from the main area of conflict. In 1863, the Confederate lieutenant, Charles Read, was operating under a roving commission to do as much damage as he could. He was supposed to destroy any Northern shipping he encountered at sea and, in addition, to enter any Northern ports of little defense that seemed feasible, there to burn the shipping in the harbor and wreck any shipyards in the vicinity. In short, his orders required him to make as much of a pest and nuisance of himself as possible, and he was conspicuously successful in carrying those instructions out.

After wreaking havoc generally all along the Atlantic seaboard, he managed to capture a Southport fishing schooner, the *Archer,* off Cape Sable. He transferred himself, his crew and his guns to her and burned his old boat, the *Tacony,* which had become too well known to the North for comfort. Thus effectively disguised, he sailed along the Maine coast to Damariscove Island, where he encountered another Maine fisherman, the *Village.* He hailed her and had a long neighborly chat with her, during which he picked up a lot of information about the disposal of the various shipping; and the officers of the *Village* picked up the impression that Read and his whole crew were drunk. So in a spirit of helpfulness, they kindly piloted the *Archer* into Portland harbor and saw her safely moored off Fish Point, a friendly courtesy they'd have extended to any fellow-fishermen in like circumstance.

Snug in the harbor, Read discovered not far away the revenue cutter *Caleb Cushing,* which was—although he probably didn't know it then—getting ready to go out and look for him in his old *Tacony.* He decided to cut her out from the fleet, take her to sea, and then come back and burn the rest of the shipping in the port. This was an ambitious and hazardous project, but at first luck was on his side. The *Cushing's* captain had just died, and most of the men had gone ashore to the funeral. The remaining skeleton crew was overpowered, and the *Archer* and the *Cushing* passed safely under the guns of the fort and out to the open sea.

But there Read's luck deserted him. The light wind died down, and he was becalmed. At seven o'clock the next morning the loss of the *Cushing* was discovered, and every steampowered vessel in the harbor set out after her. Read's two ships were surrounded very soon; and, after a rather perfunctory exchange of shots, he set fire to the *Cushing,* blew her up, and submitted to capture. And that was the end of the invasion of Maine ports.

But all participation in a war does not consist of engaging in hand-to-hand conflict. Besides sustaining crippling losses to her shipping and contributing Hannibal Hamlin to the wartime Cabinet, Maine gave $18,000,000— a lot of money for a small state in those days—and 72,945 men to the war effort. Since her entire population at the time was only a shade over 600,000, this meant that about one out of every nine persons of any age or either sex served under arms, a very high percentage. This drain on money, property, and men left Maine in an extremely weakened condition when the war ended. Then to put the finishing touch on an already discouraging situation, on the Fourth of July of the following year (1866) Portland was once more almost completely destroyed by fire, which started in a boatshop on Commercial Street and swept right across the city. The series of disastrous fires that have punctuated Portland's history since earliest days are the reason behind the disgruntled remark of a present-day tourist that "There's nothing really old to see in Portland except the cemetery."

In spite of the postwar slump and the changing times, Maine pulled herself together and continued in her old industries of lime, ice, lumber, fishing, and farming. Shipping declined somewhat with the rise and development of the railroads; but agriculture grew to take up the slack. Formerly, you remember, only corn was exported. Now as attention turned away from the sea to the development of the soil, a great many fruits and vegetables were raised on a commercial basis, the most important being apples and potatoes, still staple crops. The chief use for the potato crop at that time was to make starch, and factories were built for the purpose, the beginning of Maine's manufacturing development. The raising and selling of dairy products increased, along with the raising of sheep, cattle, pigs, and horses. Horses were, of course, used in great numbers by the logging operations; but, in addition, a Maine strain of racing horses emerged that was in wide demand everywhere. The period between the Civil War and 1900 marked Maine's beginning as an agrarian state.

It also saw the beginning of two new industries: granite quarrying and the tourist trade. The very finest quality of granite is found on the headlands and offshore islands of the Maine coast, and the quarries there have a distinct advantage over inland competitors in that the rock is on or near the surface and handy to cheap transportation by water. The first cargo to be quarried and shipped was as early as 1829, when a load went from Vinalhaven on Fox Island to Massachusetts, where it was used to build the walls of a state prison. The industry didn't really get going, though, until after the Civil War, when Maine became first of all the states in granite production. There was a building boom everywhere then, and it would be impossible to list the public buildings, state capitols, churches, and private homes all over the United States that are constructed of Maine granite, or to name the streets and avenues that are paved and curbed with it.

The largest monolith to be carved in modern times came from Vinalhaven, and it compares with the obelisks of ancient days. It was sixty feet long, had a five by five-and-a-half foot cross section, and weighed a hundred and eighty-five tons. The ship in which it was transported had to have a hole cut in her bow to accomodate it. The enormous columns in the apse of the Cathedral of St. John the Divine in New York came from Vinalhaven, too. They're more than fifty-four feet long and weigh around a hundred and twenty tons apiece.

In the great granite days, Vinalhaven was a flourishing and lively community. Over fifteen hundred men were employed in the quarries—more than the entire population of the place today. Only the men who worked on the face of the rock were called quarrymen. There were also cutters, sawyers, polishers, and carvers, as well as dynamite boys. Some of the jobs required a long apprenticeship, and for some others expert craftsmen were imported, especially from Italy. These volatile and uninhibited Italians lent zest and color to the local scene. They laughed and sang more than the restrained Yankees did, and their spontaneity enlivened life on the island so much that people still talk about them.

Transporting granite was rough and heavy work, and the ships used suffered unavoidable abuse. Some of the quarry owners built their own heavy-duty fleets, but many bought up old ships that had seen their best days and were unfit for other use. Shabby and dingy, with patched sails and flaking paint, many proud and once-famous vessels ended their days laboring along the coast with their ponderous cargoes of stone. They're gone now. Granite has given way largely to artificial stone, concrete, and other materials, just as river ice has been supplanted by electric refrigeration; and the ice schooners and the granite fleet have almost disappeared. Some granite is still quarried, but most of the quarries are now just holes in the ground, with abandoned derricks thrusting starkly above them, rusty boilers lying around them, and the huge wheels of galamanders or galumpuses—wagons used to carry the rock to the wharves—standing idly by.

The tourist trade had its inception around 1870, when Bar Harbor, which was then little more than a collection of fishing shacks, was "discovered," along with other now well-known resort towns of the coast. The railroads were by now pretty well established, and there was steamer service up and down the coast, so that access to the territory was not too difficult for out-of-staters, as they are still called. This, of course, was long before the automobile, so the summer population was of a different character from what it is now.

People came to one of the desirable locations by boat or train and, once they got there, they stayed put for a reasonable length of time. The long and rather uncomfortable trip wasn't worth while for a visit of just a few days. These conditions limited the summer people almost arbitrarily to those of some means and leisure, in contrast to today, when anybody who wants to can arrange a vacation in Maine to fit his time and purse requirements. First, in the olden days, came the large hotels, and after them came the great summer estates, built by families who had returned to the hotels year after year, and then made up their minds that they liked the Maine coast well enough to invest money and the rest of their summers in it.

Even as far back as that, the summer resorts were a serious industry, having a definite effect on the life and ways of the people. In 1890 it was reported that "the greater part of the active population was found drafted to the service of the summer hotels. The young women were waitresses. The men were drivers, hostlers and porters." They were also gardeners, maintenance men, boat-men, and crewmen on the luxury yachts that began filling the harbors of Maine. The shipyards began contracting to build these yachts and small sailing boats of all classes. Farmers readjusted their thinking on the subject of cash crops and began raising fresh vegetables for the summer trade and increasing their herds and flocks to supply butter, milk, eggs, and broilers to these people who, they found, would pay through the nose for high-grade produce. The fishermen augmented their incomes not only by sell-ing their catches at fancy prices, but also by taking out parties to fish, for a price. Farm women discovered that they could sell home-baked bread and pies and doughnuts, hooked rugs, crocheted bedspreads, and other articles of native handicraft; so that some of them built up trades that later evolved into sound businesses. The whole econ-omy of the coast was affected directly and indirectly.

It wasn't only the economy that was influenced. Whereas in the old days of the sailing ships and world trade this isolated area was saved from a narrow provincialism by ventures into the outer world, now the world came to it. Women imitated the dress, speech, and manner of the fashionable who came under their observation, and altered their habits of housekeeping, cooking, and home deco-ration in accordance with the methods employed in the hotels and great houses in which they worked. Men picked up ideas and attitudes and viewpoints from the lawyers and financiers and doctors whom they took fishing or sailing. Two men alone in a small boat on the open sea have a lot of time for the exchange of opinion. The em-ployer-employee relationship existed, of course; but it was very often—and still is—incidental to a friendship based on mutual respect and esteem.

The tourist trade wasn't—and isn't—a racket or a pin-money device, but a serious, full-time business with the ethical code of any good business. It has grown with the years, but it was flourishing already at the turn of the cen-tury, and should not be disregarded as trivial or superficial. It's as much a result of the nature of the country, and as real and important, as the lime or lumber or fish businesses.

Between the Civil War and the First World War, Maine made some internal improvements. In 1875 a compulsory education bill was passed. Many schools were erected, and the state furnished what amounted to private tutors for those children who lived in such isolated places that they could not attend a public school. This arrangement held until a very few years ago. A family I knew well had one young teacher or another living with them every winter for years, until their last child passed school age. It was very pleasant for everyone concerned. But the state decided —probably correctly—that man is a social animal and that therefore an important part of education is learning how to function in a group, how to get along with others.

So now children from offshore islands or the backwoods are sent at the state's expense to schools in towns, in all but exceptional cases. There they learn to conform; and I suppose that's good, if conformity is the ideal. The system hasn't been going on long enough so that I can draw any positive conclusions about the results; but it is my opinion that, while the individual may be happier with his corners rubbed smooth, there is going to be a shortage of one of Maine's most fascinating products, "characters," in a few decades. I could be wrong, though, and I hope I am.

In 1876 the death penalty was abolished in Maine at the request of the governor, who said that it did not deter crime. There was also a feeling that death was dangerously final and allowed no room for the correction of any possible miscarriage of justice. There still is no capital punishment in Maine.

The year 1910 was really outstanding in Maine history. The first Democratic governor in thirty-two years, Frederick W. Plaisted of Augusta, was elected; and the old argument about the northeast boundary was finally settled, through a series of conferences, we trust for keeps, although there's no way of insuring that.

In 1914 the First World War broke out and was immediately brought home to Maine by the internment in Bar Harbor of the *Kronprinzessen Cecilie,* a North German Lloyd liner loaded with gold. Even before the United States entered the war, the shipyards came to life again. Not only were modern steel ships built, but in answer to the demand for bottoms of any sort, the old skills were revived, and many wooden vessels slid down the ways. Maine contributed also 35,000 men and $116,000,000 to the war effort. The Second World War produced the same pattern—the revival of the shipyards and the contributing of men and money to the common cause.

It's incidental, but it's interesting to me that today, because of the far-flung activities of our armed forces, conversations take place that could date back a hundred and fifty years. On the street of any little coastal village you may well overhear a young man say, "That must have took place last winter when I was in Tokyo," or "Last time I run into Amassa Hatch was two years ago in Gibraltar." Or, waiting in the local laundromat for your clothes to dry, you can often listen in while one Navy wife from the nearest base tells another about shopping problems in the Philippines or gives her the recipe for a pork-pineapple dish that she picked up in Hawaii. That's the way the voyagers on the old clipper ships used to talk to each other. The wheel has come a full circle.

6 · Maine Today

TODAY the coast of Maine is going through a period of change. The only stretch of the northeastern seaboard not to have been industrialized, it is adapting to the modern world in a rather gingerly fashion. State-of-Mainers are not quick to embrace the new. The old and tried represent security to them. Anybody who doesn't like the way they manage things knows what he can do about it: go somewhere else.

However, by some sort of almost imperceptible osmosis, the new is creeping into almost all phases of coastal life. A short while ago, for example, practically nobody in any one of the tiny fishing villages east of Ellsworth owned a television set. Now virtually every little house boasts an antenna, and in the late afternoon the eight-party telephone lines hum with women's voices hashing over the latest episodes of the soap operas. The people on the programs are as real as neighbors and twice as entertaining. No one worries about getting supper. It'll only take a minute to snatch something out of the deep freezer. Modern technology has certainly lightened the housewife's load and cheered her days.

Along the coast, the old original occupations—fishing, shipbuilding, lumbering, and farming—are still pursued; but they are undergoing a metamorphosis. Where once a lobsterman or a sardiner trusted his compass, his eyesight, his instincts, and a favorable wind to bring him safe to harbor, now he depends on a gasoline or diesel motor for power and complicated depth-finders, radar, and two-way radio for guidance. No longer is he alone on the pathless prairie of the sea. At the flick of a switch, he is in communication with his kind. A very interesting way to spend fifteen minutes is to tune in on the marine wave-length, known locally as the fisherman's band. Professional matters are discussed, naturally; but there is also a lot of "Did you see that girl Herb had to the dance last night?" "Ina's expecting again, they say," and "The durned fool sold that shore lot of his for five hundred dollars." It's a very edifying experience.

Even the products of the sea differ from those of the olden days. Live lobsters and fresh fish of all kinds, scallops and clams are still staples; but with improved processing methods there is now a great market for shrimp and blue mussels, formerly not worth bothering with. The silvery scales of the small herring destined to become sardines, once a waste product, are now sometimes worth more than the balance of the catch. They are sold to manufacturers of paints, lacquers, nail polish, and artificial pearls. Even seaweed—once used only for mulching gardens or making an insipid type of milk pudding—is now gathered and marketed for cosmetic bases.

The only thing about the fishing industry that hasn't changed much is the fishermen themselves. They're still laconic, independent, and in love with their boats. They still walk around with their high boots flapping, their eyes squinched against the sun, and their heads in the air.

Ships continue to be built along the coast, although many of them now are small boats—sometimes of fiber-glass—for week-end sailors, instead of the lovely clipper ships that once sailed all over the world. The tradition of globe-girdling is not dead, though. Atomic-powered submarines are built in Maine, and they can go practically anywhere; and the special, massive ice-breaking prow of the *Manhattan* was forged by the Bath Iron Works and fitted to her in Bath, just before her historic Northwest

Passage voyage of 1969. Shipbuilding in Maine has not declined; it has simply changed.

So has lumbering. In fact, it is now a little hard to tell where lumbering stops and farming begins. The first-growth forests of magnificent pine have been gone for almost two centuries, and the hardwood second-growth of birch, maple, and oak followed. There is no real lumbering along the coast any more. Instead, there is a lively trade in Christmas trees, which until recently were cut in the woods wherever they might be found growing naturally. Obviously, the supply was not limitless, without encouragement.

So now spruce and fir trees are planted and grown as a crop, to be cut selectively from about the first of November each year until mid-December. There is a Maine Christmas Tree Growers Association, which carries on experiments in the cultivation of better Christmas trees. This has developed into a really big business, whether it classifies as lumbering or as farming. It is really a godsend to those parts of the coast—and they are extensive—where the soil is not fit to grow much of anything else. Each year thousands of trucks start trekking south and west with their towering, aromatic loads, ranging in size from two-foot table models up to twenty-five foot giants for parks and plazas. This traffic is so heavy at its peak that the Maine Turnpike Authority puts up signs each year: XMAS TREE TRUCKS USE OUTER LANE.

This controlled culture is not a bad conservation measure; and the sentimentalist in me rather likes the idea of rooms in far-off places—Baltimore, Atlanta, even Phoenix, Arizona—all fragrant and transfigured through the magic of a Maine Christmas tree that miraculously drew form and substance from the thin soil, bitter rains, and chill sunlight of the Down-East coast.

Farming along the coast always was and still is confined largely to the growing of produce for family use. The big, commercial crops—apples, potatoes, sugar beets and string beans—are raised inland. Along the coast there are some large dairy farms, but the chief agricultural product is blueberries. These are semi-cultivated. They ·grow wild on the vast barrens of Washington County, the most eastern territory of the United States, but their productiveness is encouraged by various means.

The barrens are burned over every two or three years to kill weeds and pests, they are occasionally dusted with fungicide, and during the blossoming season in early summer, hives of bees are placed at intervals to promote pollinization. These bees are rented from companies specializing in the service—an odd business to be in, I think; and a form of entertainment during bee season is to drive around the barrens looking for bears, which come out of the woods, tip over the hives, and rob them of honey, at considerable discomfort to themselves.

Aside from these measures, the blueberries are left pretty much alone until harvest time, when an army of rakers descends on them. Many of these are migrant workers, Indians from Canada. The blueberries provide seasonal occupation for coastal women in the canneries and freezing plants, giving them a little money of their own to jingle in their pockets. About 90 percent of the nation's processed blueberries come from Maine, so a serious view is taken of their culture. The University of Maine maintains an experimental blueberry farm near Jonesboro for developing new methods and strains.

The only other thing to be said about the blueberry barrens is that in late autumn they are incredibly beautiful. The rest of the year they are monotonous, featureless wastes. But in the fall the foliage of the low bushes turns a deep, glowing crimson, so that the whole earth appears bathed in wine. Under a crystal October sky and against the dark blue sea, the effect is unbelievable.

The Down-East area has always had its share or more of summer vacationers, formerly called rusticators or summer complaints, depending on the mood of the speaker. These people owned cottages on the coast and came back summer after summer to the same place. A summer cottage in Maine may be anything from a tar-paper shack on a sandspit to a twenty-room, seven-bath mansion with landscaped grounds at Bar Harbor. These visitors contributed to the local economy by employing native help and services and patronizing local businesses. This benefited some individuals considerably and probably was beneficial to the general welfare, too, in a mild way. But the whole relationship between natives and rusticators was conducted on a small, informal, and personal basis and was not exactly the stuff to satisfy avaricious dreams.

Now all that is changed. With the advent of dependable and low priced motor vehicles, the rusticator has vanished and his place has been taken by the tourist. Tourism is really Big Business along the coast and treated seriously by public and private agencies alike. The state spends a great deal of money on a system of excellent highways, attractive and convenient rest areas for motorists, and state parks and camping grounds. Almost every town has a Tourist Information booth on Main Street. Just before Memorial Day, the little local radio stations up and down the coast start adjuring the residents to be helpful and hospitable to the tourists. "Let's all band together," they say, "to give our out-of-state guests a good time." The language is slightly ambiguous, but the message comes through. Be nice to the tourists so that they'll come back with their lovely money.

Private enterprise flourishes. Motels, overnight cabins, and gift shops do a lively business. Artists, home-grown or from Away, turn out oil paintings, watercolors, and woodcuts of seagulls, stunted spruces, and derelict ships by the hundreds. Some are good and some are not, but most of them find a market among the tourists. The hooked rug originated in Maine, and the old craft along with others has been revived. Women make knitted and crocheted articles, dolls and fancy aprons, and men fashion lamps from driftwood, planters from miniature lobster traps and magazine racks from blueberry rakes. Some sell these things in their own homes and some through gift shops. Many utilize the services of H.O.M.E., in Orland. This nonprofit outlet for cottage industries was founded and is run by Franciscan nuns and serves a very useful purpose.

Ambitious home tinkerers dream of emulating Leon Leonwood Bean. His story is a classic example of Down-East inventiveness, business acuity, and drive. In 1912, Bean, a woodsman, got sick of coming home from hunting with wet, half-frozen feet. He made himself a pair of boots with a leather top stitched onto rubber feet. These were the envy of his friends, so he made a few more as a neighborly gesture. Then he borrowed $400, sent out circulars to all holders of Maine hunting licenses, and found himself in business. Today the hunting boot is only one of about six hundred items listed by L. L. Bean, Inc. of Freeport, all of which have been field-tested and approved. Bean believed in service. The store in Freeport was, until his death in 1967 at the age of ninety-four, open twenty-four hours a day 365 days a year; and it still is. The bulk of the business is mail-ordered from a folksy catalog from all fifty states and seventy foreign countries. Gen. Matthew Ridgway wore L. L. Bean hunting boots when he led the American forces in Korea, and John Wayne, Zero Mostel, Walter Cronkite, and Phyllis Diller among others are satisfied customers. By coastal reasoning, if one man could parlay $400 into a sixteen-million-dollar business, so can another. All it takes is "git-up-and-git"—and a good idea.

One result of tourism is a mushrooming of real estate values. To see this incredibly beautiful country is to covet a piece of it. The price of shore frontage has soared ridiculously. Another result, regrettably, is the proliferation of tourist traps: gift shops full of overpriced junk and falsely quaint restaurants serving poor and expensive food. These usually can be recognized for what they are. Native Down-Easters like to think that they are all operated by fly-by-nights from out-of-state, which may be partly true.

In the days of the rusticator, there was no true equality between the native and the visitor, whatever they might both pretend. They probably called each other by their first names and perhaps saw eye-to-eye on the Administration, but that was about as far as it went. They had nothing in common in experience, background, or finances. Both recognized the gulf between the mansion on the bluff and the shack on the shore and conducted themselves accordingly. There was no real communication.

The majority of modern tourists are hard working middle-class people who have saved all winter for this vacation. They understand tight budgets, difficult children, and doing their own housework. So the lines of communication are wide open. Ideas are exchanged, common problems discussed, lasting friendships formed. The lives of both parties are enriched. Tourists bring more than money to Maine and they take home more than ashtrays made of scallop shells.

There are inevitably a few rotten apples in this barrel —a few who camp on private property without permission, raid vegetable gardens, create fire hazards and make nuisances of themselves. They are the ones who impel us, against lifelong habit, to lock our doors in summer when we go away for the day. They—with their long hair, bare feet, and beads—are blamed for introducing the native young to marijuana and hard drugs, and for any vandalizing and looting of empty houses that may occur. They serve as universal scapegoats. This is doubtless unjust. Manifestations of the times in which we live are uncontrollable, seeping across state borders like an insidious virus.

To accommodate the needs of the tourists, services along the coast have expanded. It's easy now to find a car wash or a laundromat. Although there are no longer any passenger trains in Maine, bus lines cover the area adequately and extend into the Maritime Provinces and to Boston and New York. It's always possible eventually to get where you want to go.

Another influence on coastal life is the United States Navy. Since Fabbri discovered the peculiar properties of Otter Creek, many other communications bases have been built. They bring thousands of men from all parts of the country into the area. Often the single ones marry local girls. The children of the married ones attend local schools, broadening the horizons of the native children. The Navy personnel spend money in the stores, rent houses, and improve the economy significantly.

The Navy as an institution does more. It hires local civilians as office help, sends men and equipment to fires and floods, provides doctors and ambulances in emergencies, opens its adult education courses to the civilian public. Its contributions are not to be disregarded.

The Navy bases have unintentionally done the area a great service by protecting the shore. The installations usually occupy large tracts directly on the sea. The buildings take up little space, and the remaining acres of woods and ledge serve as wildlife sanctuaries. In the past, this limited appreciably the spread of shoddy development. Now at last most of the coast is subject to some form of zoning concerned with both ecological and aesthetic aspects of development; so the danger of ruination has abated.

One indication of Maine's industrial future is the atomic power plant at Wiscasset, opened in 1972. This was the subject of heated debate with some viewing it as a threat to marine life in adjacent waters and others as a great boon, the source of plentiful cheap power. To date, no catastrophes have occurred, and neither have our electricity bills shrunk perceptibly.

The people of Maine, like everybody else, have become deeply concerned about pollution. The larger rivers—the Kennebec, the Penobscot, the Androscoggin—were a few years ago little better than open sewers. No fish swam in their waters, no birds nested on their banks, no boys leaped joyously into their deep holes. Sewage and industrial waste from the mills along their banks were being discharged into their waters and their beds were clotted with detritus from the log drives. Laws have now been passed to correct these abuses, and already there is improvement in the conditions.

Concern now extends to the coast itself. Maine with her deep harbors, available land, and low taxes is very tempting to developers of industrial complexes. In 1969, such developers asked the 263 voters of Trenton, Maine, to approve the construction of a nuclear power plant and aluminum refinery within their borders. Trenton is tiny, more pastoral than coastal. There are lush meadows, large herds of cattle, and a little elm-shaded church. It's pretty but it isn't rich. A vote of yes would have been understandable.

The citizens voted no overwhelmingly, because of the danger of water, air, and land pollution. Proposed oil refineries at Searsport, Machiasport, and Eastport met with the same stubborn refusal; and so did offshore oil drillings. Money is important to the canny Down-Easter but it isn't everything.

Education in Maine was once dispensed in one-room schools. Now the little red schoolhouses have been torn down or converted into museums or community centers. Children are bussed to well-equipped consolidated schools and go on to higher educations. There are many good colleges in Maine, from Bowdoin (1794) to the recently opened (1972) College of the Atlantic at Bar Harbor, where the curriculum focuses on ecology. The University of Maine now has several campuses away from Orono, the original site.

On some remote islands, the populations are shrinking rapidly as the young people seek opportunity ashore. Therefore some of the schools have been closed because the enrollment has fallen below the requirement for state aid. The pupils are boarded in homes on the mainland at state expense, in line with a long-standing state policy.

The town of Frenchboro, several miles out to sea, dealt with the situation differently. Averse to farming their children out among strangers, the citizens persuaded the Department of Child Welfare to place orphaned or abandoned youngsters with island families. The agency was doubtful, but agreed to try the plan. The experiment has been highly successful. The children love island life, and the islanders say that having young ones under foot again has given them a new lease on life.

Once practically every crossroads and gunkhole—a small and obscure harbor—along the coast had its own post office. That, along with much else, is changing. As incumbent postmasters reach retirement age, their little post offices are being closed and their patrons are serviced by RFD. On the peninsula where I live, for example, there were seven post offices a few years ago. Now there are four. In time there will be one, at Winter Harbor. This no doubt will be more economical and efficient; but something is lost. The little post offices in the backs of stores or the kitchen ells of houses gave a village an identity, a nucleus, and served as a common gathering place.

Down-Easters have been forced by events to abandon the political premise that as Maine goes, so goes the nation. Once largely Republican, the voters are now about equally divided between the two major parties, with a growing number—including the present governor—registering as Independents. Small though she may be, Maine still manages to raise an occasional nationwide ripple, as when Margaret Chase Smith became the first woman to seek nomination for the presidency, Senator Muskie ran on the ticket with Hubert Humphrey for the vice-presidency, and Representative Cohen participated in the House hearings on the impeachment of Nixon.

Ever since the 1846 passing of the first prohibition law in the United States, the sale of alcohol has been a political issue in Maine. The Down-East character is schizophrenic. One part is idealistic, above worldly weaknesses. The other is practical and given to human folly. Teetotalism flourishes in Maine, and so does two-fisted drinking. The balance between the two is presently maintained by the State Liquor Commission, with strategically distributed stores. These sell hard liquor. The sale of beer and table wines is regulated by local option, so there are some dry towns and some where beer may be bought at grocery stores and gas stations.

The ancient Puritanical bias is hard to shake, though. Drinking men often balk at saying they want to stop at a liquor store, uniformly painted green. Instead, they want to stop at the Green Front, or even at Dr. Green's. And naturally, beer is sold at the supermarket only to accommodate hedonistic out-of-staters, who would never bring their lovely dollars to a dry state. Oddly enough, a lot of beer is sold during the nontourist season, but we won't discuss that.

This same moral ambiguity applies to the state lottery. Gambling is sinful. Period. Still and all, the lottery helps out on taxes, no one *has* to buy a ticket, folks are bound to gamble anyhow and here they get a fair shake, so state lottery tickets are sold at markets, gift shops, the liquor stores and like marts of trade. The drawings are weekly.

The status of the elderly has changed in the past decades. Formerly when a person was no longer able to take care of himself, he—or more commonly she—sold her house or signed it over to a relative or friend who would presumably be responsible for her welfare thereafter. Sometimes this worked out well, but more often it didn't. The lot of most golden agers was not a happy one.

Now things are different. With a social security check coming in every month, a senior citizen can afford the independence that is lifeblood to a Down-Easter. The checks are not large, of course; but it's amazing how far a thrifty old lady with a lifetime's experience in pinching pennies can make one go to keep her own unmortgaged roof over her head. One night, lying awake in the six-room Cape Cod cottage where I live alone, I counted the women (instead of sheep) within a two-mile radius who also live alone in houses as big or bigger than mine. There were fourteen. This is very wasteful of housing, I know, but it represents a lot of self-respect and even contentment.

The man-made aspects of the coast have changed in the past quarter century, but nothing can change the country itself. Icy green combers still hurl themselves to spectacular death against granite reefs, pointed firs still crown towering headlands, and gulls still coast screaming down invisible hills of air. Fogs still move silently in from the sea to shroud a land that will forever retain its character.

Down-East. That's what they call this land, because in the great days of the lovely ships it was reached by sailing down the prevailing westerly winds from points southwest. But where is Down-East really? To Westerners, Down-East is all of New England. To the Massachusetts man, it is anywhere beyond the Piscataqua. But once you've crossed that river, Down-East still lies ahead, beyond Portland, on the other side of Belfast, past Jonesport. It is always further along, around the next point, beyond the next bay; always the never-attained goal, the never-realized ideal.

Almost no American visitor to the Maine coast has failed to entertain a feeling that he has been here before. Even if he has never previously traveled east of the Mississippi, he experiences a sense of surprised recognition, of return to a forgotten life. Perhaps this arises from the fact that this area has been much painted and photographed and described in writing, so that the white spires of village churches and the rugged contours of the coastline are indeed familiar.

Or perhaps there really is such a thing as racial memory reaching back to our beginnings on this continent. Whatever the reason, this feeling does exist. It lends to a pilgrimage down the coast an anticipatory excitement; and to the finding of one's own Down-East the overwhelming joy of homecoming.

PART II

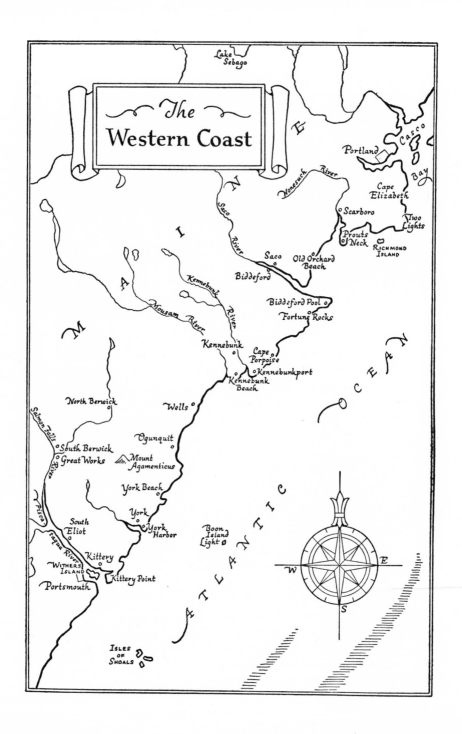

7 · The Western Coast

Kittery, Eliot, Great Works, South Berwick
North Berwick, Isles of Shoals, York, York Harbor
York Beach, Boon Island, Ogunquit, Wells, Kennebunk
Kennebunk Beach, Kennebunkport, Cape Porpoise
Biddeford, Saco, Old Orchard Beach, Scarboro

IN THE EARLY DAYS, the common means of going Down-
East was the sailing ships, which put out from the ports
of Massachusetts and coasted, with a whine of the wind
in their rigging and a whisper of broken water along their
hulls, down the prevailing westerlies. Or you could ride a
horse Down over the faint forest trails; or you could walk;
or you could combine walking and riding in a method
called "ride-and-tie."

This rather ingenious system was employed when there
weren't enough horses to go around. If two men had only
one horse, they would set out, one man riding and one
man walking. Naturally the man on horseback soon out-
stripped the man afoot. After he had covered ten miles
or so, he would dismount, tie the horse at some place
along the trail where there was good grazing and water
handy, and proceed on foot. Both men were now walking,
while the horse was relaxing and feeding. In due course
the rear man came up to the tethered horse, climbed
thankfully aboard, and took off after his friend. Somewhere in the next ten miles he would overtake and pass
his companion—probably pausing long enough to pass the

time of day—and go on until he in turn found a suitable spot to tie up the horse, to be picked up later by the man now walking. In this way everybody, including the horse, had alternate periods of working and resting. It was a practical system.

Nowadays there are any number of ways you can get Down-East. You can go by bus or by air; or by motorcycle or bicycle, I suppose. For that matter, you could if you wanted to ride a horse or walk. In fact, the only ways you can't go are by train or by boat, unless you own a boat yourself or know someone who does, or unless you happen to be working on a freighter. There used to be an overnight passenger boat from Boston to Portland, but there isn't any more. It's too bad that the classic approach to the Maine coast has fallen into limbo; and that the passenger trains have been discontinued for lack of patronage, too.

The larger number of people drive their own cars Down-East today. If you are in a tearing hurry to get to a given point, it is best to take one of the fine new four-lane highways. There is the Maine Turnpike, which is a toll road and starts at Kittery. Or there is a new free highway paralleling the coast a few miles inland, thus avoiding the congestion of such villages as Damariscotta and Wiscasset. Access to these is over the new bridge across the Piscataqua River, upstream from the old bridge. These roads are wonderful—*if* you are pressed for time. They're rather boring, though.

If you really want to see something of the coast of Maine, you'd better stick to the old U.S. 1 as the backbone of your trip, and you'd better not make a tight time schedule for yourself, because there are a great many side sallies and incidental diversions that are going to shoot it full of holes. The thing to do is to stop worrying about time the minute you cross on the old bridge over the Piscataqua from Portsmouth, New Hampshire, to Kittery, Maine, and let yourself be carried willy-nilly on the currents of your own interests and curiosity.

This bridge is quite a handsome structure and a long

one, erected as a memorial to the New Hampshire and Maine dead of World War I. About midway along it on one of the uprights is a plaque marking the state line, and I for one always begin to feel wonderful the minute I've passed that marker. The air starts smelling better, and the trees across the river on Maine soil look greener. When I come off the end of the bridge, I always think, "There! Now at last I'm in Maine!" and everything is suddenly brighter. Crossing the new bridge opened in 1973 has the same salubrious effect.

The coast of Maine is divided by geographical accident into four distinct natural parts: the Western Coast, Casco Bay (which is in a class by itself), the Middle Coast, and the Eastern Coast. We'll discuss the character of each as we come to it, starting right now with the Western, which extends from the Piscataqua River to Cape Elizabeth, just below Portland.

When Whittier spoke of "O hundred-harbored Maine!", he wasn't using poetic license by any means, but conspicuous understatement. However, the description does not apply to this section of the coast. A sailing friend of mine tells me that there isn't a really first-class harbor in the whole sixty miles of the Western Coast and that the only feature it has to recommend it to the navigator is Mount Agamenticus. Agamenticus isn't really a mountain at all, but a 673-foot green hill in York. Nevertheless it is one of the oldest and best-known seamarks and guides of the coast, rising as it does from flat country.

There are a few jutting promontories of granite on this Western Coast, but in general the land is level or gently rolling. Long beaches of gleaming white sand alternate with stretches of sea marsh, where brackish little creeks meander and the salt hay ripples and shines almost metallically in the sun. The water is comparatively warm here, and the beaches shelve gradually, so that the swimming is wonderful—both comfortable and safe. The same cannot be said of the coast east of Casco Bay, where the water is always icy and conditions are often dangerous.

All along here is some of the prettiest and best farming country in the State of Maine, with rolling fields, well-built stone walls, and prosperous-looking herds and barns and acreage. Dark woodlots intersperse the green meadows, and in the damp places along the roadside grow brilliant red and bell-shaped orange wild lilies. In the spring, the leafless rhodora blazes magenta on the barrens, too beautiful to believe. This was the part of the coast first settled and is still the most thickly inhabited, so that it has a tamed and groomed appearance, lacking further along.

Let me be perfectly honest. It is not my favorite section of the Maine coast. Making such a statement is as easy a way as I know to start an argument, because a great many people love it dearly, and apparently no one can take a detached attitude in a discussion of the merits of his own, personally staked-out claim Down-East. Everyone has one spot that he considers perfect, the honor of which he will defend with his life's blood, if necessary. So I will concede readily that the Western Coast has some distinct advantages over other sections and that parts of it are lovely; but there are other places that I myself like better.

My chief complaint is that there are too many people on the Western Coast. This is inevitable, the result of those undenied advantages. It is the most easily available section, has the best beaches, and is the least frequently fogbound, so that chances of good vacation weather are better there than they are further along. There are better shopping centers and more theaters, movies, and golf courses. All this means more people. I like people all right. What I object to is what happens when too many of them occupy a small space, especially if they have come there to have a good time.

This has happened to the Western Coast. Too many areas have sprouted mushroom growths of filling stations, flimsy overnight camps, hot-dog stands, billboards, garish roadside stands, and cluttery eating places. You can find localities where this is not true, but you have to hunt for them, and to me this spoils the section. But very likely

I'm a fussbudgetty type whose opinions can safely be disregarded.

But let's get back. The nature of this part of the coast
is not particularly favorable for the establishment of shipyards. However, in the early days it was the only part
that was settled, lumber was available, and ships were
necessary to the way of life; so a great many yards came
into being at river mouths and on the islands. Many of
them exist to this day, the first one that we encounter
being at Kittery, right on the New Hampshire line.

Originally the land on which Kittery stands came under
the Great Patent of New England, issued by King James
in 1620 to a council of Plymouth, England, the same grant
under which the Pilgrims colonized. Two years later, in
1622, the land was transferred to the grant of Sir Ferdinando Gorges, the Father of Maine, and the next year,
1623, came the first settler, one Thompson of Richard
Vines's company. (The Vines group, you remember, spent
the winter of 1616-17 at Winter Harbor, now Fortune
Rocks, near Biddeford Pool to prove that the Maine climate was not too severe for Europeans.) The town was
incorporated in 1647 as Piscataqua Plantation and included the Berwicks and Eliots. All through the French
and Indian Wars, Kittery suffered terribly from frequent
raids, but it was either tougher or had better defenses than
most of its neigbors, because it was one of the four towns
in Maine that hadn't been completely abandoned at the
low ebb of affairs in 1691.

Kittery was once the most important and prosperous
commercial center in Maine. That was in the days of Sir
William Pepperell's father, who came early to New England in a fishing vessel, built up a lively fish business,
and ultimately settled at Kittery Point, where his famous
son was born. The Pepperells branched out into shipbuilding and accumulated the first sizable fortune in the
New World, solely through their own honest efforts. Sir
William, who you will remember was the leader of the

Siege of Louisbourg, came home to die in Kittery at a comparatively early age, his health undermined and ruined by the hardship and exposure undergone during the fabulous campaign. But his house, which faces the sea, can still be seen.

Kittery has always been a shipbuilding center. One of the early builders, Thomas Withers, had his home and yard on Withers Island and there sent down the ways the first ship to fly the flag of the United States of America, John Paul Jones's *Ranger*. The *America*, a gift of the French government during the Revolution, the first line-of-battle ship ever to be built in this country and a regular dreadnaught of her time, was launched at Kittery; and so was the celebrated *Kearsarge* of Civil War fame, whose victory over the *Alabama* helped turn the tide of the war. You cannot separate Kittery from shipbuilding.

That's as true today as it has ever been. Now the islands in the river that once were used for the drying of fish are occupied by the Portsmouth Navy Yard, which is in Kittery as much as it is in Portsmouth and which is open to the public. This yard was established as a government base in 1806, and it is still a very busy installation. Although the village of Kittery is a pleasant and unspoiled place, it is given an air of activity and liveliness by the presence of the navy yard, which—aside from launching a great fleet of ships—has figured conspicuously in world events.

For example, when, during the Spanish-American War, Admiral Cervera and his staff were captured at Santiago de Cuba, they were brought to Kittery and put into technical custody for a while on one of the islands, until they might be returned to Spain. While they were there, people came from all over in the hope of actually seeing with their own eyes a real live Spanish admiral, who might or might not be at least indirectly responsible for the sinking of the *Maine*. (You must remember that feeling ran pretty high at the time over that affair, and Sweet Reason was more or less in abeyance for a while.)

*The colonial instinct for beauty is preserved in the lines
and balance of the First Congregational Church at Kittery.*

Then not much later, in 1905, the attention of the world was centered on the delegates who met to draw up and sign the Treaty of Portsmouth, which ended the Russo-Japanese War. In spite of its name, the treaty was actually signed in Kittery, in the Supply Department Building, which happens to be in the part of the Navy yard that is in Maine.

To arrive at the village of Kittery you turn to the right off U.S. 1 at a point about half a mile from the end of the old drawbridge. Almost immediately you find yourself in the type of town always—although sometimes mistakenly —pictured when anyone says "little New England village." There are the great old trees; the beautiful, well-kept, ancient houses; the white spire of the church; and the pervading air of peace. It's a nice place.

The First Congregational Church is worth inspecting. Although it was remodeled in 1874, the pulpit dates back to the original building, erected in 1730. It is very delicate and graceful, and I was impressed here, as I frequently am in old buildings, by the unerring feeling for line and balance that the long-ago artisans possessed. Nobody told them what was good and what wasn't. Few of them had had any formal training in design and architecture. Most were just carpenters and cabinet makers, really. But they just couldn't seem to go wrong, possibly because they were unaware of any book of rules which might confuse their instinct for beauty.

Next door to the church is the Sparhawk House, built in 1742 by Sir William Pepperell for his son-in-law and considered one of the few really fine Georgian houses in America. The doorway is particularly interesting to the connoisseur. Across the road is the Lady Pepperell House, built for Sir William's widow. It's an elaborate Georgian structure, rather heavy and pretentious, and here the widow Pepperell lived until her death in 1789. Even after the Revolution, which invalidated her or anybody else's right to a title, she insisted upon being addressed as Lady Pepperell and upon being treated with great deference. I don't imagine she was very popular with her neighbors.

The house where Sir William was born is out at Kittery Point, which is the earliest settled section of the town, on the sea and reached over a short, woodsy road. This house was built by Sir William's father in 1682—it's a *really* old house—and I like it better than the more sophisticated mansions for which his famous son was responsible. It's a weather-beaten, two-and-a-half-story Colonial with a gambrel roof. A gambrel roof is so named because it is shaped on two planes like the hock or gambrel of a horse. The door and window casings show the marks of the broad-ax used to smooth them, and the windows have their original lights, unbroken through all these years. There are lilac bushes around the house, and it looks like a place where people worked hard and lived honestly—a roomy, simple, dignified house.

At Kittery Point there is also Fort McClary, dating from 1690, when it was used as a rallying point for mutual protection against Indian raiding parties. At that time it was called Pepperell's Fort, because it was near Pepperell's house and probably built mostly by Pepperell funds and labor. Then for a while it was called Fort William, for America's only baronet, Sir William Pepperell; and at the time of the Revolution the fort received its present name, for Major Andrew McClary, who was killed at Bunker Hill.

Fort McClary fell into disuse for a while, but was repaired and regarrisoned during the Civil War, to protect the shipyards against southern marauders. It's partly in ruins now, although you can still see the old powder magazine and rifle pits, and the old hexagonal blockhouse with its deep overhang is in pretty good condition. The blockhouse is a very good example of the standard type built during the French and Indian Wars all along the coast.

The site of the fort is now a state memorial, a part of Maine's public park and picnic ground system. Maine, realizing that the tourist trade is a serious business, has spent a lot of thought and money on setting aside and improving sites for camp and lunch grounds. This not only contributes to the comfort and well-being of the tourist, but also serves to reduce the forest fire hazard created by indiscriminate campfire building. The state is dotted with these sites, and it is possible to have a very happy and inexpensive vacation by taking advantage of them. In some places there is a nominal charge for the use of the facilities, and in others there is no fee at all. In either case, using a campground is a lot cheaper than staying at a hotel; and, if you like camping, you can have a wonderful time on very little money.

The Fort McClary Memorial happens to be one of the free sites. There is a custodian in charge to help you, if necessary, and to answer questions; and there are fireplaces, picnic tables, tested drinking water, rest rooms, a beach and bathhouse, diving boards, and swings and slides for children. And, in addition, there is a view.

In and around Kittery, and in fact all along the Western Coast, there are plenty of good hotels, motels, overnight cabins, tourist homes, and eating places to accommodate the visitor. Some are reasonable and some are expensive, but you can usually tell which is which by inspecting them from a safe distance.

Up the Piscataqua River from Kittery is the town of Eliot, a lovely, quiet place, once famous as the home of Greenacre Colony. This was one of those communal experiments devoted to plain living and high thinking which have marked New England's intellectual progress at intervals, probably all arising in protest against the narrow religious thought and shackling conventions of the day.

Greenacre was founded by a Miss Farmer, daughter of the man who first turned electricity to the practical use of lighting bulbs and running trolley cars. The purpose of the colony was to provide a congenial climate and favorable environment for intellectual growth and unhampered thinking, all on a high plane, of course. At first it was really successful, and some of the best minds of the time lectured and conversed there—men like John Fiske, Edward Everett Hale, and William Dean Howells. But as is too often true when idealism is unsupported by hard-boiled realism, the colony later fell into the hands of crackpots and self-interested promoters—actually, I suppose, a type of racketeer—and gradually lost prestige until it was abandoned.

About ten miles above Eliot is the site of one of the very early sawmills, built in 1650, when this country was blanketed by dense forest and the big trees were being felled and sawed up for use in the shipyards below. This mill used gang saws, which were an innovation at the time, and was consequently capable of turning out large quantities of planks, or in the language of the day, of "performing great works." The little settlement that grew up around the mill was therefore called—either derisively or boastfully—Great Works; and it is known by that name to this day.

But the real reason we are taking this side trip is to visit South Berwick, two miles above Great Works, on the Salmon Falls River. Sarah Orne Jewett was born here in 1849, in a house which is now open for inspection during the summer for an inconsequential fee. It was built in 1774 and is in a remarkably fine state of preservation, with a center hall that is considered by experts to be one of the loveliest in New England. The whole house is beautifully proportioned and very well built, and it has a secret staircase winding from cellar to attic. And that isn't all. The old furnishings still remain—magnificent old tables and chairs and four-posters, and fine old willowware, and fascinating bric-a-brac of ivory and silver. It's worth seeing, if you like old things.

Miss Jewett was the daughter of a country doctor; and when she was a child, she used to accompany her father on his calls. These took him to lonely farms far out in the country, and to the cottages of the seafaring men and their families. She saw a lot of life and heard a great many tales of adventure and of the past, as she waited with members of a family while her father delivered a baby or saw a pneumonia case through the crisis. Inevitably she began to write these stories and to sell them.

At the time, most writers were devoting their efforts to subjects rather removed from the common round of daily life; and because Miss Jewett portrayed characters whom everyone knew and because she described familiar scenes and experiences, she attained immense popularity. In 1901, Bowdoin College awarded her the degree of Doctor of Letters, the first honor they'd ever conferred upon a woman. She deserved it. Her novels are still good, especially *A Country Doctor* and *The Country of the Pointed Firs*. If you want to get the feeling of Maine and a little background material, you could do worse than read the writings of Sarah Orne Jewett.

The South Berwick area is also the scene of the novels of Gladys Hasty Carroll, who—like Miss Jewett— draws on her own experience and observations. For several years, a dramatization of *As the Earth Turns* was presented by a hometown cast. Clearly this prophetess is not without honor locally.

North Berwick, seven miles away, was settled in 1630 as a part of Kittery, and became a separate town in 1831. For over a hundred years, plows have been manufactured there, but the quiet little village is best remembered as the place where Berwick sponge cake originated. In 1842, when the railroad came to North Berwick, a man named Walter Briggs, who was a cripple, saw an opportunity to make some money. His wife was famous all through the region for the excellence of her sponge cake; so Walter opened up in the railroad station what he called a "restorer."

This may well have been the original station lunch counter. Travelers soon learned of the wonderful cake you could buy at the North Berwick station, and it became known as Berwick sponge cake. You can find the recipe under that name in any good standard cookbook. When Charles Dickens visited America, he made a point of taking a little girl of his acquaintance, a Katie Smith, into the station and "restoring" her with a piece of cake. She grew up to become famous as Kate Douglas Wiggin.

Before leaving the Kittery area, we really should mention the Isles of Shoals, because of their past significance and because they are the first of the hundreds of Maine coast islands that we shall see. There are seven of them, four in Maine and three in New Hampshire; seen from the mainland, they lie hazy and cloudlike on the eastern horizon. John Smith was not the first white man to behold them, by any means, but he was the first to describe and chart them, calling them Smith's Isles. Around the islands was splendid fishing territory, since the fish schooled or "shoaled" there. The early European fishermen fell into the habit of referring to them as the islands where the fish shoaled, or the Isles of Shoals. They could have been so named because of the many dangerous reefs and shoals that lie all around them, but it just happens that they weren't.

The total area of all the islands is only about three hundred and fifty acres, a large part of which is rock. They are wild and weather-torn and lonely, with very little vegetation except low-growing flowers and blueberry and bayberry bushes. The biggest island of a hundred and thirty acres is Appledore, on which Sir William Pepperell's father first settled, before he moved to Kittery Point, because the rocks, far from being a discouragement, furnished a perfect drying space for the choice dunfish on which he founded his fortune. Appledore was also one of the four towns of Maine not abandoned when the Indian raids were worst.

In spite of their insignificance and barrenness, the Isles of Shoals have had a colorful and varied history. Following the days of early industriousness, at about the time of the Revolution, they had a bad reputation. The islanders were regarded by the people on the mainland as being about half civilized or less, a bunch of drunken outlaws with the lowest of moral standards. Pirates were supposed to use the islands as a base, and a lot of time has been wasted in hunting for pirate loot hidden on them. But in the 1800's, things took a turn for the better, and the Shoals entered into a period of respectability and prosperity.

This was largely due to the arrival of Thomas Leighton and his family to keep the Isles of Shoals Light. Keeping a lighthouse on a remote Maine island leaves you with plenty of time on your hands, so Leighton improved his leisure by building a hotel on Appledore. When his daughter Celia married Levi Thaxter of the islands and began writing poetry which appeared in the *Atlantic Monthly,* the islands enjoyed a literary vogue. They were visited by such people as Hawthorne, Whittier, Lowell, Frances Hodgson Burnett, and Thomas Bailey Aldrich, who in turn attracted the non-literary. Other hotels were built, and the place flourished as a popular summer resort. Business declined, however, with the increasing use of the automobile, until today it is far from brisk. But you can still get to the Isles on a boat from Portsmouth, and you can still find accommodations there.

At present there are a lighthouse and a Coast Guard station on the Isles of Shoals, some of which are now privately owned. On one of these, Lunging Island, food and clothing are kept throughout the year in an open cottage, for possible use of anyone who may be shipwrecked there.

Star Island is the most thickly built up. It and a part of Appledore are the property now of the Isles of Shoals Unitarian Association, and are used during the summer for religious conferences, sponsored by the Unitarian Church but open to people of any faith or creed. This is quite a change from the days when these islands were commonly referred to as "the Godless isles," where children were usually born out of wedlock, the young grew up in ignorance, men and women even forgot their own ages, and the inhabitants made a bonfire of the deserted church.

East along the coast from Kittery on alternate route 1 are the Yorks—York, York Harbor and York Beach. York was first settled as Agamenticus, a fur-trading post, by the Pilgrims around 1624. In 1639, all that territory was given over by a royal charter to Sir Ferdinando Gorges. The wording of the charter reads "shall forever be called the Province and County of Maine and not by any other name whatsoever." This was the first time that the name *Maine* was ever officially used anywhere.

Gorges sent out a company under his nephew, Thomas Gorges, and they established a "city" with a full set of officials, including a mayor and board of aldermen. They called it Gorgeana, in honor of their sponsor, and it was the first chartered English city in North America. But in 1652, common sense reasserted itself, and the "city" of Gorgeana was reorganized as a town and renamed simply York. So now Gorges has nothing named after him except an empty, tumble-down fort in Portland Harbor.

York suffered bitterly during the French and Indian Wars, and was finally wiped out in a raid during which all the buildings were burned, all the men killed and scalped, and seventy-three women and children carried off to Canada by the Abenakis. This was in the middle of the winter's cruel cold, but almost all of the captives survived the four-hundred-mile march through the wilderness. Some of them made their way back, and new settlers came in to take up land at this promising spot, so that by 1775, York was again a thriving community.

During the Revolution, feeling ran high in York. The citizens even had their own tea party, when Captain James Donnell anchored his sloop *Cynthia*, carrying a hundred and fifty pounds of tea (among other things), at Keating's wharf. The local branch of the Sons of Liberty was highly incensed. Full of righteous wrath, the members confiscated the tea, lugged it up to Edward Grow's store for safe keeping, and went home to change their clothes. After dark, now dressed as Pequawket Indians, they broke into the store and carried away all the tea. I don't know what they did with it, but I doubt if they threw it away.

Most of all the Yorks are unusually attractive and unspoiled places, and this is by no means an accident. They could easily have gone the way of so many towns which have been ruined by commercialism. This was prevented by the wisdom and foresight of some of the early visitors.

In 1892, a group of distinguished summer residents from Boston, New York, and Philadelphia formed a Men's Club, built a clubhouse, and became incorporated as the York Harbor Reading Room. There wasn't much reading done in the Reading Room. It was really the equivalent of the old country store, where the citizens meet to talk things over while killing time. Out of this talk grew the York Harbor Village Corporation and the zoning ordinances which the corporation sponsored. This was probably the first instance of zoning in New England, and certainly in Maine. The result is an orderly group of villages surrounded by well-kept summer residences, uncommercialized but lacking none of the necessary shops and services. More towns should follow the example of the Yorks.

In York itself is Sewall's Bridge, built in 1761 and still in use, the first pile drawbridge in America. Opposite a beautiful white church with a cock weather vane is the Old York Cemetery, where there is a grave completely covered by an enormous boulder so that the occupant, a certified witch, can't escape. There are a great many fine old houses in York, one of them, the Wilcox House, standing on land that was leased for nine hundred years. Three hundred of them have elapsed, but there's still plenty of time before anyone has to start worrying about renewing or moving.

The York Gaol is really a museum, a gambrel-roofed building enclosing the ancient stone jail, built in 1653. The old jail itself is enough to make your blood run cold.

*The gambrel-roofed York Gaol contains the old stone jail,
built in 1653.*

The cells are horrible, dark, cramped holes, like caves in
the granite, with windows barred by sawmill blades, teeth
up, a disheartening sight to a would-be escape artist. Down
below is a pit for discipline cases, a damp, dreadful place.
In the museum are Indian relics, items of historical interest, and examples of Colonial handiwork.

I think I had better make clear right now my attitude
toward museums, old houses, and the like. Some people
are bored to tears by a collection of old junk, and some
people are fascinated by it. I am one of the latter, and I'll
tell you why.

We aren't the first people who ever set foot on the
Maine coast. Other folk *lived* here. They came here in
search of something they couldn't find elsewhere—independence, or religious freedom, or wealth, or a home of
their own, or a good job, or escape from any one of a number of things, including the arm of the law. They worked
hard here, suffered, loved and hated, fought their various
enemies, and enjoyed the company of their friends. They
cheated and stole, perhaps, or were fair and generous.
They did both brave and cowardly things; they sang,
laughed, wept, cried out in anguish, or were silent. They
found what they were looking for here, or they failed to
find it. In the end, they died and were buried here, their
blood and bones returning to the earth that had nourished
them. A few of them are remembered by name for the
things they did and were, but most of them are not. They
might as well never have existed at all, for all we know
of them.

The old houses and the museums are tangible evidence
that those people really were here. They are full of things
that they made with their own hands and used every day
of their lives, full of articles that they found beautiful or
indispensable. They are real things, and solid; things we
can see and touch. They look the same to our eyes as they
did to eyes long closed and forgotten, and they feel the
same to the nerves of our fingers and palms as they did to

the hands that closed around them in the long ago—bright and heavy, or gray and cool. They are the bridge—the durable structure that connects the past with the present; they are the visible thread leading back into an invisible time and bearing witness to its reality.

The two beaches serving the Yorks are Long Beach and York Beach, both excellent, with smooth white sand. York Beach has concessions, a campground, and picnicking facilities; it is, in brief, a typical popular public amusement beach. York Harbor has good anchorage for small boats, and there you can also hire a tuna boat and guide. Tuna fishing is a popular sport all along this coast. If you are interested in golf, the York Country Club allows guest players.

In each one of the Yorks there is, as in almost all Maine coast towns today, a tourist information bureau; and, as is invariably the case at every one I have ever had occasion to consult, the person in charge is not only courteous, but extremely helpful. These attendants go out of their way to be of assistance, offering suggestions if you really don't know yourself what you're after, and creating a warming impression of being personally interested in your problems. This may just be a part of their job and training, but it makes you feel good, just the same.

Off the Yorks is a small, low, rocky island, hardly more than a reef, bearing a tall lighthouse. In 1682, a ship trading between Plymouth and Pemaquid, the *Increase,* was wrecked here. Four survivors, an Indian and three whites, managed to drag themselves ashore on this desolate island. For almost a month they lived on fish and gulls' eggs, waiting vainly for rescue. No ship passed, and they saw no signs of life on the mainland. They were about ready to give up hope when one day they observed a great and inexplicable column of smoke rising from the summit of the low green hill known as Mount Agamenticus. They thanked God heartily and set about collecting driftwood to build their own signal fire.

In actual fact, they had reason to thank God, because this fire was directly traceable to the circulation of His Word among the Indians. Here on the Western Coast, close to Massachusetts' Puritan colonies, the religious education of the savage was in the hands of John Eliot, who converted the tribes of southern Maine to Protestantism. One of his converts was Aspinquid, who embraced the teaching of Eliot so wholeheartedly and lived so faithfully by the concept of Christianity that he was called by the Indians Saint Aspinquid. After his death and burial high on Mount Agamenticus, hundreds of Indians from all over Maine went annually to his grave to build a huge memorial fire, into which they threw the flesh of deer and moose and fish and even a few snakes. It was their way of honoring Aspinquid's memory.

This fire was the source of the smoke seen by the castaways. The Indians observed the signal from the island and came out to rescue the four men. So great was their gratitude for the miraculous boon conferred on them in the hour of their extremity that the survivors chistened the island Boon Island, a name which it retains to this day. The Boon Island light is familiar to all coastal shipping.

A few miles along the coast from York Beach is one of the rare rocky formations of this area, Bald Head Cliff, an eighty-foot granite precipice against the base of which the sea crashes and boils thunderously. There's a footpath along the top of the cliffs, and although in spots it is rather rough and brambly, it is worth walking over for the succession of beautiful and impressive vistas that it offers. It leads eventually into Ogunquit.

For many years, Ogunquit was simply a fishing village in an unusually lovely location. Then a few artists discovered it, then more and more, until now it is widely known for its artists' colony and its summer theater group.

The early artists had a rather rough time. They used to go out into coves along the coast to do a little painting at odd hours of the day. Word got around that these de-

A wooden footbridge is a picturesque path to Ogunquit, fishing-village-turned-artist colony.

praved characters (because *naturally* all artists and writers are dissolute) were seeking solitude in order to portray the female form in the nude. Indignation ran high. An artist could scarcely set up his easel before a fleet of small boats, manned by binocular-carrying citizens, would come sneaking around the nearest point to catch him at his unspeakable orgies. This was fair-to-middling nerve-racking for the serious painter, who was trying to get down onto canvas nothing more shocking than the peculiar play of the light across a stretch of the sea. Oddly enough, the artists became no more popular when the innocence of their activities was firmly established. My land, no. Everybody was furious with them for falling short of expectation in the matter of nudes. It just proved that they were sly as well as wicked.

But artists are so common now in Ogunquit that nobody, except perhaps tourists, bothers any more even to look over their shoulders.

A great many of them live at Perkins Cove, a pretty little harbor that offers safe mooring for small boats. The settlement at Perkins Cove centers around the Art School. The little cottages have been decorated individualistically by their art-practicing owners, and the place has a certain unreal and studied charm, like a fanciful stage set. There are art and antiques shops all over the place, and an abundance of carefully quaint Tea Shoppes. In spite of a synthetic appearance, Perkins Cove has appeal; but it certainly isn't authentic Maine coast.

Ogunquit now is a crowded and busy center, with many good hotels and shops. The Indian name means "Beautiful Place by the Sea," and it is just that. In addition to the picturesque rocks, there is a two-mile stretch of very fine beach, with every facility for water sports. All the country along here is characterized by great sand dunes and also, I'm sorry to say, by a high degree of commercialism in the form of roadside stands and overnight cabins. But after all, people do have to have some place to eat and sleep if they are going to visit this area.

Perhaps Ogunquit is best known, though, for its summer theater, which is one of the largest and oldest in Maine. During the June-to-September season, a new play is presented each week, with nationally known screen and stage stars as guest artists. In conjunction with the theater is The Workshop, which presents several plays during the summer and attracts students of the theater from all over the country.

Ogunquit is really a part of Wells Township. Between it and Wells is the Joseph Storer Garrison House, where for two days in 1692 fifteen Englishmen withstood a siege by several hundred French and Indians. The Lindsay Tavern, built in 1799, was a stagecoach stop on the old post road. It is still in business as a tourist home and still retains some of its original features, such as the handmade door hinges, the Dutch oven in the dining room, and the stenciled wallpaper in the front hall.

In the early days there was a salt works in Wells, where thirty bushels a week of salt was produced by the evaporation of sea water. The town also has the distinction of having held, in 1798, the first dancing school north of Boston. But, for most of its existence, farming has been the chief occupation of its inhabitants; and it still is, since the large number of tourists and summer people furnish an excellent market for farm produce.

Beyond Wells are the Kennebunks—Kennebunk Beach, Kennebunkport, and Kennebunk itself. Kennebunk used to be the chief shipbuilding center in York County, but it is now mostly famous as a summer resort. The Garrick Playhouse is located there, and plays are presented during the summer as tryouts before the New York season opens. Some very well-known writers have summered there. among them Kenneth Roberts, Margaret Deland, and the late Booth Tarkington. The schooner *Regina*, which Tarkington used as a studio, may be seen today tied up at the wharf. The town is a lovely, elm-shaded place, with some beautiful old houses. On Mill Lane is the old Perkins

Mill, which has been grinding grain since 1749. Today it is a restaurant, but you can still see the primitive and ingenious old machinery, just as it was when it was installed over two hundred years ago.

Between the Port and Kennebunk is Cape Porpoise, the most conspicuous promontory south of Cape Elizabeth. It was described by both Champlain and Gosnold and named by John Smith, because he saw a school of porpoise there. It was settled early in the history of Maine, but in 1690 the little hamlet was completely wiped out by the Indians. The surviving inhabitants took refuge on nearby Stage Island, where they were besieged for days. Finally, when their ammunition and provisions were running low, Nicholas Morey, a cripple, undertook the hopeless assignment of escaping in a leaky dory under cover of night and rowing thirty miles to Portsmouth, to enlist aid. Against all probability, he succeeded. I'd like to know what he was thinking about out there all alone on the ocean, as he rowed painfully down the unlighted coast. He must have felt terribly small and lost and lonely. But maybe that's the way all heroes feel, a part of the price of heroism.

The little colony of Cape Porpoise was continually harassed by the Indians for years after that. No sooner would the stubborn settlers re-establish themselves than another raid would wipe out all their possessions. They never managed to accrue any wealth at all; so they had no church, no school, nothing. I don't know why they didn't just give up. To add insult to injury, some busybody reported them to the General Court in Boston for negligence to their citizens, because of the lack of school and church, and they were censured officially and ordered to provide same. In time they did, but it took some managing.

Today Cape Porpoise is a prosperous year-round fishing village and summer resort, with a good little harbor and some inns that are famous for their seafood dinners.

Kennebunk proper is notable for some beautiful old houses, and for its fine, ancient elms. Five of these, on Main Street near Fletcher Street, are believed to have been

Stately elms shade the streets of Kennebunkport.

Ornate scrollwork adorns the Wedding Cake House in Kennebunk, allegedly a sea captain's gift to his bride.

set out on the very day of the Battle of Concord and Lexington; and another, on Storer Street, is called the Lafayette elm because when Lafayette visited his friend General Joseph Storer in 1825, he stood under this tree at a public outdoor reception given him by the people of Kennebunk. General Storer's house is the first building on Storer Street. Kenneth Roberts was born in it, and as anyone who has read his very fine historical novels knows, grew up to use much of this territory as background for his books.

In Kennebunk, as I have said, there are a great many lovely old houses, and a church, the First Parish Unitarian Church, in whose steeple hangs a bell cast by Paul Revere. But a house that receives probably more attention than any other is extraordinary rather than beautiful. In my opinion, at least, it *was* a pretty good-looking house—simple, two-storied, well-proportioned, with a graceful Palladian window over the entrance—before someone started messing around with it.

The story is that a sea captain who was planning to be married was suddenly ordered to sea; so he had to move his wedding day forward or postpone it indefinitely. He and his betrothed chose to get married, but the notice was too short to permit the baking and decorating of a wedding cake. To make up this loss to his bride, the captain decided to transform his whole house into a wedding cake, with the aid of a lot of scroll-saw work, painted white.

This tale may be apocryphal, but the house certainly looks like a wedding cake, and it is called the Wedding Cake House. Elaborate fretwork pinnacles rise from each corner to points well above the roof and are joined by fancy arches at the first and second story levels. Lacy peaks rise over the doorway, obscuring the nice lines and the Palladian window, and I should think they'd tend to make the interior gloomy. I hope the bride appreciated this gesture. Personally I'd scalp any man who did that to any house he expected me to live in. But I don't have to live there, and I don't—thank the Lord—have to be responsible for the upkeep of this frippery, either.

Biddeford and Saco, beyond Kennebunk and the only two large cities on the Western Coast, are always thought of and usually spoken of together. (Saco is pronounced "Socko," by the way.) Although they are separate cities on opposite banks of the Saco River, they form an industrial unit, most of the industries being in Biddeford, while Saco is predominantly residential. The chief industry is the manufacture of cotton goods, and the largest mill is the Pepperell Manufacturing Company, whose plant may be visited by permit. In both towns there are modern shopping and service centers.

The two cities were settled around 1630, so they are really old. They don't look it, although you can find some old houses if you hunt for them. The old Saco Jail, built in 1653, still stands and is a museum today. On Main Street in Saco, too, is the York Institute, a museum housing a good collection of Colonial costumes and furnishings, paintings, Maine minerals, Indian relics, and historical documents. The first court in Maine—and some say in the United States—was held in Saco in 1640.

All this territory was explored by Richard Vines during that winter he spent down at Fortune Rocks near Biddeford Pool. Biddeford Pool isn't in Biddeford, but a few miles down the river, at the mouth. Both the Pool and Fortune Rocks are summer colonies now, rather quiet. Between the two are Three Freshwater Ponds, a group of little ponds of fresh water not much more than fifty feet from the salt ocean.

In order to get from Biddeford and Saco to Scarboro on the Nonesuch River, you pass behind Old Orchard Beach. If you take my advice, you will stay in back of it, and you will keep right on going. It's one of the longest beaches on the Atlantic coast, and the beach itself is really superb. Or it would be, if people had let it alone. However it has been a popular amusement resort for over a century, during which a tawdry collection of roller coasters, fun houses, merry-go-rounds, cottages, hotels, dance halls and the Lord knows what-all has accumulated. But once when I was making disparaging remarks about Old Orchard my teen-age daughter informed me that you could have a whale of a good time there during an evening, *if* you were young. All I have to say to that is, I *never* was that young.

Old Orchard Beach's rather lovely name comes from the fact that there used to be an old orchard on the shore. This brings to mind a picture of apple-blossom petals blowing out over the surf. The picture is strictly mental. The place isn't like that at all today, if it ever was.

There's some dispute, too, about the origin of the name of the Nonesuch River. One school of thought claims it was so named because it winds in such an exaggerated manner; and the other says that it gets its name from the remarkable richness of the soil along its banks. There are grounds for either contention. The soil really is good; and the river is so crooked that in the early days of shipping it was impossible to bring a boat up it, and to accommodate vessels a canal had to be built, roughly paralleling its course.

Scarboro was settled in 1633 by Thomas Cammock and his wife Margaret. Shortly afterward, Henry Josselyn, who became the first Deputy Governor and the only Royal Chief Justice that Maine ever had, followed them. At that time the place was called Black Point, but the name was changed to Scarboro fairly early in its history. It was here, you will remember, that William King, the first Governor of Maine, spent his youth, before he set out barefoot for Bath.

Scarboro was twice abandoned because of the frequency and savagery of Indian attacks upon it. During one of these a little girl of eight, Mary Scammon, who was visiting relatives, was captured and carried away to Canada. She was an unusually bright and pretty little thing, and the family of Governor Vaudreil of Quebec was so charmed with her that they assumed responsibility for her and brought her up as one of their own children. She was given an education and other advantages that she probably would never have had if she had remained at home. In time she grew up and made an excellent marriage to a Monsieur Disnincour, a wealthy Frenchman of Quebec.

After many years had elapsed, her brother Humphrey Scammon heard through devious channels that she was still alive, a fact of which no one had been aware. He set out to look for her and finally found her living happily and more than comfortably. She was glad to see him and to hear all the news from a home she could scarcely remember; but when he asked her to return to Maine with him and take her place among her own people, she refused. Her people were the French Catholics of Quebec, who had been good to her and among whom she had grown up.

It seems to me that she showed very good sense. She would have been perfectly miserable back on a Maine frontier farm; and after the first excitement of seeing their long-lost baby again had worn off, I feel sure that her family would have been first irritated, then resentful, then embittered by her city manner and French ways. I doubt if the story would have ended with everyone living happily ever after.

In Scarboro is the Black Point Preserve and Game Farm, where small game enjoys life in a wooded area set aside by local residents; and down near the Prout's Neck Yacht Club is the Prouts Neck Bird Sanctuary, given to the village of Scarboro by Charles Homer in memory of his brother, Winslow Homer, whose marine paintings are, I suppose, as well known and generally admired as those of any other artist. This seems to me to be a very fitting memorial for a man who obviously knew so well and loved so much the coast of Maine.

Massacre Pond, near the village, is so named because in 1713 Richard Hunnewell and nineteen companions were slaughtered there by the Indians; and at the east end of a beautiful cove called Garrison Cove—because there used to be a garrison house there for protection against Indian raids—is a marker indicating the spot where Chief Mogg Heigone, the subject of Whittier's poem "Mogg Megone," was slain. Scarboro is calm and peaceful today, but this is the quiet of an old age that was preceded by an unusually violent and troubled youth. Still, the same thing is true of this whole Western Coast. There isn't a town on it that hasn't been bathed in blood.

The Scarboro Salt Marsh is the largest salt marsh in Maine. The Maine Audubon Society maintains a lookout station there from which it conducts guided canoe trips through the marsh. These are of special interest to ornithologists, ecologists, limnologists, and nature lovers in general.

A few miles beyond Scarboro lies Portland, and the end of the Western Coast. A great many people consider that they aren't even approaching the mystic boundary of the land known as Down-East until they have passed beyond this city; but to a great many others the Western Coast *is* Down-East. Neither I nor anyone else can say who is right and who is wrong. Down-East is where you yourself find it, and if you haven't found it on the Western Coast, there's still plenty of time. It's somewhere down-along, just where I can't tell you. But you'll be able to tell yourself the moment you enter into it.

8 · Portland

BECAUSE I and my ancestors for over three hundred years before me were country born and country bred, I have an almost psychopathic aversion to cities and city life. I have always considered it one of man's unalienable rights to be able to step out of the door of his house directly onto the living earth, to own a tree under which to sit and think, and to proceed along a public thoroughfare at his own sweet pace, be it fast or slow, without bumping elbows with fellow walkers. I'd rather be dead than sentenced without chance of reprieve to spend the rest of my life in a city.

There is one exception to this rather sweeping and possibly childish statement: Portland, Maine. It's the one city I know in which I believe I would be content to live for any length of time. It's a city where— But before we go into that, perhaps we'd better give its background a brief run-down.

Portland's rather hectic history is the direct result of her unique geography. The city lies back of Cape Elizabeth to the south, on a peninsula roughly rectangular in outline and saddle-shaped in contour, with Munjoy's Hill at the eastern end and Bramhall's Hill at the west. The city's center occupies a sagging ridge between the two. It is almost surrounded by the waters of Casco Bay, Back Cove, and Fore River, being connected with the mainland only on the northwest. It's a sweet natural site, protected from storms from the sea and enemy invasion from the land,

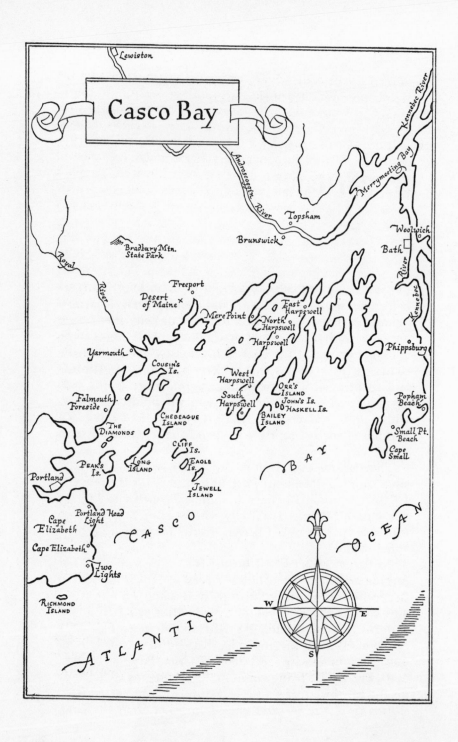

and with a climate whose temperature is modified by the stabilizing influence of the surrounding ocean.

Out in front stretches the great oval of Casco Bay with its many, many beautiful islands and deep-water channels; and back of the city lies a vast area of softly rolling, rich, and lovely farming country. If you sat down and tried to make a blueprint of an ideal location for a city, I don't think you could come up with anything better than what Portland possesses. But this is, of course, just one woman's opinion.

Portland's first settler was Christopher Levitt, "the King's Woodward of the County of Somersetshire in New England." In 1623 he built a stone house on House Island, where he and his company spent the winter. The following spring, he left on the island a garrison of ten men and returned to England to raise interest in and money for the forming of a city on the mainland, presumably where Portland now stands. For some reason he never came back. What happened to his ten men is uncertain, but I don't think we need concern ourselves too much about them. At that time Maine waters were full of European fishing boats, so probably, when they got tried of waiting for Levitt, the members of the garrison flagged one in and made their way home on her.

The next settler in the locality didn't stay very long, either. This was a man named Walter Bagnall, called "The Great Walt," both because of his physical size and because of the magnitude of his operations. He was what the young of today call a Big Wheel, nothing more nor less than a seventeenth-century racketeer. In 1628, he based himself on Richmond Island near the mouth of the Spurwink River and carried on a trade with the Indians that was really remarkable for its dishonesty, even in a day when fair-trade principles, as applied to the Indians, were nonexistent. Governor Winthrop of Massachusetts himself censured Bagnall as "a wicked fellow who much wronged the Indians," and the Lord knows Winthrop was sufficiently accustomed to sharp practice in dealings with the natives not to be shocked by any ordinary cheating.

The Great Walt exchanged worthless trinkets for valuable furs and amassed a considerable fortune by the standards of the day. However, he carried things a bit too far when he charged Chief Squidraset a tidy sum for the well-water he used to dilute some rum involved in a deal between the two men. Squidraset, understandably incensed, came back with a party of warriors, killed the Great Walt, and burned his buildings to the ground. And that ended his tenancy, after a period of three or four years.

This Richmond Island is the island that Champlain called Isle de Bacchus when he was making his exploration of the coast, because of the many excellent wild grapes he found there. At the time he was looking for a good site for the great fortress and city that France was planning to establish in the New World. I can't understand why he rejected Portland. He was enthusiastic about the whole territory, and must have made a favorable report on its advantages. Possibly a higher brass rendered the decision. At any rate, the fortress was finally established at Quebec, a fact which may well have changed the entire history of the coast.

The first permanent settlement in the Portland area was made in 1632, when George Cleeve and Richard Tucker moved their families to the part of the peninsula now called Munjoy's Hill. At that time it was known as Machigonne, and it was subsequently called Indigreat, Elbow, the Neck, Casco, and Falmouth, a name which stuck for quite a while. Originally the English name Portland was applied to Portland Head on Cape Elizabeth; and it wasn't until July 4, 1786, that the town officially assumed its present name. In the intervening century-and-a-half, it certainly had its ups and downs.

They started with bad title trouble for Cleeve. He'd first settled with his partner down near Richmond Island; but a title dispute arose there, and rather than fuss around with it, Cleeve and Tucker moved along to Machigonne, which was a better site anyhow. They probably thought they were leaving their troubles behind them, but they couldn't have been more mistaken. It would take pages to outline the fine points of the various litigations that harassed them, but the general idea is that several patent holders claimed the land. Boundary lines and landmarks were indefinite at the time, and patents were issued in a very offhand manner, so confusion was bound to arise, especially in the case of as desirable a land grant as the Casco Bay area.

One of the claimants was Sir Ferdinando Gorges, who held the New Somersetshire patent, and for a while Cleeve served as his deputy. But then a group of religious fanatics called the Husbandmen, who had in 1630 been issued a grant known as the Patent of the Plough after their ship, the *Plough,* contended that Machigonne fell within their boundaries. Cleeve, not wanting to move again, went to England and persuaded a Colonel Rigby to buy up the Patent of the Plough, which was renamed the Province of Lygonia. Cleeve was put in charge as Deputy President and returned to take over his proprietorship.

There followed a long and tedious quarrel between the Gorges agents and Cleeve's patron Rigby over rights and titles, which for years dragged through the courts first of Boston and then of England. Finally both Gorges and Rigby died, and Massachusetts took over their disputed territory, putting it under her government and leaving poor Cleeve more or less out in the cold. He died in poverty, ruined by the protracted litigations, all his work gone for nothing.

It's a little hard now to determine just what sort of man he was. He was described by some of his contemporaries as being jealous, contentious, dishonest, grasping, and hard to get along with. But these are the words of his enemies, who were trying to gain possession of what he had. Actually, as far as I can learn, he conducted himself always in an upright and honest manner; and, while he pursued his ends vigorously and persistently, his dealings were invariably open and above-board. It was no time or place for weakness or vacillation, and Cleeve, alone and without available funds, had only his own ability and initiative to back him. I can't quite see him as the blackguard of the piece, but rather as the prototype of the intelligent, determined pioneer.

By 1675 Falmouth, as it was then called, had grown to be a sizable and prosperous little town of four hundred, with a meetinghouse of its own and a good trade in masts, furs, and fish established. But that was the year the Indian Wars broke out; and within twelve months the village had been burned and plundered, and those of its inhabitants who were not killed had either gone back to Massachusetts or retreated to Jewell's Island, far out at the end of the bay. Not until 1716 was any further attempt made to settle permanently on what was dangerous and disputed territory.

In that year Samuel Moody received permission from the Massachusetts government to take up land at Falmouth, and the first thing he did was to build a fort at his own expense. Then he induced enough people to join him so that three garrisons were established in the township. Perhaps because forehandedness is as good an insurance as any against disaster, the place was never again seriously molested by the French or the Indians and grew quickly into a prosperous settlement. One of the striking things about Portland's history is that it has so often and so quickly recovered from a number of assorted catastrophes. Of course its location and topography make it too valuable a site for a great port and city to be given up easily.

For fifty years the development continued, until by 1770 Falmouth was as flourishing as any Colonial city, not excepting Boston. It was a natural outlet for the fish, furs, and lumber of the surrounding territory, and a receiving port for the rum, sugar, molasses, spices, and other trade goods required by the entire coast. To meet the shipping demands, the shipyards boomed; and until the outbreak of the Revolution the exporting of masts for the British

Navy and Merchant Marine was a very lucrative business. The city was both busy and prosperous.

It was the masts that were responsible for the second destruction of Falmouth. In 1775 the feeling of the citizenry was generally against England. They'd already demonstrated this by seizing from the customhouse the stamps required by the Stamp Act, carrying them through the streets on the end of a long pole—probably to prove that they wouldn't touch the things with a mere ten-foot pole—and finally burning them.

But there were in Falmouth, as elsewhere, those who remained loyal to the King. One of these was a Captain Coulson, a shipbuilder. He was engaged in outfitting a vessel for the shipping of masts to England when a local committee attempted to restrain him on the grounds that masts were vital war supplies and therefore should not be exported.

He appealed for aid to Henry Mowatt, captain of the British sloop-of-war *Canseau,* which happened to be in the harbor. Things hadn't developed to the state of a shooting war yet, and Captain Mowatt apparently didn't realize the amount of excitement this affair of the masts had aroused locally. He and his surgeon went for a stroll through the streets on Munjoy Hill, quite possibly just to get some air and exercise. But a group of Colonials decided that Mowatt was spying on their activities, seized him, and threw him into jail. He was shortly released, after promising to return when summoned.

He didn't show up when he was supposed to. Instead, five months later, accompanied by a small fleet and breathing a fire that had been growing steadily as he had been brooding on the indignities which Falmouth had imposed on him, he hove to off the harbor. He sent word ashore that the residents of the city had two hours in which to evacuate themselves and their valuables before he opened fire. There followed a certain amount of frantic parleying, to no avail. At 9:30 on the morning of October 18, 1775, Mowatt let loose with everything he had—bombs, cannon balls and grapeshot—and that night landing parties came ashore to put to the torch whatever structures had not already been destroyed. The custom house, the new courthouse, the town hall, all the warehouses, and over four hundred dwellings went up in smoke, and two thousand people were left homeless. The wonder is that nobody was badly hurt. Only one citizen was slightly wounded in the fracas, although some of the British were supposed to have been killed or at least grievously injured. But this may have been just wishful thinking.

One person for whom I have a decidedly soft spot emerges from the holocaust. That is the Widow Alice Greely (or Greele), who kept a tavern in the center of the city. Any woman capable of running a public house in those robust days had to be made of stout stuff, and Dame Alice was no exception. She refused to leave the city on Mowatt's warning, but instead filled all her buckets with water and waited inside her place of business. Whenever a flame broke out on her roof, she tore outside, climbed up, and threw water on it, joking grimly all the while. As a result, her tavern was one of the few public buildings to survive the bombardment, and for lack of better quarters, County Court was held there all through the Revolution and until a new courthouse was built in 1787. I hope she was handsomely paid for this accommodation, but I don't imagine I have to worry unduly about the welfare of a woman of her spirit. Her tavern was a landmark in Portland until quite recent years.

Falmouth was left pretty well alone by the British after that, since the wharves and warehouses were too completely ruined to make occupation worthwhile. The local industries and commerce suffered, too, through the general devastation; so a large part of the population moved elsewhere, rather than starve. However, the place was never completely abandoned, because it served as an assembly point for military recruits. About seven hundred citizens managed to hang on and scratch out a poor living until the Revolution was over and the city could again start to rebuild.

This it did with its customary gusto. The name was changed to Portland in 1786, possibly in an attempt to change the luck, and a period of great commercial and civic activity ensued. Forts and bridges were built, roads were extended into the surrounding country, and Maine's first bank and its first newspaper—the *Falmouth Gazette*—were established. Commerce with England became more profitable than it had ever been, and the French Revolution gave great impetus to American shipping. The defeat of the Barbary pirates by Portland's son, Commodore Edward Preble, served to make commerce safe as well as lively, with a consequent boom in shipbuilding. In 1800, Portland's population was over 3700, a surprisingly large number when you consider that ninety-seven per cent of the entire population of our country at that time was rural.

The War of 1812 did nothing to impair Portland's prosperity. Fortunes were made overnight in privateering, and the shipyards worked at fever pitch. Even those periods when the British blockade hindered or altogether halted the sea traffic were disguised, long-view blessings. Barred from the sea and disinclined simply to sit and suck their thumbs until conditions improved, men turned to the land. Back of Portland lay vast areas of excellent farm land, hitherto neglected. Now this was cleared farther and farther inland and put to the plow. Roads were built and new land-type industries developed. The hinterland was given a chance to catch up with the waterfront. A fine area of solid productivity backed up the city, which served as its market and center; and so it was only natural that when at last in 1820 Maine received statehood, Portland was chosen as the capital, a position it held until the removal to Augusta in 1831.

Portland was incorporated as a city in 1832 and enjoyed a period of progress and rapid development. Steamboats began to ply between the harbor and the islands of Casco

Bay. The first one was the ferry *Kennebec,* more commonly known as the *Groundhog,* because of a tendency of her primitive engines to fail in crises. Since she had neither sails nor oars, the passengers then had a choice of sitting quietly for an unpredictable length of time, or of turning the paddlewheels themselves by jumping on its blades in shifts. They usually chose the latter course; and I don't know whether their fares were refunded in this event or not. Railroads, too, came into Portland; and, with the arrival of the steamer *Sarah Sands* from Liverpool in 1853, the city became an international steamshipping point and port. She was doing all right until the great fire of July 4, 1866, which we have mentioned before.

Again the city was laid waste with a financial loss amounting to millions, but miraculously without the loss of a life. Again the city groggily pulled itself together and started rebuilding immediately. The result was an improvement. Streets were straightened and widened, areas of congestion were removed, and the park system that makes Portland so beautiful today was inaugurated. The city fathers, with a wisdom and vision a little unusual in that era, set aside certain sites of great commercial value as public squares and parks for "protection against the spread of fire and to promote the general health." These parks, twenty-six in number, range in size from small, tree-shaded plots to Deering's Oaks's beautiful fifty-four acres; and they are scattered all through the city. You are always within easy walking distance of one or another, so you never can forget about trees and grass and nesting birds. That's one of the reasons I like Portland.

From that point on, the city's fortunes followed those of the rest of the coast. When the lumbering and shipbuilding industries declined generally, their places were taken by the handling of agricultural products, by the manufacture of a variety of articles, and by the development of the tourist trade. Portland's shipping has been of first importance since Colonial days, and it still is. Being 116 miles nearer Europe than any other port in the United States is a distinct advantage. In addition, the traffic in the harbor has been increased by the laying of the Montreal-Portland pipe line. This line carries crude oil to refineries in Canada, saving tankers a two-thousand-mile trip around Nova Scotia and up the St. Lawrence River. You can almost always see a tanker tied up at the dock in Fore River with the great black hose pumping the oil to begin its two-hundred-mile trip.

Portland was until the 1950s a rail center with two stations. They have been razed. Formerly all mail entering Maine and much of New England and the Maritime Provinces passed through Portland. At Christmas the piles of mail sacks and express packages on the station platforms were mountainous. Then in July when the summer camps abounding throughout Maine opened, the rafters echoed with shouts of children and slightly frantic exhortations of counselors. On Labor Day the flow of youth reversed as bigger, browner veterans of a season outdoors took home their skinned knees and memories. Today passenger service on Maine railroads is nonexistent. As elsewhere, buses, planes, and private cars have taken over. Something has been lost. The pokey little trains were almost community forums. Between the tiny stations, women gossiped with their next-town neighbors and men settled the fate of the Nation.

Portland's economic, industrial, and commercial record and standing are impressive; but the city is prouder, I think, of her cultural accomplishments and of her many famous sons and daughters. I've never been in a place where the citizens in general seem so aware of local history and of the great figures of the past. Usually in a strange city you go out of your way to visit the birthplace of a character in whom you are interested, and when you get there, no one has ever heard of the man or has the faintest idea where—or if—he was born. That is not the case in Portland. There are people who will tell you that in 1912 they heard Lillian Nordica, when she made her last appearance in Maine, sing encore after encore of

"Home, Sweet Home," and their eyes will grow dreamy in the remembrance of that triumph; and they'll show you the service station which occupies the site of the old Jefferson Theater, named for Joseph Jefferson, who appeared there. It's a matter of civic pride that in 1796, when she was nine years old, Elizabeth Arnold sang in Portland at an evening performance in which her mother played the lead. Elizabeth Arnold later grew up to become the mother of Edgar Allan Poe.

The list of Portland's great children is much too long to treat in full, but there are a few who must be mentioned. There is Commodore Edward Preble, who has a street named after him. He received a medal from Congress for his services to the country, and he was commended by Pope Pius VII, after he had subdued the pirates of the Barbary Coast, as having "done more for Christianity in a small space of time than the most powerful nations have done in ages." That's quite a citation for a Portland boy.

Then there was Thomas Brackett Reed, a direct descendant of George Cleeve, who became a brilliant lawyer and politician and one of the greatest men in Congress. He is generally remembered as being one of the firmest and most able Speakers that the House of Representatives ever had. My personal reason for thinking highly of him is a retort he made to what I have long considered to be America's outstanding example of smugness and pomposity. When a certain gentleman pronounced self-righteously, "I would rather be right than President," Reed commented drily, "The gentleman need not worry. He will never be either."

Nobody has to be told that Henry Wadsworth Longfellow's home was Portland. His best poem, "My Lost Youth," is all about the city as he knew it when he was a boy. Paul Akers, the sculptor, was originally a Portland sign painter; and Franklin Simmons, who sculptured the statue of the poet in Longfellow Square, was a Portland man, too. He has a great many famous works to his credit; and for one, the statue of General Logan, he was knighted by King Humbert of Italy. In Colonial days, men like William Phipps and William Pepperell were frequently raised to the peerage by English rulers, but I don't remember anybody else who ever became an Italian knight.

There was also Deacon Willis, a newspaperman of Portland who was jailed for his outspokeness and upon release went up to Boston to found the *Youth's Companion* on which I, along with most Americans of my age group, was brought up; and William Fessenden, the Secretary of the Treasury under Lincoln; and Elizabeth Oakes Smith, the first American woman ever to take the platform in behalf of women's rights; and Cyrus H. K. Curtis, founder of the *Ladies' Home Journal* and head of the Curtis Publishing Company. Then there was the Rev. Francis E. Clark, pastor of the Williston Church. In 1881 he formed a little club of young people, which he called the Christian Endeavor Society. It started as a strictly parochial affair, but eventually spread all over this country and the world, so that there were Christian Endeavor Societies everywhere. I used to belong to one myself. It has been called the most important religious advance movement of the century.

Still another example of this Maine talent for putting original ideas into operation is General Neal Dow. He's the man responsible for the whole prohibition movement. He started locally by forming the first temperance society in America and causing a prohibition law to be written into the Maine statutes. This was such an unusual thing at the time that for years any prohibition law was known as a Maine law. Dow's views spread widely with national and even international results. He has been damned as a busybody and praised as a crusader. Apparently he was actually a rather lovable and kindly man, as even those who didn't see eye to eye with him freely admitted; and whether you agree with his ideas or not, you will certainly have to award him points for moral courage and tenacity of purpose.

Then, to bring the matter of Portland's initiative up to modern times, the city has the distinction of having established over her broadcasting station the first radio parish in America and probably the first in the world.

But let's go back to Cyrus H. K. Curtis for a minute. When he was a boy growing up in Portland, he had a very good friend, a man whom he admired very much, Hermann Kotzschmar, a composer and the organist for forty-seven years at the First Parish Church. Curtis left Portland to make an almost phenomenal success in the publishing world; but he never outgrew his love for Maine, and he made his summer home there. When he saw Portland's fine new City Hall and Municipal Auditorium (1909-12), he presented to the city one of the largest and best organs in the world, to be installed in memory of his old friend and namesake. This is a truly impressive instrument, with an air chest fifty-three feet long and sixty-five hundred pipes, varying in length from one-half inch to thirty-two feet. Only an engineer or a musican can appreciate its intricacy and responsiveness, but anyone who isn't completely tone deaf will enjoy the music it makes. And during the summer there are free concerts four nights of the week, from Tuesday through Friday, on the Kotzschmar Memorial Organ, with world-famous organists as guest artists. They are very well worth attending.

The First Parish Church, of which Kotzschmar was organist, is very old and extremely lovely, in the simple, austere style of early worship. Just looking at it is a religious experience. The pews are especially interesting. They are "slip pews," built with a slight downward slope so that anyone who dozes during service will wake up to find himself flat on the floor. It also has an exquisite crystal chandelier, suspended from a cannon ball which was found embedded in the walls of the church after Mowatt's bombardment of 1775. But let's not get sidetracked again. Let's get on to the present.

Today Portland is the second port in New England (after Boston), Maine's largest manufacturing city, an important agricultural and fishing center, and a vital rail junction. It doesn't seem like any of those things, with their connotations of noise, crowds, bustle and grime. It seems like a leisurely, inexhaustibly charming, large village. Part of this is due to the fact that all the buildings are decently low and comfortably old—although not ancient in most cases—with a minimum of chrome finish and glass blocks; many are made of nicely faded brick. Part of the effect is due to the many parks and to the big trees that shade the streets, even in the business section. They are so predominant that Portland is sometimes called the Forest City; and the trees, as well as the proximity to the ocean, help to keep Portland's average summer temperature in the sixties. Then a great many of the sidewalks are paved with brick, warm and colorful, slightly uneven, and delightfully reminiscent of another day.

Congress street is the main drag; and there you will find the movie houses, the really excellent department stores, the specialty shops, and the bulk of the traffic. But if you turn almost any corner off Congress, you'll find yourself walking along over the brick under arching boughs in a cool green shade. Exchange Street is especially interesting. Here is the Old Portland Exchange, designated a landmark area. This is Old Portland, preserved and restored to its original purpose and charm. Some of the best shops of all are here. They are worth a visit.

I can't begin to tell you all the things there are to do and see in Portland. But I don't really have to, because the Chamber of Commerce issues from time to time a little free booklet and guide to current and permanent attractions, which is available at any hotel, at many drugstores, and at the tourist information booths. From it you can choose your own diversion. It tells you where you can play golf or tennis, fish, bowl, or go dancing. It tells you what's at the various movie houses and what's playing on the straw-hat circuit in the neighboring resorts. It lists special events, like temporary art exhibits, concerts, ball games, tuna tournaments, and open houses, as well as the hours of service at the many churches. It also includes an outline of points of historic or scenic interest and a map of the city.

So, if you visit Portland, pick up a copy of this guide the very first thing you do.

Still, I'd like to tell you about a few things in Portland that you shouldn't miss. One of them is a very simple pleasure, that of walking along State Street. State Street is considered by many to be one of the really famous and outstandingly beautiful streets in America. It isn't spectacular. It's wide and quiet, with brick sidewalks and an air of lazy somnolence; and the houses that face onto it are gracious and simple and dignified. A favorite of mine is the old Shepley House, now the Portland Club, which has an especially lovely doorway, with leaded fanlight and sidelights and a very nice Palladian window over it. This house has a public dining room, so if you are interested in fine old interiors, you can inspect this one.

State Street starts down at Deering's Oaks, which is the Deering's Woods of Longfellow's poem, "My Lost Youth." You remember:

> *And Deering's Woods are fresh and fair,*
> *And with joy that is almost pain*
> *My heart goes back to wander there . . .*

Deering's Oaks is now the largest of the city's public parks, but it's still fresh and fair. It's almost like a well-groomed forest, with a pond where you can go boating in summer or skating in winter; and you can play tennis there, or bowl on the green, while your children take advantage of the excellent playground facilities. But it's a nice place just to walk around, exercising your dog, if you have one. You can sit on a bench and read your book, too, without having your feet stepped on, and if you walk on the grass, no one shouts at you. It's almost like walking through a country wood.

Two of the other larger parks are the Eastern and Western Promenades, at opposite ends of the peninsula. The Western Promenade is located on Bramhall's Hill, the site of George Bramhall's tannery in the early days, and is

backed by the best residential section of the city. The flow-
erbeds and lawns are unusually beautiful and well kept,
and it's a nice place to go at any time of day. But it's especially nice on a clear evening, at sunset. From it you get
a panoramic view of the entire Presidential Range, far off
in New Hampshire, dark against the flaming sky. There
are very few eastern cities in which, when you feel like
looking at some mountains, you can do so simply by taking
a short walk.

From the Eastern Promenade, on Munjoy's Hill where
Cleeve settled, you get an excellent and unobstructed view
of Casco Bay and all the islands. Any time of day will do
for this. The old Fort Ethan Allen, erected at the time of
the War of 1812, is over there, too, as well as a large sum-
merhouse, where band concerts are held in summer. It's
pleasant to walk around under the trees, listening to the
music and looking at the lights off on the islands. If you
want a larger perspective, you can for a nominal fee climb
to the top of the Portland Observatory, which is nearby,
and really get a bird's-eye view of the city and much of
the coast. It was from this tower that watchers followed
the progress of the *Boxer-Enterprise* fight.

Unhappily the municipal beach out by the Eastern
Promenade has been closed. This is due largely to pollution, much of which has been contributed by oil spills.
Portland Harbor is the natural port for tankers supplying oil to northern New England. In the past, spills
have been frequent and disastrous. New laws governing responsibility for spills and better cleanup methods
are improving the situation. Perhaps one day soon the
city will have back its beach.

But to get back to State Street. As you walk up from
Deering's Oaks, you come to Longfellow Square, where
State crosses Congress. In the Square is Simmons' seven-
foot bronze statue of the poet, seated in an armchair and
clasping a roll of manuscript. My favorite occupation in all
the world doesn't happen to be looking at statues. In fact, I

*The Wadsworth-Longfellow House, now a museum, still
feels like a place where people live.*

can ordinarily take them or leave them. This is one, however, that even I take pleasure in looking at. It's supposed to be a really faithful portrait of the poet, and I think that it must be. His personality—kind, gentle, sunny-natured—comes through so clearly. It looks alive, and not like a well-wrought mass of metal.

For the same reason, it's a pleasure to visit the Wadsworth-Longfellow House on Congress Street. It doesn't feel like a shrine or museum, but like a place where people live. There is a small admission fee to the premises, which entitles you to go into every room and closet and into the garden behind. This is not Longfellow's birthplace, which is no longer in existence, but his grandfather's house, in which he grew up. The furnishings are just the way they used to be, and it's so easy to imagine the kind of life lived in these rooms. It must have been a happy life, with the large family running in and out and the rooms full of talk and laughter. It's really a tribute to those in charge of maintaining the place today that the visitor feels just like moving in, closing the door against the public, and setting up housekeeping without rearranging a single stick of furniture or even having to dust the bric-a-brac.

The garden out in back is one of the most peaceful places I have ever visited. This is particularly amazing, since you walk off busy Congress Street, enter the front door of the house, and walk straight through a short hall and out the back door into a green quiet. The traffic isn't more than a hundred feet behind you, and yet its noise is completely blocked off. The walls of the surrounding business buildings rise high above an oasis of trees and shade-loving ground-plantings. Water falls lightly from a wall fountain into a little pool, and birds splash in a birdbath. It's a marvelous spot to find in the very heart of a busy city.

There are loads of houses in Portland that are open to visitors. I'm not going to list them or take you on a tour

of them. You can find the list in the guide. But I do have
to tell you about my favorite of them all, the Victoria
Mansion on Danforth Street. This may not be everyone's
dish of tea, since everyone doesn't share my enthusiasm for
things Victorian. But if you do, this is the place in which
to go quietly crazy. It's the perfect Victorian setting at its
most elegant, rococo, and spare-no-expensiveness. Even the
hinges of all the doors, to say nothing of the knobs and
latch plates, are silver-plated; and the washbowls of the
five lavatories are not only made of the finest imported
Italian marble, but are delicately painted with ferns and
flowers, so that they resemble Dresden china. The one that
serves the master bedroom, moreover, is double, so that
two people can brush their teeth at the same time.

In the big reception hall there's a flying staircase that
floats effortlessly to the top of the house, two stories above.
The rails, of San Domingo mahogany, are supported by
three hundred and thirty-seven hand-carved balusters, each
one of which meant a week's job for a skilled workman.
At the rear of the hall under the staircase is the most beautiful square grand piano I ever saw, with mother-of-pearl
keys and a solid front of pearl, shell, and ivory inlay of
great richness and delicacy. It was a gift of ex-Governor
and Mrs. William Tudor Gardiner. There are two other
pianos as well in the house, one in the music room and
one in the drawing room, in addition to a lovely harp and
a very rare glass harmonica. This, in case you wonder,
sounds like a harmonica but looks like a box full of crystal goblets of graduated sizes.

The bedroom designed for a young girl is perfect, all
frothy lace and ruffles, light blue and cream satin pillows,
ivory satin and blue velvet upholstery, gilt mirrors and
carved cupids. I can't quite imagine one of today's tennis-
playing, shorts-wearing, rhythm-and-blues-loving teen-
agers being at home in it, but it was a lovely room for the
girl it was planned for, with her maidenly doubts and
fears, her budding hopes and shy questionings, and her

modest deportment. It is a room which must certainly have encouraged ladylike behavior.

The best room of all, though, is the parlor. The ceiling is completely covered with hand-painted roses, and it has a gorgeous carved marble mantel and a great, ornate chandelier decorated with carved cherubim. The draperies are crimson brocade, and the upholstery of the rosewood furniture is needlepoint or black satin. It's a huge room, with a high, high ceiling; and you can't enter it without immediately longing to give a party in it—the kind of party where everyone wears long white gloves and off-shoulder gowns, sips claret cup decorously, and listens to a string quartet playing in the background of the music room across the hall. This is considered one of the very finest formal rooms in all America.

But forgive me if I seem to go overboard about this house. In my own defense let me say that it is commonly acknowledged to be the best and most authentic of its kind in the Western Hemisphere, and even the curator of a London museum found it worth his while to come over and visit it. What's more, King George VI was enough interested in it to dictate a letter about the house, which is framed and hangs in the hallway.

The history of the house illustrates very nicely some moral and historical points. The builder was Ruggles Sylvester Morse, a Maine man born in 1817. His coming of age coincided with the era of great trade with the South, and he became established in business in New Orleans, where he married. He did very well indeed, so well that he built this mansion merely as a summer place and used to come North, probably on one of the sailing ships, to spend the hot season.

When the Civil War broke out, the people of New Orleans became suspicious of him because of his northern origin, so he moved to Portland. Here, however, he was equally suspect because of his long residence in the South. Morse was really a man without a home and a good example of what we mentioned before—the mental agony suffered by many Maine coasters through a division of loyalties.

His wife, partly because she was not accepted in Portland and partly because she was genuinely homesick, was unhappy. She is reported to have exclaimed frequently, "Oh, if I could only return to my beautiful home in New Orleans!" This illustrates the homely tenet that wealth does not necessarily insure a heart at ease. Moreover, the lovely young girl's room was not tenanted by the Morses' own flesh and blood. Much as they desired a family, they were childless. To fill this empty space in their lives, they took into their home a niece, Olive Higgins, whom they loved and cherished as their own daughter, upon whom they showered every luxury and advantage, and who would doubtless have been heiress to all this wealth. However, she died young.

This is, to me, a very sad story; and it seems particularly poignant when you think about it in the house itself, with all its elegance and high style. So I hope it doesn't seem heartless of me to remark that it's precisely the right story to go with the background. They are both period pieces.

I wasn't going to say too much about houses, but I'll have to mention the old Wingate House, because it **is** now a part of the L.D.M. Sweat Museum. The house itself, at the corner of Spring and High Streets, is a fine post-colonial mansion with its original furnishings, and is open to visitors free of charge. Its last owners, the Sweats, left it to the Portland Society of Arts, along with funds for the erection of an art-gallery wing to the rear. In this gallery are some excellent paintings, including canvases by Gilbert Stuart, Douglas Volk, Winslow Homer, Andrew Wyeth, and John Singer Sargent. There is one Sargent that I'm mad about—the lighted face of a man against a black background. What intrigues me—aside from the superb brushwork and composition—is that you can't decide whether he was a rake-hellion or an aesthete.

There are collections of tapestries, pottery, sculpture,

and other art forms, too. Paul Akers' "The Pearl Diver"
is there, a beautiful and meticulous piece of sculpture,
portraying a handsome drowned youth with all his pearl-
gathering equipment, presumably lying on the floor of the
sea. Hawthorne saw this while Akers was working on it in
Rome and mentions it in his *Marble Faun*. Possibly
I'm naive and easily impressed, but I just can't get over
the wonder of *me* standing and admiring the very identical
figure that Nathaniel Hawthorne stood and admired half
a world and a full century away.

The Sweat Museum holds monthly exhibits of contemporary paintings. The day I was there, it featured an exhibit of water colors by Maine artists, chiefly of the coast.
A few of them were extremely modern and atrocious to
this untaught eye; but some of them were really wonderful. There are also Visitors' Teas held at the Museum
occasionally, and they are very pleasant affairs indeed.

That's enough about houses and museums. There are
more, but you can easily find them for yourself.

Because I have always been affected by the story of the
deaths of the two young captains of the *Boxer* and the
Enterprise, I thought, once when I was in Portland with
a little time on my hands, that I'd go and see their graves.
This was a purely sentimental errand in the sloppiest
tradition, but I'm glad I went. The boys are buried in
the old Eastern Cemetery, which you reach by walking
along Congress Street to the Munjoy Hill section of the
city.

The cemetery is a quiet, sun-dappled knoll, surrounded
by a high old iron fence, and a little unkempt. In fact,
the grass at the rear where the heroes are buried was
knee-high on the day I went there. Somehow it didn't
seem neglectful or disrespectful, but rather fitting, that
they should lie in peace without power mowers racketing
over their heads.

Yet the thing I found there that made the walk worth
my while was a third grave, beside the other two, with
this inscription:—

Beneath this marble
By the side of his Gallant Commander
rest the remains of

Lieut. Kervin Waters

A native of Georgetown, District of Columbia
who received a mortal wound
Sept. 5th, 1813
While a midshipman on board
The U.S. Brig Enterprise
in an action with his British Majesty's Brig Boxer
which terminated in the capture of the latter.

He languished in severe pain
until Sept. 25th, 1815
When he died with Christian calmness and resignation.

Age 18

The young men of Portland Erect this stone
as a testimony of their respect for his valour and virtues.

Maybe it's because I am the mother of an eighteen-year-old boy myself that I find my heart so deeply touched by that worn old stone. But just imagine that poor kid, only sixteen and a long way from home, wounded terribly, and then spending two interminable years dying in a strange place. And imagine the young men of this alien city, probably no more endowed with compassion and imagination than most of the young men of any time or place, banding together to preserve his memory so that a century and a half later a stray tourist such as I stops in the tall grass in the sunny quiet, with the islands of the bay spread out at her feet, to grieve for his lost life and wasted quality.

Out beyond the west end, but still a part of Portland, is a section called Stroudwater Village. This is an amazing place to find within the limits of any modern city. It's a true colonial village, really rural, almost as it was when George Tate, the King's Mast Agent, lived in a house still standing there and open to the public now. The village is not a restoration or a real-estate developement done in careful Period. It's a survival. In fact, the Tate House is supposed to be Portland's oldest dwelling, preserved but not "improved." It has never had a coat of paint since the day it was built, two hundred years ago, and I don't know what has protected the surface all this time. I only wish I did.

Nearby are some old wooden bridges and an old dam across the Stroudwater River, which probably marks the site of the first paper mill in Maine, established two centuries ago by Colonel Westbrook. Stroudwater Village isn't a showplace or tourist exhibit, but it's an interesting place to go, just the same, if you want to get some idea of what Portland was like before the Revolution.

Of course, you really shouldn't leave Portland without visiting the waterfront. It's just down the ridge from the center of the city. In fact, one of the things I like about Portland is that it is small enough so you can walk all over it very easily, and it's my experience that you really see a lot more and appreciate what you see, if you're progressing at foot pace. This applies anywhere, country as well as city.

You should visit the waterfront, if for no other reason, to eat a lobster dinner at one of the places specializing in seafood. It's an experience. A sign on one restaurant reads:

The lobster that we serve today
Slept last night in Casco Bay.

And I feel pretty sure it did, at that. Another, on Custom House Wharf, is one of the famous restaurants of the nation, although at first glance it looks more like a warehouse—meaning no disrespect. Nobody could be disrespectful in the presence of such food.

But if you're allergic to seafood, the waterfront is still

The Portland waterfront is lined with boats that ply the islands of Casco Bay.

interesting. There are still "Spanish sailors with bearded lips," as there were in the days recalled in "My Lost Youth," as well as sailors speaking other strange tongues and ships flying alien colors. There are ocean-going vessels tied up at the piers, and if you go aboard and ask for the Chief Officer, telling him frankly that you are just a tourist, he will—if he isn't busy at the moment—gladly show you around and answer your silly questions. At the Maine State Pier the Coast Guard cutters dock, and they have visiting hours on Sunday afternoons. At the top of the gangplank you ask for the Officer of the Deck, and he deputizes someone to take you over the boat and explain everything to you. This pays off, I guess because, I once took a young friend of my son on one of these visits, and the minute he was old enough, he joined the Coast Guard. He's still in it.

The waterfront has especially fascinating pawnshops, crammed with very unlikely articles. After reading for years about brass knuckles, I saw my first in a Portland waterfront pawnshop. I was compelled to buy them. So far the only use I have found for them has been as a paperweight, but you never know what the future will bring. There are plenty more, if you want some, too, put into hock by sailors who have either decided to eschew violence or who are in reduced circumstances.

Pawnshops are generically rather grubby places, full of testimony to lost hopes and dire emergencies. But if you can stand a little grime, they can be extremely interesting and even enlightening. Even if you don't want to buy anything, it's absorbing just to nose around the pawnshops and speculate on the origin and history of some of the articles here.

The boats that ply among the islands are berthed on the waterfront, and it is from here that you set out on a tour of exploration of the second of the great natural divisions of the Maine coast—Casco Bay. But that's another chapter.

I'm very well aware that I have by no means exhausted the possibilities of Portland; but I've surely given you enough to start on. You take it from here. The things that you discover for yourself you will enjoy much more than the things I have told you about, because they will be your own private property.

9 · The Islands of Casco Bay

Peak's Island, The Diamonds
Long Island, The Chebeagues, Cliff Island
Jewell Island, Harpswell

CASCO BAY, the second great natural division of the Maine coast, is cradled in the sea-reaching arms of Cape Elizabeth to the west and Cape Small on the east. There are two theories concerning the origin of its name. Some believe that it is a corruption of the Indian *Aucocisco,* or Place of Herons; but I hold with those who think that the name survives from the days when the sixteenth-century Spaniard Esteban Gomez called it the Bahia de Casco, the Bay of the Helmet or Skull.

In any event it's an enormous bay, measuring about eighteen miles across the entrance, having an average width of twelve miles, and covering an area of approximately two hundred square miles. The average tide range in the bay is about ten feet. Four small but deep rivers empty into it, flowing from freshwater ponds which dot a countryside that is more rugged than that of the Western Coast. The shining stretches of white sand begin to disappear here, and the beaches are more often composed of shingle. The whole broad surface of the indentation is covered with islands, like a great fleet lying at anchor.

It is the islands that give the bay its unique and fascinating character. They are called the Calendar Islands, because there are supposed to be three hundred and sixty-five of them, or one for every day in the year. This is a nice tidy idea, but whoever counted them originally must have been seeing double if not triple. The *United States Coast Pilot* gives the number as one hundred and thirty-six. It really doesn't make any difference what the exact number is. They are still almost unbelievably lovely as seen from the city, or viewed at closer range from the deck of a boat, or—the final test—debarked upon and scrutinized at the closest range of all, that of the foot traveler.

The islands are of glacial origin, a fact that increases their resemblance to a flotilla of ships all lying with their bows to the wind and tide. Since the glacier traveled on a southwesterly course, ploughing great furrows in the face of the land as it went its ponderous way, all the islands run in that direction. There are three parallel rows of them, known as the Outer, Middle, and Inner ranges, the Inner Range clear and sharp in the bay, the Middle Range dimmed by haze, and the outermost floating along the horizon like clouds in a dream.

Some of them have the most intriguing names, like Junk of Pork—because it is blunt and square like a pound of salt pork at the butcher's; and Pound of Tea—because that was its purchase price in the olden days; and Pumpkin Nob and East Brown Cow and Burnt Coat and Clapboard and The Brothers and Thrumcap.

Along the coast of Maine there are at least six islands and one ledge named Thrumcap. Long ago, weavers used to make little caps of the thrums, or tag ends of the warp; so any island that resembled a toboggan cap was likely to be called Thrumcap. There are more Sheep, Cow, and Hog islands than you could shake a stick at. Sometimes their outlines vaguely resemble the animal in question; but more often the island was used as pasture for livestock, since sheep or pigs on an island need no fencing and are safe from wolves or thieves.

The largest of the islands of Casco Bay is Great Che-

More than 200 islands can be seen from the tower of Portland Head Light, built in 1791.

beague, the Isle of Many Springs, which measures two and a half by five miles. I don't know what the smallest one is, because no two people I have encountered can agree on where you draw the line between a true island and a reef. The most thickly populated is Peak's Island, perhaps because it is the nearest of the larger islands to the city of Portland. Some, like Hope Island, are privately owned, large estates with only the owners' residences on them; and a few are unpopulated except by gulls and seals.

A few islanders, especially those on the most easterly of the islands, still pursue the old fishing-and-farming way of life, very nearly as it was lived a century and a half ago. About two-thirds of the people, however, are simply commuters who work in the city. The boats which ply between the waterfront of Portland and the islands of Casco Bay are merely the Down-East equivalent of the 8:17 and 5:23 trains serving any inland suburb, except that to me, at least, it is much more romantic to catch the local boat home after a hard day at the office than it is to ride a commuting train. In summer, of course, the population on most of the islands is greatly swollen by vacationists who either own cottages or stay at the hotels and tourist homes.

The best way to get a good picture of Casco Bay is to take a boat trip from Portland through the islands. This is very easily arranged. The boats leave fairly frequently from the Customhouse Wharf, off Commercial Street. There are all-day trips to Bailey and Orr's islands at the eastern end of the bay, allowing you a long enough stopover so that you can treat yourself to a shore dinner, if you want to; and there are shorter trips of about three hours to Great Chebeague and Cliff Island. There are even shorter ones too, but I wouldn't recommend them, as they go only to the more suburban-type islands and don't really give you a fair idea of the territory. The boats aren't operated primarily as sightseeing tours for the visitor, but are the inter-island freight, mail, and passenger service. They run regularly all the year round, whether there are any tourists or not.

It's fun to go on a boat ride. Within fifteen minutes of leaving the dock, you feel miles away from paved streets and crowded business blocks. The islands slide past, with the sea breaking like lace against their tree-crowned ramparts. The gulls coast over, delicately poised on nothing, their arched wings sensitive to the invisible currents of the air. They mew and scream incessantly, their bold eyes peering down their cruel beaks deep into the water below. Sighting a fish, they fold their wings and plunge like plummets into the depths, then rise to shake the water from their feathers in a curiously fussy gesture. Families of seals bask on ledges and watch the boat go by, the older ones a little worried, the pups merely inquisitive and not at all frightened. They are the most appealing little things you ever saw in your life.

As the boat approaches the landing of any of the islands, the whistle is blown, and you can see all those who have nothing better to do converging down the roads that lead to the dock. Some are meeting guests and some come to inquire if the merchandise they ordered from the mainland is aboard today, but more treat the occasion as a form of entertainment or a social event. The boat crew and their friends ashore exchange greetings and current gossip at the tops of their lungs, and everything is very relaxed and informal. You find yourself chatting cosily with complete strangers about practically anything at all.

Islands have always seemed to exert a peculiar fascination on most people. Even those who really wouldn't care to live on one find themselves in love with the *idea* of an island. An island seems to be the symbol of independence and individuality, of freedom and integration and safety, of a world of one's own, where all is ordered according to one's heart's desire, large enough to encompass every personal ambition and dream, but small enough for complete knowledge. In a way, an island is a state of mind almost as much as it is a topographical feature of a landscape, and I think that this has always been so. Certainly for hundreds of years the idea of an island has been used constantly in literature and even religion to represent any number of diverse philosophies and view points. Possibly it is because of these extensive literary connotations that islands seem so romantic, although not necessarily. I know people who can barely read, who still love islands.

In the early days, however, the islands of Casco Bay were among the first places to be settled for much less fancy reasons than these. Romance didn't enter into the picture at all. They were quite simply the safest places to live, the least open to attack from enemies. The early colonists were voyagers and fishermen, and the sea was never a barrier to them. Rather it was an open highway which they used safely and confidently and a wide moat between them and the savages of the mainland, whom they had some occasion to fear. Therefore when the first settler of the Casco Bay area, Christopher Levitt, decided to spend the winter of 1623 in the New World, it was House Island that he chose for his base. After all, he had only ten men, and they undoubtedly felt more comfortable with the open sea around them, instead of being surrounded by a dark, close-crowding forest.

The House Island of Levitt's garrison was not the same island that is called by that name today. It was probably either York or Cushing Island. The modern House Island is one of the first to be seen after leaving Portland Harbor, a small, low island with the granite walls of Fort Scammell, which is disused, at one end. There are also on this little island the ruin of a stone house erected by fishermen almost three centuries ago in 1661, and the empty buildings of the former immigration center.

On the other side of the channel is Fort Gorges, named for the Father of Maine. It is a low, octagonal stone structure occupying almost the whole of a marshy island, and it is one of the most depressing things I have ever seen— why, I'm not sure. Possibly if I didn't know that it is the only monument in the world to a man whose vision and labor were very largely responsible for the initial devel-

opment of the Maine coast, I wouldn't find it so sorry
a sight. But it's mighty cold and bleak and it gives you the
shivers.

The first stop the boat makes is at Peak's Island, a
large, thickly populated place where many of Portland's
workers live. It is one of the insular wards of the city, and
the boys and girls of Peak's attend high school in Portland,
taking the boat morning and night instead of a school bus.
Several hundred people live on this island the year round,
and in summer the population is many times multiplied
by visitors. The place combines the advantages of a shore
resort with easy access to city conveniences and entertainment.

Before colonization, Peak's Island was a rendezvous of
the Indians, who went there for their clambakes and summer excursions to the sea, and Indian relics have been
found here in great numbers, and still occasionally come
to light. Later the whole island was divided among four
families—Sterlings, Bracketts, Trotts, and Skillings—each
having its own strip and family landing. Then, when the
steam ferries came into being, Peak's enjoyed a great boom.
At that time, every city worth its salt had an amusement
park, with roller coasters, vaudeville, roller-skating rinks,
and fireworks every evening; so Greenwood Park sprang
up on Peak's. There was also a repertory theater, and it
was quite the vogue to ride the ferry over to the island
and take in the show, an outing that cost twenty-five cents.
This included transportation both ways *and* admission.

Almost all of us were taught "The Wreck of the Hes-
perus," way back in grade school, but perhaps you didn't
know that Longfellow based his poem on the wreck of the
schooner *Helen Eliza,* which was driven onto Peak's Island
in the great storm of 1869. She broke up on the rocks,
and only one member of the crew was rescued, a young
man who had not long before been the sole survivor of
a ship which foundered during a hurricane off the West
Indies. Prudently he decided that enough was enough, and
in order to make sure that he wasn't caught in a third

and possibly final wreck, he moved well away from the sea to a farm in New Hampshire. He should have taken the further precaution of learning how to swim; for, shortly after taking up residence on his inland acres, he started to cross a small stream on a slippery log, fell off, and drowned.

From Peak's the boat proceeds up a deep channel between the double island of Little and Great Diamond on the one side, and Long Island on the other. This is where the scenery starts to grow more and more beautiful. The Diamonds are really rugged, with crags plunging down into the water, dark woods outlined against the sky, and sudden fields open to the sun. They are both almost entirely summer colonies, although on Great Diamond you will find Fort McKinley, which is part of the Portland harbor defense system. The fort is open to visitors, and in the summer it is used as a training post for the R.O.T.C., the O.R.C., and the C.M.T.C.

Great Diamond used to be called Hog Island because it was used as a great, safe hog pen; and in addition, it was the source of tons of hay, which was cut, loaded onto boats, and sold in Portland. This was in the horse-drawn era. The horse gave way to the gasoline motor, the hog gave way to the summer resident, the hay fields grew up to brush, and the summer people renamed the island, because the original name laid them open to too many obvious and not very funny jokes. "Hog Island" was inappropriate to such a lovely spot, anyhow.

Long Island also is unusually beautiful, and it is a most satisfactory place to spend a vacation, since it has been quite well developed. There are excellent roads, many lovely footpaths winding through pine groves, and some good inns and hotels, some of which boast their own mineral springs, supposed to have great medicinal properties. Long Island—and this is not true of all the islands—possesses some good sandy beaches for those who like to swim. One of these, on the ocean side, is called Singing Beach, because when the wind and tide are ex-

actly right, a curious musical tone arises from it. It's a
rather eerie effect, but very interesting. I should have
thought the sound would have scared the superstitious
Indians half to death, but apparently it didn't, since they
used the island as a picnic ground, and there still exist
great shell heaps around which you can sometimes find
flint arrowheads.

The navy has a fueling depot on Long Island, which
served the North Atlantic Fleet during World War II. At
that time there were often as many as fifty or sixty ships
riding at anchor in Hussey's Sound, waiting to refuel. It
must have been an impressive sight. The last time I was
there, there were no vessels at all. Instead, on every one
of the twenty-four posts of the fueling pier sat an enormous gull. I thought that some artistic soul had carved
and painted them, and stuck them up there for picturesque reasons, and my off-hand opinion was that he'd over-
done it a little. In Nature, there wouldn't be one on *every*
post, and they wouldn't all be facing in the same direction.
At this point of my reveries, one of them took off on a
private errand, and his place was immediately taken by
another who materialized out of the blue, made a two-
point landing, and promptly struck the exact pose of all
the rest. I was left with the need to revise my thinking on
the relationship between Art and Nature.

My favorites among the islands of Casco Bay are the
two Chebeagues, Great and Little. Nobody lives on Little
Chebeague now, more's the pity. In the center of it is a
grove of trees, sheltering some abandoned houses, and all
around the perimeter open fields run down to the rocks
and beaches. Somehow it looks just right, just like the
kind of an island you would like to own—not too big, but
big enough, and with a nice balance of meadow and wood
on its seventy-five acres.

There used to be a fair-sized colony on Little Chebeague, but during World War II the government took
over the island as a naval recreation center and evacuated
all the inhabitants. After the war, the navy in turn moved

out, and for a while the island was occupied only by a
caretaker and his family. As is the case of some of the
other islands that are privately occupied, the boat discontinued regular service and stopped only if there was
freight to deliver or if someone wanted to get off, in which
event a signal was hung at the end of the dock. Usually
this is a red flag or a lantern or some similar device.

But Little Chebeague is one of the Middle Range of
islands, which at some seasons of the year are so shrouded
in fog that an ordinary signal is hard to discern. When
that happened the caretaker, who raised sheep, caught one
of his flock and tied it to the end of the wharf. Naturally
the sheep didn't like this very much, so it plunged around,
baa-ing at the top of its lungs. It was big and active and
noisy enough so that the helmsman, unless he was totally
deaf and blind, couldn't miss it and obediently put in. The
caretaker is gone now, though, so the boat never stops
at Little Chebeague any more. Only vandals go there to
break windows and carry away whatever isn't nailed down.

At low tide a sandspit connects Little Chebeague with
Great Chebeague. When the tide is in, the sandspit is
covered with water, leaving a point called Indian Point
at the Great Chebeague end. Very conspicuous on Indian
Point is a lone tree, standing all by itself on the wind-
swept barren. Well over a century and a half ago, way
back in 1791, a man named Wentworth Ricker came to
settle on Great Chebeague. He took up land at Indian
Point and started a garden there. One day he discovered
a tiny oak growing in his garden patch. He tended and
encouraged it, and eventually it grew to be a landmark—
and seamark, well known to all navigators of the bay. Early
in this century a Philadelphian, Ellis Ames Ballard, bought
Indian Point and built a summer home there. He too
took a proprietary interest in the tree and spent a great
deal of money on tree surgeons, to keep it in good health.
Then came our recent series of hurricanes, during which
hundreds of younger trees on Great Chebeague suc-

cumbed. But not the Indian Point tree. It still serves as a point of reference to Chebeague Islanders.

There are about three hundred permanent residents of Great Chebeague, most of whom make their living by fishing, lobstering, farming, and acting as caretakers of the summer places. In summer the population reaches about two thousand, and so in love with the island do some of the visitors become that not infrequently they stay later and later into the fall and end by becoming permanent residents themselves. This is not surprising. Great Chebeague is a perfectly beautiful island, with rocky points, little sandy beaches, shining stands of spruce and fir and pine, and spreading fields full of daisies and buttercups and ferns and wild berries. The winding roads are bright with crushed clam shells and, as you follow them, you have opened to your delighted eyes vista after vista of the bay with its sprinkling of islands. Even when you're out of sight of the sea, you know it is there by the sound of it and by some quality of the air—something more than saltiness and purity. I can't tell you what that quality is; but you seem to be immersed in peace, so that it soaks into your very blood and bones. This isn't a poetic fancy on my part. It's the truth. There is probably a physiological explanation for this, but the effect is almost spiritual.

Nowadays the summer people furnish the chief source of the islanders' income, but this was not always so. During the latter part of the nineteenth century, when the granite quarries farther up the coast were in their heyday of production, much of the granite was transported in sloops built and owned on Chebeague and usually manned by Chebeague men. The Chebeague stone sloops were familiar sights in Maine waters, and very comfortable fortunes were built up through their operations. This accounts for some of the unusually fine houses other than those built by summer people which you will see on the island. "Stone sloop money" is a common term used to account for any evidences of undue splurging in the past.

It sounds a little bit like double talk the first time you hear it delivered in the dead-pan Maine manner, before you know what it means.

Great Chebeague has hotels, bathing and boating facilities, fishing, tennis courts, croquet grounds, and a nine-hole golf course which I believe must be one of the most scenic anywhere. It lies on the ocean side of the island, and I fail to see how anyone can concentrate on his game with all that beauty spread out before him.

Beyond Great Chebeague is Cliff Island, once called Crotch Island. Either name describes it well. This, too, is a ward of Portland, although it seems a million miles away from Congress Street, and the sons and daughters of the three hundred residents make the daily round trip to the city to attend high school. A great many of the inhabitants are Seventh Day Adventists and observe the Sabbath on Saturday, which makes for a little confusion in business matters. Lobstering, fishing, and summer people are the chief occupations, as on most of these islands of the Outer Range.

Cliff Island was once the bailiwick of a villain, Captain Keiff, who lived there alone in a log hut. On stormy nights, he used to tie a lantern around the neck of his horse and ride up and down the shore. Ships at sea would be misguided by this light and be wrecked on the very dangerous reefs and ledges that surround the island. Captain Keiff would then salvage the cargo and kill off any survivors, whom he buried in a grassy meadow that is still known as Keiff's Garden. It is located near the ravine that splits the island. He is supposed to have become rich as a result of this evil practice, but I'm not sure how that was managed. Too many practical difficulties would seem to lie in the way of converting the water-damaged goods into cash without having the nature of his activities uncovered. I imagine that all he really got out of it was articles that might come in handy around the log cabin, and whatever perverted satisfaction this form of endeavor offered his warped mind.

Near Cliff Island is Eagle Island, where Admiral Robert
E. Peary, the discoverer of the North Pole, lived; and beyond that is Jewell Island, the outermost of the large
islands, named for George Jewell, who settled there in
1636. This is the island to which some of the settlers of
Portland (then Falmouth) retreated when the town was
wiped out by the French and the Indians in 1675; and
the Lord knows they should have been safe enough in
this remote and sea-girt spot.

Possibly its remoteness and wildness is the reason why
Jewell Island was picked over two centuries ago as a likely
place for Captain Kidd to have buried his treasure.
Actually, Kidd never went anywhere near it, but people
who are romantic and sanguine enough to go searching
for pirate loot sometimes are too out-of-this-world to
bother ascertaining the facts. However that may be, the
legend of buried treasure has persisted on Jewell, and
seekers have gone to great lengths above and beyond
simply digging in promising places to find it.

Sacrificial lambs have been slaughtered and their blood
poured on likely locations; divining rods have been employed; soothsayers have been consulted; mesmerists have
hypnotized subjects and instructed them to indicate the
spot; mediums have been in touch with Kidd's ghost; and
the witless babblings of the feeble-minded have been
heeded as possible expressions of second sight. In brief, an
all-out effort to get something for nothing has been made
on Jewell Island. To date, no one has found a red cent.

There is a tale, of course, that a Captain Jonathan
Chase found the treasure, killing and burying a helper in
the process. This yarn is backed up by a great deal of
circumstantial evidence which varies widely in the telling, and is enlivened by a lot of lurid embroidery. It's only
one of many legends, all of which lean heavily on mystery
and lightly on fact. As far as I am concerned, there is
no treasure on Jewell Island and never was. But don't let
me discourage you. I could be wrong.

Harpswell, which includes Bailey Island and Orr's

Island, is the most broken and tattered township in Maine, and it is said to have more and a greater variety of islands than any town in North America. It consists of a series of ragged peninsulas and points, the longest of which measures nine miles, flanked on either side by chains of small islands. Sea waters wind in a maze through the town, giving it a disunited and rugged beauty. Because many of these channels are narrow, they are bridged, and it is possible to drive onto some of the islands without realizing that you have actually left the mainland behind you. The boat lands at South Harpswell, in Potts Harbor, on the narrow strip of mainland known as Harpswell Neck. But it's very hard here to distinguish mainland from island. This entire township is a fishing and vacationing area, popular because of its great beauty and its availability by either land or sea.

One of the smaller islands, Ragged Island, has a great literary tradition. For many years it was the summer home of Edna St. Vincent Millay, whom many consider one of America's finest poets; and before that it served as the scene of the Elm Island series of books for boys (and tomboys) by Elijah Kellogg. I don't suppose children read them now, but I used to love them when I was a child. Elijah Kellogg himself was the first pastor of the Congregational Church (1843) still standing in Harpswell Center, a man much beloved by everyone. He is perhaps best known for his "Spartacus to the Gladiators," a true classic of its kind. When I was young, we always devoted Friday afternoons in school to recitations; and someone invariably chose to do Spartacus. I can hear it now:— "If ye are men, follow me! Strike down your guard, gain the mountain passes, and then do bloody work!" It used to chill my blood.

Another island, Pond Island, was the boyhood home of Robert Peter Tristram Coffin and the scene of his book *The Lost Paradise,* one of the best books of childhood recollections I have ever read. It gives the feeling of island life in an almost uncanny manner. Orr's Island also has literary connotations. Harriet Beecher Stowe, who wrote *Uncle Tom's Cabin,* spent a summer there, out of which came her early American classic, *The Pearl of Orr's Island.* You can still see the little white cottage that served as setting for the story.

Between Orr's Island and Bailey Island is an unusual and beautiful bridge. It is made of huge granite blocks laid in the fashion of a honeycomb, to permit the strong tides to flow freely through it. Otherwise it might easily be swept away. There was one other bridge in the world like it, in Scotland, but the Scottish bridge was destroyed by bombing in the Second World War. Bailey Island has a small year-round population, which is greatly increased during the summer. It's a nice place to spend a vacation.

It's also one of the few places along the Maine coast where there is a well-authenticated story of pirate treasure actually having been found. A poor farmer named John Wilson was out duck hunting one day when, in an attempt to retrieve a fallen bird, he slipped into a crevasse between two ledges. In his scramble to climb out, he uncovered an iron pot filled with pieces of Spanish gold. Apparently there was no curse on this money, which he exchanged for twelve-thousand dollars in coin of the realm, a comfortable fortune at the time. He used it to buy a handsome sloop and the best farm on Bailey, married, produced a fine family, and became one of the leaders of the community.

Another pirate story of the locality is much less probable, but much more colorful. It concerns little John's Island, where Gene Tunney and the members of the Lauder family summer. Long ago there was a tavern on the north end of the island, a hangout of sailors. One of these was a Portuguese who never did any work but always had plenty of gold and silver to spend, when he blew in from parts unknown. This went on for years.

Finally the Portuguese died in a foreign land, but, before he breathed his last, he gave a shipmate a map of John's Island, showing the location of a hidden well. At the bottom of this, he said, was more gold and silver than half a dozen men could carry away. He knew (he said) because he'd helped put it there.

The next time the recipient of these confidences returned to the Maine coast he enlisted the aid of a trusted friend, took his map, and went looking for the treasure. They waited for a good dark night, having no desire to share their good fortune. They found the well, all right, and were just getting down to business when out of the woods tore a great black stallion, eyes ablaze, hoofs flying, nostrils red and flaring. The diggers dropped their tools and ran for their lives. The next day they returned to look the scene over. The horse's hoofprints were all over the place, but they couldn't find the horse. Encouraged, they came back again that night, and again the same thing happened. A third time they tried to recover the loot, with the same result; so then they gave up. No one else ever saw the crazy stallion; and I don't suppose it's necessary to add that no one ever found the treasure, either.

These islands of Harpswell are full of stories, some of them true. There is the story of Haskell Island, of which Jimmy Doolittle was at one time part owner. It seems that a little less than a century ago an old lobsterman named Humphrey was the only inhabitant of Haskell. He lived there alone except for a plague of rats that overran the island, stealing fish from his bait barrel and causing him great annoyance. His friends wanted him to move into Harpswell, but he was set in his ways and refused to go. So they kept a loose watch over him by checking each morning to be sure smoke was rising from his chimney, a sign that he was all right.

One morning no smoke was visible, so a group went over to investigate. To their horror, they found that the poor old man had died and been almost eaten by the rats. They went to work with clubs and sticks to exterminate the vermin; but the next spring they were as thick as ever, so Haskell was given up for a time.

Then two young fishermen named Mills from North

Harpswell decided that they could lick the problem. They established themselves on Haskell with a dozen of the biggest and toughest cats they could collect. It was a nip-and-tuck fight, but the cats finally emerged triumphant. They wiped out the rats. The Mills had been smart, but not quite smart enough. They hadn't had the foresight to confine their pets to one sex, and soon the island was overrun in turn by cats. The brothers were kept busy catching fish to feed them, now that the rat supply was exhausted. But they didn't care. They loved their cats, and their cats loved them.

This wave of good feeling was strictly confined to the Mills family. It was impossible for anyone else to land without being attacked by great packs of really vicious cats. The owner of the island—for the Mills boys were actually only squatters—at last had a chance to sell it; but, when he tried to go ashore with his prospective customer, they were driven off by the cats. So he told the boys they'd have to do something about the nuisance. They did nothing.

Then one morning they awoke to find the whole island covered with dead cats. Someone had come in the night and spread poison for them. The brothers were heartbroken, and went away never to return. The story ends with the statement that never to this day has there been another cat or rat on Haskell Island, but I don't know whether this is true or not.

A yarn that I find extremely disturbing concerns John Darling of Harpswell. Probably this bothers me because it happened, if not within my memory, at least within my lifetime, and therefore seems more real and immediate than some of the other tales to which remoteness in time gives the quality of the legendary.

John Darling was an undesirable citizen—not a criminal or a menace to society, but just a ne'er-do-well or bum. He was a nuisance around town, so the citizens finally decided that they'd have to cope with him. If they put him in jail, they'd be saddled with his support for an indefinite term.

So they concluded that the best course would be to maroon him. They picked out a barren, treeless islet within their boundaries that wasn't much good for anything else, placed Darling and a few of the rude necessities of life upon it, and left him to his own devices.

There he lived for twenty years, in a hut he built of driftwood, exposed to the hot suns of summer and the bitter winds of winter, drinking brackish water, and subsisting largely on lobster, shellfish, and the flesh of sea gulls. From time to time, when it occurred to them, the citizens brought him such staples as flour, sugar, and cast-off clothing; but for the most part he scratched his own living and made do with his own company. He really lived like an animal, or under worse conditions than most animals, whether wild or domesticated, endure. Animals usually have either decent food, or freedom to go where they please, or both.

The surprising part of this is that in spite of foul water, food that was often spoiled, exposure to the elements, filth, and great physical hardship, Darling not only survived but developed enormous strength and perfect health. I should think he would have gone mad. It must be far worse to be a castaway on an island from which you can see boats passing all the time and smoke rising from chimneys across a strip of water and even hear the voices of your fellow man floating over the sea, than on an island surrounded by emptiness. But he didn't go mad. He just lived on and on with himself for two decades.

Finally, one bitter day, no smoke was seen rising from his chimney. Investigators found him frozen on the pile of rags he called a bed. I think that is a horrible story, and the reason I include it here is that I don't want to give the impression that the islands of Casco Bay are an earthly paradise. They are just like any other place in the world, where things happen both good and bad.

This whole sea-threaded world of islands and capes is a wonderful place to walk or drive. You are almost never out of sight of the sea, and the view changes with almost every step you take, never becoming monotonous or less lovely. There are snug houses to see, and picturesque wharves, and lobster shacks hung with multicolored buoys used to mark the location of traps, and all the vivid life of the fishing towns. There are swimming and tuna fishing and picnic grounds conveniently placed, with facilities for cooking your own shore dinner. One of these, at Cundy's Harbor, is especially nice. Cundy's Harbor is a tiny place that caters to devotees of deep-sea fishing. All over this area there are plenty of places to stay for a longer or shorter period, and plenty of places where you can get a good meal.

On the return to Portland, the boat takes a course along the inner edge of the bay, passing through a maze of small and medium-sized islands. There is Cousin's Island, which was settled as early as 1628, or only eight years after the Plymouth Pilgrims, and Basket Island, where the Admiral Pearys lived before they moved to Eagle, and Mackworth Island, which was given to the state of Maine by ex-Governor Baxter to be used as the site of a school for the deaf and dumb.

The boat goes in close to the shore of the mainland, a shore that was, during the great days of the wonderful sailing ships and the busy days of the old wars of our country, so thick with shipyards that they almost overlapped each other, and the sound of the caulking hammer rang all up and down its length. Now the boat owners' requirements may be met at one large and bustling yard called the Handy Boat Service. Near it is the Portland Yacht Club, a meticulously groomed establishment with dozens of beautiful pleasure boats of all classes moored in the basin in front.

This section of the waterfront just north of Portland is called Falmouth Foreside, and it is a residential area of lovely houses and estates. Here, at Mussel Cove, is the site of the first tidal mill in Maine: a mill on a dam which caused the water to flow alternately in opposite directions as the tide rose and fell, so that a constant flow of power was maintained. This was a useful innovation in a country where there are no good natural falls and no suitable sites for the usual type of power dam requiring a large water-storage basin.

Here also near Falmouth Foreside at a place now called Waite's Landing was the old Fort Casco, which served as the buffer between Portland and the French and Indians to the north. Now white houses stand among great old trees, and long shadows fall across velvety green lawns. Spotless small boats are tied up at trim docks, and the waters of the bay look crisp in the sun and break gently on the shingle. It is hard to believe that this was once the scene of great violence and terror—of fire and bloodshed and scalping and sudden death.

If there is time, if the weather is auspicious, and if there are enough tourists aboard to make it worth while, the boat often takes a short swing down along the coast of Cape Elizabeth, the lower limit of Casco Bay, before returning to her dock in the harbor. John Smith named the cape in honor of his queen. Part of it is in South Portland, a fine parklike residential section; and the rest is in the township of Cape Elizabeth, an excellent agricultural area with many fine farms. They specialize in cabbage and squash, which are famous far outside New England, although all manner of other garden produce is raised, too, for the markets of the city.

The rugged and scenic immediate coast of the cape is largely given over to the tourist trade. It isn't too suitable for farming anyhow. It boasts Portland Head Light, which was ordered built by George Washington himself in 1790. The original tower still stands and is now the oldest light in operation on the entire Atlantic coast. It is probably also the most familiar to people who have never been within a thousand miles of the sea, since it has been painted and photographed innumerable times, and its likeness appears in a great many places, including museums, art calendars, school books, and the backs of playing cards.

It stands behind Fort Williams, the military headquarters of Maine and New Hampshire.

At the tip of the cape is the Cape Elizabeth Light and Coast Guard station. It's worth while to go out there on a windy or stormy day, even if you do suffer some discomfort, to see the surf break on the rocks. It comes thundering in from the open ocean, tons and tons of water in each breaker, and simply hurls itself onto the reefs. Such a display of mindless power and force is almost frightening, and you can become hypnotized watching it. It's a most impressive sight, and one tending to restore to proper perspective any picayune worries that have been troubling you.

Winslow Homer, who has been called by those who should know one of the few real geniuses in the history of American painting, lived at Prouts Neck in nearby Scarboro. He was not exclusively a marine artist, of course, but his pictures of the sea and coast are probably his best known. This country and shore served as subjects for many of his canvases; and, as a result, the strange sense of return is very strong to many—like me—who know very well that they have never before in their lives set foot on Cape Elizabeth, and yet can't quite believe it in the presence of so much that seems familiar. It's an odd feeling.

Seascapes near his home at Prouts Neck served as subjects for Winslow Homer's canvases.

10 · The Shore of Casco Bay

Desert of Maine, Freeport, Bradbury
Mountain State Park, Brunswick, Bath, Cape Small

NORTH of Portland on U.S. 1, between Yarmouth and Freeport, is a natural oddity known as the Desert of Maine. This now covers several hundred acres, and it is growing larger all the time. It actually is a small desert, complete with shifting dunes and sand storms. When it was first noticed, back in the '90's, it was only about thirty feet square. The top soil is very thin here over a layer of sand which may have been the bed of an ancient lake, and when something—either fire or the close cropping of sheep— killed the grass roots, there was nothing to hold the loam in place. It blew away and the sand took over. The tops of trees that were seventy feet tall now show through the sand as low bushes. Strangely enough, they are still alive, and one apple tree still blossoms and bears small fruit. Eventually it too will probably be covered.

One need not, however, feel sorry for the owners of the land. It's no good for farming any more, of course; but they must make a far better and easier living from the gate receipts charged for the viewing of this natural wonder than anyone ever did by cultivating the soil.

There is a village called Freeport in more than half the states of the Union. Usually they are so named because in the olden days they were free ports; or because their settlers migrated from one of the original, true Freeports. Freeport, Maine, is different. When the town was incorporated in 1789, it was named for Sir Andrew Freeport, a character in Addison's *Spectator* Papers. The town is also known as the Birthplace of Maine because, when the Province of Maine separated from Massachusetts and achieved independent statehood in 1820, the final papers supposedly were signed by the commissioners of both places at Freeport, in Jameson's Tavern, built in 1779 and still standing.

Freeport is noted today as the home of L. L. Bean, Inc. Bean items are mail-ordered from all over the world, and the name is practically sacred among sportsmen. The end result of a plain Maine woodsman's notion of a good hunting boot, the sprawling store is open twenty-four hours a day, including Christmas. In early days, Freeport suffered greatly from Indian attacks. All coastal towns have their Indian raid tales, but the story of Molly Phinney of Freeport is more like Hollywood than history.

It seems that in 1756 there lived at Flying Point a family named Means. The household consisted of Thomas Means and his wife, their several small children, and Mrs. Means's sister, Molly Phinney. They lived close to the community block house, so they felt fairly safe and became careless about heeding warnings of parties on the warpath. As a result, a band of Indians surprised them one day. Except for one small girl who hid, all the Meanses were killed, and Molly Phinney was carried off to captivity in Canada.

She was less fortunate than Mary Scammon of Scarboro, who, you will remember, was adopted by an influential French family. Molly Phinney was not a child, but a strong young woman, capable of turning out a good day's work; so she was placed in the family of one of the feudal lords of Quebec as little better than a slave.

But back in Freeport, she'd had an admirer, a Yankee skipper by the name of William McLellan, who happened to be away at the time of the raid. When he came back and found his girl gone, he was fit to be tied. He made up his mind that he was going to get her back, no matter what, so he promptly set sail for Quebec. Posing as a neutral trader, he hung around the taverns, listening to the gossip, until he learned where Molly was. That was all he needed to know.

Captain McLellan certainly had plenty of initiative, but I think that Molly should be given her share of the credit for what happened next. If she hadn't possessed remarkable self-control and quick wits, she'd have spent the rest of her life in durance. One of her duties was answering the door; and, when she opened it one afternoon and found her suitor on the step, she'd have been only human if she had shrieked, fainted, or at least exclaimed "Well, for heaven's sake!" But not Molly. Wooden-faced, she accepted the note he passed her, hid it in her bodice, and reported to the family that it was just someone who'd got the wrong address.

At midnight, Captain McLellan returned, equipped with a rope ladder, to find Molly ready to go. They made their escape, boarded his ship, and sailed back to Maine, where they were married and—I suppose—lived as happily ever after as most people do.

Way back on the dim fringes of my memory of my extreme youth is the recollection of spending what seemed like a year (but was probably about a week) of terror. The reason for this was that the mother of a family living near us told my sister and me that the world was coming to an end very soon. She knew the hour and the day; and she herself so obviously believed this that we were forced to believe it too. She didn't bother any more to do her washing and ironing, since no one would be there to wear the clean clothes, and my sister and I couldn't understand our own mother's foolishness in putting in provisions for a week end which we knew never would arrive. But the world didn't end, of course, and I forgot all about the whole thing until I went to Freeport and heard about Shiloh.

Shiloh was the headquarters of one of those cults that flourished in New England from time to time. This one, called the Holy Ghost and Us Society, was a religious sect with Adventist beliefs. It was founded and headed during the 1900's by Reverend Frank W. Sandford, who preferred to be called Elijah. People from all over were converted, sold their worldly goods, turned the proceeds over to Sandford, and lived at Shiloh on what he chose to dole out to them. He exerted a great deal of influence—which extended, as I have said, even to my sister and me—and for a time the colony flourished. But he overplayed his hand when he predicted a Judgment Day that never arrived. After that, the colony declined and was for many years abandoned.

Now, there is little activity at Shiloh. The elaborate buildings have been renovated, but they are occupied only by the son of the founder and a group of caretakers and dependents.

About five miles from Freeport, just beyond Pownal Center, is the Bradbury Mountain State Park. This is a tract of about 250 acres, with a camp ground, picnic areas, fireplaces, rest rooms, and other conveniences. There is a well-preserved cattle pound there which was probably built in the 1700's, and an abandoned feldspar quarry that geologists find of great interest. But best of all is a 485-foot granite bluff, reached by a good, though steep, trail. From the top is a beautiful panoramic view of Casco Bay, spread out like a map below.

The shopping center for this East Casco Bay area is Brunswick, a manufacturing city of about eight thousand souls and the seat of Bowdoin College. It is an unusually attractive city, with wide, well-planned streets and a great many old trees and houses. Its principal street, Maine Street, was laid out in 1717, when the citizens voted to construct a thoroughfare that would be twelve rods wide. This was an unusual thing to do in a time when cities were not generally planned, but grew up higgledy-piggledy. Maine Street retains its original width and is the second widest street in New England, the widest being in Keene, New Hampshire. Brunswick lies on the Androscoggin River, just above where it joins the Kennebec to form Merrymeeting Bay, on a dam at the falls of the Androscoggin, the source of power for the various mills.

Brunswick started life as a fur-trading post called by the Indian name Pejepscot and run by a Thomas Purchase. He developed a superior method of curing the salmon that he caught at the falls and built up such a good business in exporting fish along with his furs that others were attracted to the vicinity, and quite a thriving little settlement evolved. However, Purchase consistently cheated the Indians, so that the first violence of King Philip's War in Maine was the destruction of the Purchase block house. The place was constantly harassed all during the French and Indian Wars, in spite of the building of forts and the placing of garrisons to protect it. The Indians called the region *Ahmelahcogneturcook,* which means "Place of Much Fish, Fowl, and Beasts," and it was one of their best and favorite hunting grounds. So quite aside from their grudge against Purchase, they naturally resented the presence of white men there even more than they did in other places along the coast. However, around 1730 the settlement began its uninterrupted development, which has continued to this day.

Early in its history it was a great lumbering and ship-building center, but those industries no longer exist in Brunswick. Instead we have textile mills and paper box factories. Brunswick claims the first cotton mill in Maine, established in 1809; and in 1843 Aaron Dennison began experimenting in the back of his father's house with the making of paper boxes. This was the beginning of the great Dennison Manufacturing Company, now of Massachusetts, which is known all over the world today. This same Aaron Dennison, who seems to have been one of the breed of ingenious Yankee cusses, tinkered around with watches until he perfected a means of making clockwork by machinery. He then, as a side line, established the Boston Watch Company, now the Waltham Watch Company, famous for mass production of watches.

Possibly Brunswick is best known as the seat of Bowdoin College, an institution that has had and still has an immeasurable effect on both the cultural tone and the general atmosphere of the city. It is not large as colleges go, but it has always been an extremely good one, with a very high scholastic standard. Bowdoin has an impressive list of illustrious graduates in all fields of subsequent endeavor. Among them are Nathaniel Hawthorne and Henry Wadsworth Longfellow; Admiral Peary, who discovered the North Pole, and Commander Donald B. MacMillan, who explored polar regions; and a great many men in public life, like Thomas B. Reed, Senator William P. Frye, Chief Justice Melville W. Fuller, William Fessenden, Hannibal Hamlin, and the fourteenth President of the United States, Franklin Pierce. This is hardly a start on the list, and Bowdoin is still turning them out.

The college was founded in 1794, but it didn't actually open its doors until 1802. It ran into several difficulties along the way. First came the problem of choosing a site for the proposed fount of learning. Portland was suggested, but the committee reported that it offered too many "Temptations to Dissipation, Extravagance, Vanity, and Various Vices of Sea-port Towns." Then the quiet little town of New Gloucester was considered, since it was well away from the sea with its vanity, various vices, et cetera. However, the farmer who owned the desired land refused to sell it for fear the students would stone his apple trees. Finally Brunswick was decided upon.

When the idea was first broached, the founders decided to name the college after James Bowdoin, governor of Massachusetts. (Maine was, of course, still a part of Massachusetts at the time.) This seemed like a wise decision.

Although Governor Bowdoin was the grandson of Pierre Baudouin, a penniless refugee from religious persecution who had landed at Casco in 1687, the family had attained both wealth and influence since and could probably be counted on for financial and political support of a school named in its honor.

However, by the time a site had been chosen, Bowdoin was dead and John Hancock, who hated him bitterly, had become governor. Hancock was loath to sign a document to establish an institution perpetuating a name so abhorrent to him, so he delayed taking the necessary step for two or three years, and it wasn't until after his death that the next governor, Samuel Adams, finally signed.

The name still proved a practical choice, though, since the governor's son, Honorable James Bowdoin, minister to Spain and France, contributed generously to the support of the college and, in addition, left it his collection of Dutch and Italian masters, the first collection of European art ever to be brought to this country by an American.

The college was at first far from flourishing. Everything was in one building, Massachusetts Hall: classrooms, dormitories, dining quarters, and the president's home. There was no paint on the woodwork and no paper on the walls, and the drafty rooms were heated only by fireplaces, which are *not* adequate during a Maine winter. Moreover, there was no bell system, so the president pounded on the stairs with his cane when he wanted to summon the student body or indicate the beginning or end of a class period. The first graduating class consisted of eight men; and it's rather a wonder to me that even that many toughed it out for the four years.

That first commencement really must have been something, to judge from an account written by Elijah Kellogg, the same man who wrote "Spartacus to the Gladiators." In the first place, it rained torrentially. General Knox was the guest of honor, but he was very late, since his carriage tipped over in one of the village streets, which had been washed out by the rain. The exercises were scheduled to be held outdoors, but had to be moved into an unfinished church. The roof leaked so badly that President McKeen was obliged to hold an umbrella all the while he was delivering his address, a circumstance which cramped his oratorical style considerably by immobilizing one of his hands.

Nevertheless, commencements were so rare in that day and particularly in Maine that the affair was a howling success. Not only the interested parties, but the whole countryside as well, attended. It was like a state fair. Professional gamblers and snake charmers set up their pitches on the campus, which was ringed with the booths of vendors of all sorts of food, gadgets, and souvenirs. Horse racing was held on a nearby flat, and I guess a good time was had by all. It was more like a carnival than a milestone in educational history.

Today the Bowdoin campus, near the center of the city, is an impressively beautiful area which may be entered through any one of several memorial gateways. A guide may be picked up at the college office in Massachusetts Hall. The office of the president still contains an open fireplace, equipped with a swinging crane and some old black cauldrons, relics of the day when this room was the college kitchen. The guide will give you information about any of the buildings, but I should like to urge you to visit especially the Walker Art Gallery, which has been called the best small museum in the country. Founded as we have seen by the Honorable James Bowdoin, it contains some notable European drawings and paintings, such as a Rembrandt, a Breughel, and a Tintoretto, as well as some famous American works. The original of Gilbert Stuart's portrait of Thomas Jefferson is there, and Stuart took four separate trips to Bowdoin to make copies of this masterpiece.

Just across from the college on U.S. 1 is the First Parish Congregational Church. At the time preceding the Civil War, the minister was Dr. Calvin E. Stowe. One Sunday while he was preaching, he was rather dismayed to see his

wife, Harriet, get up and leave in the middle of the ser-
mon. I don't believe she could have been paying particularly close attention to what her husband was saying,
because she later claimed that suddenly a vision appeared
to her, more real and clear than the worshipers in the
pews. It showed in bright colors, bathed in a celestial light,
an old Negro dying after having been lashed by a slave
overseer, while a lovely child looked down from heaven.

Taking this as a sign, she quitted the church, went
home, and immediately started writing *Uncle Tom's
Cabin.* The pew in which the idea was born is indicated
by a plaque, and the house where the book was written
still stands on Federal Street. It is open to the public, and
there is a gift shop in the rear.

Nearly opposite the First Parish Church is the house in
which Longfellow lived when he taught at Bowdoin, and
on Federal Street you may find the house in which Hawthorne roomed while he was a student there. On School
Street, in what was formerly a church, is the Pejepscot
Historical Museum which, though small and unpretentious, houses an excellent collection of historical material.
But to me the best monument in Brunswick is none of
these man-made things, but the Bowdoin Pines.

The Bowdoin Pines lie along U.S. 1 to Bath, on Bath
Street. They are the small remnant of the dense forest of
white pine that once covered this whole country. These
are the pines that were called the mast pines, the pines on
which the whole great shipbuilding industry of Maine was
based, the pines that caused much of our trouble with
England. This great natural resource was squandered
prodigally, until only this little grove remains, saved
through the foresight of the college. Some of the trees rise
straight up for seventy feet before the branches begin, and
many of them stood there before the first white man came
to America. The floor of the forest is carpeted with several
centuries' accumulation of needles, soft and resilient under foot. It is a dim, lovely, quiet place to walk, scented
with the indescribably clean and heady odor of pine, and

*Harriet Beecher Stowe's house in Brunswick is now an
inn of thirty rooms.*

full of the susurrus of the wind in the arrogant tops overhead. The people of Brunswick are justifiably proud of the Bowdoin Pines.

About seven miles from Brunswick, south on Maine Street, is Mere Point, on Casco Bay, where there is a summer colony. Near it is a boulder bearing a tablet to commemorate the round-the-world flight of the U.S. Army pilots in 1924. It was in this field that the airmen, who had started westward from Seattle, Washington, first landed again on American soil. In making their landfall along the coast of Maine the very ships of the air continued the tradition of the ancient ships of the sea.

About seven miles from Brunswick is Bath, once the greatest shipbuilding port of the entire world and still a shipbuilding city. It lies on the Kennebec, one of the historical rivers of America.

Bath itself was settled in 1660, but previously the old Plymouth Company had established a fur trading post on Arrowsic, an island across the river from Bath. And, although it was destroyed several times by the Indians, it was the first permanent settlement on the Kennebec. In Bath's early days, it was known as Long Reach, because of the straight three-mile stretch of river out in front. A poor colony, it was referred to contemptuously as "a twenty-cow parish," which was worse than calling it a one-horse town. The seafaring colonists didn't bother much with horses in those days. They didn't need them. But *everybody* was supposed to have two or more cows.

It was the Long Reach that changed Bath from a poor little hamlet to a flourishing shipbuilding city. This stretch of water is judged by many to be unequaled in the world as a site for shipyards. The easily sloping shores are just right for the laying of keels; the deep, wide channel of the river permits safe and easy launching, and the sea is accessible but far enough away so that its great storms cannot destroy shipping at anchor. Moreover, the Kennebec and the Androscoggin rivers penetrate to the very heart of the dense forest country to the north, so that what seemed to be a limitless supply of lumber was available by the simple method of cutting it and driving it down the streams, long after the coastal stands had been exhausted. Twelve tidal mills sprang up to saw the logs into timbers and planking. As a result of this happy combination of circumstances, more ships have been built and launched on the strip of shore at Bath than in any equal area on the face of the globe.

The first Bath ship was a schooner built by Jonathan Philbrick and his two sons in 1743, near where the custom-house now stands. This, however, was a family enterprise. Shipbuilding as a business was not established until 1762, when Captain William Swanton built and launched on contract the *Earl of Bute,* the first full-rigged ship to go down Bath ways. This began Bath's history as a shipbuilding city, a history that extends to this day, when ships and the methods and materials of constructing them are far different from what they were in the era of the wooden hulls.

Those were the days! Bath ships were familiar in every port in the world, and respected wherever they went. Every old house in the city contains blue and white Canton ginger jars, glowing Paisley shawls, heavy teakwood chests, strange shells, and bronze gongs from heathen temples. They were souvenirs of the time when Bath citizens were as much at home in Shanghai or Manila or Lisbon as they were walking along Front Street.

Sailors rollicked along the waterfront then, and once, when one had offended the proprieties and was put into stocks as punishment. his shipmates refused to sail without him, when the time came that the tide was right. They couldn't talk the authorities into letting their friend loose, so they just picked him up, stocks and all, took him aboard ship, and sailed away with him. Bath was a lively place, all right.

At the time of the California Gold Rush, the yards of Bath originated the half-clipper ship, remarkable for its great speed. Old seafarers loved this daring type, but they weren't very good carriers, and so they passed away. Bath yards didn't lose their skill in making fast boats, though. The successful America Cup Defender of 1937, the Class J *Ranger,* was Bath-built. Bath also launched the largest wooden ship afloat, the six-masted *Wyoming,* as well as the only seven-masted schooner ever built, the all-steel *Thomas W. Lawson.* Not only were private vessels constructed, but many navy ships as well. There were the early gunboats *Castine* and *Machias,* many monitors, cruisers and destroyers, and the great *Georgia,* one of the most formidable fighting machines in the world until modern times.

When steam replaced sail and iron hulls replaced wooden ships, Bath went into a decline. But in 1890, General Thomas Hyde founded the Bath Iron Works, which has become one of Maine's most satisfactory enterprises. The switch to the new type of shipbuilding was a success, and Bath continues to build all types of vessels except the very largest. The launching of a ship is still an important event in Bath, just as it used to be in by-gone days.

Nowadays the ships are usually christened with a bottle of champagne In the early days it was rum, the common beverage on all social levels, distilled locally on Winnegance Creek. Rum continued to be customary until the dreary days of national prohibition, when the distraught builders had to look about for a suitable substitute. They hit upon Poland Spring Water, as at least being of Maine origin. This strikes me as a sorry and emasculate travesty of a once robust and symbolic ceremony. Poland Spring Water indeed! Some day when I have nothing better to do, I'm going to check on the records of some of the ships launched under this feeble auspice. I'll bet none of them ever amounted to much.

Bath today is a pleasant, modern, industrial city with a

busy shopping center, comfortable hotels, and good restaurants. In the Davenport Memorial Building are not only
the municipal offices, but also the Davenport Memorial
Museum, a collection of paintings, half models of ships,
early tools and other articles connected with the maritime
history of Maine. In the tower of the building is a bell
cast by Paul Revere. Nearby, in the City Park, there is a
cannon taken from the British man-of-war *Somerset*, the
same ship that was "swinging wide at her moorings" in
Boston harbor on the very night when the same Revere
took his famous ride to Concord and Lexington.

The operatic star Emma Eames, later married to the
baritone Emilio De Gogorza, was brought up in Bath by
her grandmother. She would have been born there, too,
except that the Eameses were one of the peripatetic families
so common in the era of the clipper ships; so Mme. De
Gogorza first saw the light of day in Shanghai. In her later
years she returned to Bath to live in a house on North
Street.

A short distance north of the city center, on the bank
of the river, is an interesting old building, the Peterson
House. This was built in 1770 for the King's mast agent
by a ship's carpenter. It's an odd-looking structure, fash-
ioned something like a ship, wide at the bottom and narrow at the top, with the door jambs and window frames
following the general outline of the house. Apparently the
carpenter couldn't cut loose from the type of construction
to which he was accustomed. The modern front lawn used
to be the landing place of the great sticks of pine marked
with the King's Broad Arrow for use by His Majesty's
Navy.

A house that should be visited by any naturalist is the
home of Herbert L. Spinney, at 75 Court Street. Mr. Spinney was associated for many years with the Smithsonian
Institution, and there is in his home an excellent collection of native fauna and flora. I know that this sort of
thing leaves many people cold; but some of us find it really

worth while, and I don't think that Mr. Spinney's house is too well known or widely patronized.

From Bath, route 209 leads down Cape Small, the easternmost limit of Casco Bay. Cape Small is much less thickly populated than the peninsulas that comprise the Harpswell-Bailey Island area, visible across an arm of the bay. It's very pretty country, with a great deal of unstudied charm. Old farmhouses stand in thickets of lilac and snowball bushes, with fields full of wildflowers spread all around them. The colors are unusually vivid, due—so they tell me—to the salt sea air. I guess they tell me right, because along the whole coast the blossoms are much brighter than those of the same species inland. All of this cape, after you have crossed the Bath city line near Winnegance, lies in the township of Phippsburg, which was named in honor of Sir William Phipps, the bold bravo who captured Port Royal for the English during the French and Indian Wars.

In Phippsburg Center is the James McCobb House, built in 1774. The town's first post office was located in its kitchen. It's a private house now, but you can look at the interesting old hinges and bull's-eye glass of the front door without bothering the occupants.

A little way out from the town is the Fort Baldwin Memorial Park, on the side of Sabino Hill. This has no facilities for picnicking or camping, but it is significant as being the site of the Popham colony of 1607-1608, whose members, you recall, turned in a report that New England was an impossible place. If they'd stuck it out, Popham could have shared with Jamestown the honor of being the first permanent English settlement in the New World. However, the "pretty Pynnace" *Virginia* of thirty tons, the first ship ever to be launched in America and the mother of the great Maine shipbuilding tradition, was built here that winter. So the efforts of the colonists weren't entirely wasted.

Near the end of Cape Small are the active summer

colony of Popham Beach and the Fort Popham Memorial Park. Here there are facilities for picnickers. The original Fort Popham was erected during the Revolution, but it has nothing to do with the present fort. This was started in 1861 and never finished. It was just an expensive idea someone had, which turned out not to be practical. The old fort makes a fascinating ruin, though, impressive, picturesque, and mysterious. It looks a great deal older than it is, like a stone age survival, and it's rather fun to explore. From the top there is a fine view up the Kennebec valley and out to sea.

On an island off the mouth of the Kennebec is the Seguin Island Light. It is the highest above the sea on the Maine coast, although not the highest tower, and it stands 180 feet above high tide. It is open to visitors, and you can usually find a lobsterman or fisherman who is willing to take you out there for a consideration. The size of the consideration depends on how the lobsterman is feeling, whether he likes your looks, how busy he is at the time, and whether or not he really wants to go or would rather stay ashore and tie bait bags. That's something you have to work out for yourself.

Cape Small marks the end of Casco Bay, and the Kennebec River defines the limit of its sphere of influence ashore. You need take but a minute to cross the river on the Carlton Bridge at Bath, but the Kennebec can't be dismissed as lightly as all that. It is far from the longest or the deepest or the widest river in the United States, but greatness is not always determined by size. I insist that it is one of the great rivers of our country. Therefore I think that before we proceed farther along Down-East, we'd better take a little time out to consider the Kennebec.

11 · The Kennebec

Merrymeeting, Gardiner, Hallowell
Augusta, Woolwich, The Five Islands District

RIVERS have played an almost incalculable part in the story of mankind.

In prehistoric days, human life originated and flourished along their banks, so that river valleys have frequently been likened to cradles. The valley of the Tigris and Euphrates, for instance, has been called the cradle of Babylonian culture. Rivers have been termed highways, opening up large areas to exploration and cultivation. The Mississippi is a good example of this. Rivers have also served as barriers and boundaries separating groups, as in the case of the Rio Grande; a river may be the common factor binding groups together, the economic backbone supporting a civilization, as in the case of the Nile. Some rivers, like the Ganges, have been regarded as sacred objects of worship; and some have been used as symbols, so that there are people who refer to dying as "crossing over the River Jordan." A surprising number of wars boil down to jealous disagreement over the control of a river basin, no matter what other contributory causes for fighting there may be. The Saar illustrates this point.

In fact, it would be impossible to expunge the mention of rivers from any history, just as it would be impossible to maintain life, whether plant or animal, on the face of the globe without rivers; and it would be extremely difficult, if not actually impossible, even with modern technology, to continue our present rate of agricultural and industrial productivity. Rivers are the veins and arteries of the world.

What makes a river great? Why is a comparatively small stream like the Kennebec a greater river than the Amazon, which is the longest in the world? The greatness of a river is judged entirely by its degree of service to mankind and by the extent of its influence on history. The Kennebec has been both a cradle and a boundary. It has been worshiped as a god. It has watered crops and turned the wheels of mills and factories. It has been a vast shipyard and a clear road into the wilderness. Wars have been fought because of it, and whole ways of living determined by its characteristics. The Kennebec is truly great.

Actually it is only 164 miles long; but it and its largest tributary, the 174-mile Androscoggin, drain more than half of Maine. Their myriad brooks and creeks and ponds lie like a huge silver net over the whole central portion of the state. The Kennebec, which the Indians called the Quinnebequi, the river god, comes down from Maine's largest lake, Moosehead, deep in the heart of the state; and the Androscoggin rises in the Rangeley Lakes, that lonely and lovely chain far over in the northwest corner. Deviously but surely they find their way down from the hills to mingle in Merrymeeting Bay, a large shoal body of water into which three other rivers, the Abagadasset, the Cathance, and the East River, also flow.

That's popularly supposed to be the reason for the bay's name—so many streams meet there so merrily. I myself am not satisfied with that explanation. The name originally was spelled Maremiten, which I think could be translated roughly to mean "inland sea"; and I believe Merrymeeting to be only a rather charming corruption. As always, I could be wrong, however.

The seventeen-mile stretch of river between Merrymeeting Bay and the ocean, made up of the waters of so many branches, has just one name, the Kennebec.

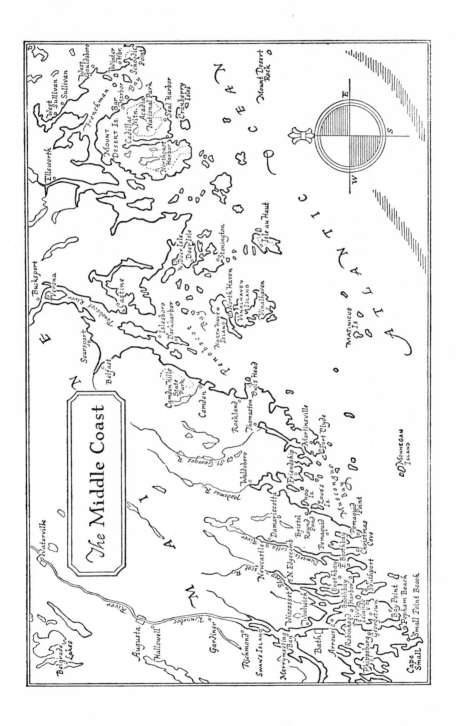

The Middle Coast

Before the white man came, the Kennebec basin was the hunting ground and hallowed property of that tribe of the Abenakis known as the Norridgewocks. Their permanent homes were up-river, where they farmed their small plots of land, hunted along the wooded shores, and used the stream as a thoroughfare by which to reach their vacation spots along the coast and visit their Canadian relatives. It was then and for many years after the advent of the Europeans a territory rich in fish and game, and the Abenakis lived there very happily.

On January 18, 1608, the Popham colony made the first known report on the Kennebec weather. According to their log, there was in the space of seven hours "thunder, lightning, raine, frost, snow in all abundance, the last continuing." They assumed that this was typical, and they were right. Their mistake lay in letting it discourage them to the extent that they abandoned their colony. If they'd stuck it out, they would have discovered that they were merely experiencing routine New England weather, variable and unpredictable but, to those of us who are accustomed to it, invigorating and stimulating beyond compare. If it's rougher than average at times, we are more than compensated when it decides to show what a really gorgeous day can be like. Nevertheless, that particular eighteenth of January delayed the settling of the Kennebec valley for many years.

The first successful settlement was the fur-trading post which the Plymouth Pilgrims established in 1628 on the site of present-day Augusta, to raise money to pay for the *Mayflower*. The Indians called the place Cushnoc, which means "the tide runs no further up the river"; and Augusta is in fact the tide head, being thirty-nine miles from the sea and having an average tidal range of four feet. Perhaps because of its tidal significance, Cushnoc was considered a sacred spot by the Indians, and they held annual powwows there, of a religious nature.

In spite of the fact that this was, to the Indians, hallowed territory, the traders had no trouble with the natives for thirty-two years, or until the French and Indian Wars broke out. By that time, the *Mayflower* had been paid for several times over, so the English gave up the post at Cushnoc as being too dangerous to hold. But during their occupation, the only violence which broke out was– typically enough—of their own making.

This is what happened. The first factor of the trading post was John Howland, a young man who had previously distinguished himself by falling overboard from the *Mayflower* in mid-ocean and almost being lost forever. Shortly after he took charge of Cushnoc, a free-lance fur trapper named Hocking moved into the region and started running his own independent trap lines. There was actually room enough for everybody, but here as elsewhere the Pilgrims took an extremely dim view of anyone's muscling in on their territory. To look at the famous and familiar painting of them wending their way to church through the snowy woods, you'd think butter wouldn't melt in their mouths. But an investigation of their activities and methods on weekdays seems to reveal that the picture shows only their Sunday faces. The rest of the time they were fairly hard-boiled and ruthless operators.

Acting as agent for the Plymouth Company, Howland attempted to dislodge Hocking, and in the fracas that followed, Hocking was shot through the head and killed. And here is where things begin to get a little bit confused. I can't give you the logic behind what follows, but I will report the sequence of events, for what that's worth.

At the time of the shooting, John Alden was captain of a ship which happened to be anchored in the Kennebec opposite the post, waiting for a load of furs. This was the same John Alden who later married Priscilla Mullens, as told in Longfellow's *The Courtship of Miles Standish*. Hocking was buried (I assume), and Alden sailed back to Boston with his cargo, where—simply as a matter of mild general interest—he passed on news of the killing. Although he'd had nothing to do with the affair other than having had the bad fortune to be in the general vicinity at the time, he was clapped into jail as a material witness and possible suspect.

When the Pilgrim Fathers of Plymouth heard about this, they were furious. They sent Miles Standish, of all people, up to Boston to get John Alden out of custody. Standish was never noted for his mildness and forbearance, and he raised such a hullabaloo that Alden was set free. However, the captain so annoyed Governor Dudley by the intemperance of his language that Standish himself was bound over to appear in court at the next term, to answer to the charges leveled against Alden. Of course, he knew even less about the facts of the case than Alden did, if that were possible; but this didn't seem to make any difference. By then the main issue, fixing responsibility for the death of Hocking, had been completely lost in the shuffle, and the affair had deteriorated into a jealous squabble between Boston and Plymouth.

I guess Plymouth won, because Standish never did appear in court, and the whole matter was dropped. Alden married Standish's girl, and fur trading with the Indians along the Kennebec continued peaceably until the French and Indians Wars caused the closing of Cushnoc.

However, the brief existence of the post had one very far-reaching effect. The Canadian Indians, who came down the easy way over the great concourse of the Kennebec to trade their furs at Cushnoc, reported back to the Jesuit missionaries of Canada that their friends along the Maine coast were being converted to Protestantism by the traders. This was something that the Catholic Fathers couldn't in good conscience disregard; so in 1646, Father Gabriel Druilletes set out down the Kennebec to establish the mission at Norridgewock. He was the first white to follow the course of the river and to set eyes on Katahdin; and it was over the trail blazed by Druilletes that Benedict Arnold many years later led his forces against Quebec.

Druilletes was evidently a capable and selfless man who worked hard and understandingly among the savages. At the same time he was able to maintain amicable relationships with the Protestant whites of the territory. The Indians idolized him; and he was on sufficiently friendly terms with John Winslow, then the factor at Cushnoc, so that once when Druilletes had business in Massachusetts he stayed at Winslow's home in Plymouth.

This season of good feeling ended with the French and Indian Wars, which were, in fact, waged all the more violently because of the fanatical element often bred by a religious difference. Now for a long time the Kennebec basin became a scene of bloodshed and terror. The river was a political sore point anyhow, since the French claimed it as the boundary of their domain. But perhaps the Indians would not have entered into hostilities so whole-heartedly if the English hadn't caused Father Râle, a successor of Father Druilletes at the Norridgewock mission, to be murdered. The actual blow was delivered by an Indian, but he was in English pay. Jaquish Island near the mouth of the Kennebec, a bleak and desolate place, is named for the murderer, incidentally.

After the war ended, the Kennebec came into its own. Bath and Brunswick were settled, and the shipbuilding era began. Ships fanned out all over the world from the estuary of the Kennebec, and the name of the river was as familiar everywhere as were the tall masts of the vessels launched on her reaches. To meet the demand for lumber, woods crews worked farther and farther up her course into the far hinterland, and millions of feet of pine were driven down on the spring freshets.

The valley of the Kennebec was for a time the world's principal source of the tall mast pines; and in the cutting of those pines a whole new breed of men, the Maine lumberjacks, came into being. It was in their logging camps, far up on the tributaries of the Kennebec and of Maine's other great river, the Penobscot, that the legend of Paul Bunyan was created; and when the pine was exhausted and the sons of the old lumberjacks moved West, they took their hero with them, so that tales of his prowess and his blue ox Babe were told from coast to coast.

After the pine was gone, there still remained the spruce, which to me is the most beautiful of northern conifers. Although not as desirable as pine for some purposes, spruce is nevertheless a good utility wood for building boards, railroad ties, and similar uses. So every spring still saw the Kennebec jammed from shore to shore with the long logs. Then once the best of the spruce was cut off, there still remained the pulpwood, which is being cut to this day. Anything can be used for pulp—scrub spruce, small fir, even poplar, an otherwise trash wood. The stuff is cut into four-foot lengths and trucked down the Kennebec to the paper mills along its banks almost to the mouth. Until recent times the pulpwood was driven down the river, but it became apparent—rather late in the day—that sunken logs and bark, rotting on the river bottom, contributed enormously to water pollution and extermination of fish by ruining spawning beds. Log drives are now prohibited by law.

It was the growth of the pulp industry that ruined the Kennebec as anything but a working river. A river should be beautiful—and the Kennebec is still that—and useful, which the Kennebec has always been. But in addition, it should be a source of pleasure, which the Kennebec is no longer. The sawdust from the mills has covered the feeding grounds of the fish, and the chemicals used in the manufacture of paper have polluted and poisoned the water. However, legislation governing industrial waste disposal has been passed, and it is to be hoped that the Kennebec will eventually be restored to beauty.

Once the land was cleared by the loggers and opened to the sun, it was discovered to be of unusual richness. So the farmers followed the lumberjacks, building their snug houses and great barns farther and farther up the river. You couldn't say of a man, however, that he was a farmer or a logger or a shipbuilder. Most men were all three, changing occupations with the seasons of the year; and in the latter 1800's a fourth occupation helped balance the close budgets of the Kennebec families.

They went into the ice business. All along the coast, ice
was cut in winter for shipping to the tropics, but the bulk
of the business was done on the Kennebec. Kennebec ice
was supposed to be purer and better than any other ice,
and it commanded a better price abroad. Actually I don't
imagine there was too much difference in ice at the time.
All the rivers were unpolluted and zero weather is zero
weather wherever you encounter it. However, there are on
record instances where unscrupulous captains maintained
to their customers in Cairo or Manila that theirs was the
true, bona-fide Kennebec ice, when really it had been cut
on the Penobscot or even on the Hudson. This was downright dishonest; but when you come right down to it, I
don't imagine very much real harm was done.

The ice business is dead on the Kennebec today, and so
is the old long-log business, but it's still a great river. The
shipyards remain at Bath, the mills flourish all along its
length, the farms continue to produce abundantly, and the
Kennebec is still a busy highway along its lower reaches.
It's still a river to be taken into account.

Since this is supposed to be a book about the coast of
Maine, we can't explore the Kennebec to its sources. To
do so would mean exploring a large part of the state. We
should, however, go as far upstream as the tides go, to Augusta, the capital of the State of Maine and the site of the
first occupation of the valley.

The drive up the west shore of the Kennebec from
Brunswick is through some really beautiful farming country, gently rolling and prosperous-appearing. The houses
stand along the road, and the fields slope down behind to
the shores of Merrymeeting Bay. The view is gorgeous, especially when the autumn frosts have turned the leaves of
the maples to scarlet and crimson and gold against the
deep blue of the bay.

Merrymeeting is now considered to be one of the best
duck-hunting regions on the entire Atlantic coast. A Captain Samuel Nickerson started planting wild rice there in

1890, and this was so successful in attracting enormous flocks of migrating waterfowl that the State Inland Fish and Game Commission has taken over the rice planting, with the result that the place has become a sportsman's dream world. A little further up the river Swan's Island, in the middle of the stream below Richmond, is a State Game Preserve for the further encouragement of wild life.

Gardiner, about six miles below Augusta, is today a manufacturing city, but it didn't start out to be that. Back in the 1700's, through a series of land grants, Dr. Sylvester Gardiner managed to gain possession of a hundred thousand acres of this rich and beautiful country. His idea was to set up a little feudal empire which he and his descendants would control completely and forever. The Revolution ruined this scheme. However, one of his direct descendants, ex-Governor William Tudor Gardiner, still owns land here: "Oaklands," considered one of the finest estates in Maine.

The city of Gardiner is famous, too, as having been the boyhood home of Edwin Arlington Robinson, one of America's great modern poets, whose "Tilbury Town" *is* Gardiner and its people. Mrs. Laura E. Richards is also a Gardiner writer who has used the Maine coast as the background for many of her books, among them *Captain January.*

It's possible for ships to go as far up the Kennebec as Augusta, but very few of them do so now. Most of them stop two miles short, at Hallowell, and these are largely tankers delivering oil at the docks of Oil Cloth Point. Hallowell is legally a city, although its population is less than three thousand and it looks more like a pretty town. It is set in a bowl in the hills facing the river, and you have to turn off the highway to really appreciate its charm.

There are some fine old houses in the town, as well as the Worster House, an inn built in 1832 and still very much in business. Such distinguished Americans as William Lloyd Garrison, Horace Greeley, President James Polk,

Daniel Webster and Ralph Waldo Emerson have stayed there. In those days Gardiner was the starting point of the historic old Coos Trail to New Hampshire; and although I can find very few people who will believe this, Gardiner was also the starting point of the automotive industry. The first workable steam automobile in America was built here in 1858, eight years before Henry Alonzo House drove his marvel from Bridgeport to Stratford, Connecticut.

As we have said before, Augusta was originally the site of the trading post of Cushnoc, subsequently abandoned. In 1754, Fort Western, one of a string of forts serving as buffers between Canada and Massachusetts, was erected on the spot. Five years later, Montcalm surrendered at Quebec and the fort was no longer needed, so it was dismantled. However, the fort's commander, Captain James Howard, liked the country well enough to stay on and become the first permanent settler of Augusta. At the time, Fort Western was within the boundaries of Hallowell and was included when that town was incorporated in 1771. Hallowell was known as The Hook—a contraction of the Indian "Bombahook"—and what is now Augusta was known as The Fort, to distinguish the two sections of the same place.

A certain amount of jealousy grew up between the hamlets, which was brought to a head when the first bridge over the Kennebec was built at The Fort. The Fort withdrew from the alliance in 1797 and set itself up as an independent town under the name of Harrington, after Lord Harrington. Hallowell citizens persisted in calling the rival settlement Herring-town, which made the Herring-towners so mad that they changed the name in less than four months to Augusta, probably as a compliment to the daughter of General Dearborn, a Revolutionary hero.

With the growth of the shipbuilding industry on the lower Kennebec, Augusta bloomed. Deep-water vessels

The noble edifice of the state Capitol, begun in 1829, was designed by Charles Bulfinch of Boston.

could come up as far as her waterfront, and it was therefore the natural point at which to transfer cargoes from
the big ships to long-boats of shallow draft for distribution
throughout the vast territory up-river. A whole fleet of
schooners and packets plied regularly between Augusta
and Boston, and a healthy commercial traffic developed. It
was not at all unusual to see twenty-five or more ships
docked at the Augusta wharves, even though she did seem
to be an inland city. This lasted until the arrival of the
railroad and then trailer trucks, which put the ships out
of business.

However, by this time (1827) Augusta had become the
capital of the state; and although she is an industrial city
with over forty enterprises, it is as the capital that she is
best known today.

The Capitol was begun in 1829. It's a noble and beautiful edifice designed by Charles Bulfinch of Boston and
constructed of Hallowell granite, which is unusually fine—
a clear gray marked with black tourmaline specks and
bearing very little mica. The gold figure on top of the
dome represents Wisdom, a hopeful choice for any building housing a governing body, I would say. The Capitol
contains a Hall of Flags, as well as the very excellent State
Library, which performs an unusually good and efficient
service in supplying books to people in isolated areas
away from the ordinary sources. I used to live in the backwoods myself, and I don't know how I would have got
through the long, snowbound winters without the book
boxes from the State Library.

State Park, a well-kept and well-landscaped area of about
twenty acres, extends down the knoll in front of the Capitol. This park is also an arboretum, where the State For-
estry Department experiments to determine what plants
and trees will grow in this climate. Students of horticulture and dendrology will find a great deal to interest them
here; and for the rest of us, it's a pleasant and quiet place
to walk or sit in the shade.

Augusta has several good parks, the best and largest of

which is 475-acre Ganneston Park, privately owned by Mr. Brooks Brown, Jr., but open to the public. No motoring is allowed there, so you feel as if you were in a real wood. There are facilities for picnicking, hiking, horseback riding, and winter sports; and since it is also a game preserve and bird sanctuary, it's a good place to go bird-watching in the very early morning before there are too many people around.

Across Capitol Street from the Capitol is the Blaine House, a large and good example of the Classic Revival school of architecture. It was formerly the home of James G. Blaine, who ran unsuccessfully for the Presidency of the United States in 1884. In 1919, his daughter, Mrs. Harriet Blaine Beale, presented the house to the state as a memorial to her son, who was killed in World War I. She intended it to be the official residence of the governor of the state of Maine. And that's what it is today. In the state dining room is a silver service which was recovered from the cruiser *Maine* ten years after she was sunk in Havana harbor.

Another interesting old Augusta house, at the corner of Stone and Cony Streets, is the Reuel Williams House. This is sometimes open by permission of the owner, and it is worth visiting if you happen to be in town on an open day. The architecture is very fine, and the house is full of beautiful antiques and objects of art. One fascinating room is octagonal in shape, and its hand-painted wall paper depicts scenes in the Hawaiian Islands. This paper is in perfect condition, although it was painted in Paris in 1806, or a century and half ago; and while the New York Metropolitan Museum and a Philadelphia museum possess some of the panels, the Williams House is the only place where you can see the whole series. It was given to the original owner by the same James Bowdoin. who left his art collection to Bowdoin College.

You can cross the Kennebec at Augusta and go back down to the coast proper on route 9. Again you drive

*Across from the Capitol, the executive mansion was once
the home of James G. Blaine.*

through a beautiful farming country and rejoin U.S. 1 at Woolwich, across the river from Bath. Woolwich, which was the home of that poor boy who became Sir William Phipps and the Royal Governor of Massachusetts, is now a farming and dairying village whose chief industry is the canning of corn, peas, and beans. As is usual in many Maine agricultural communities, a representative of one of the large commercial canning houses arranges with the farmer in the spring the amount and type of crop he shall plant, and guarantees to purchase his entire production, to be processed in the company's local branch plant. This works out very well, not only assuring the farmer a market, but also assuring his family a short period of seasonal occupation in the fields or the cannery just about when a little extra money for new shoes for school will come in very handy.

Seaward from Woolwich lies the eastern half of the Kennebec delta, an almost unspoiled region of islands, like its counterpart over across in the Harpswells. Here in this sea-threaded world of woods and farms, many people live much as their fathers did, using kerosene lamps, pumping water by hand from their wells, and gaining their living from the land and the sea—and the summer people, of course. The section is known as the Five Islands district, because there are five principal islands there—Georgetown, Malden, Crow, Mink, and Hen. But there are scores of smaller islands, and the number is increasing all the time.

The gradual sinking of the coast is very evident here. Almost from year to year you can see what is happening as peninsulas become islands and marshes turn into stretches of open sea. It's really a fascinating country, lying between the mouths of the Kennebec and the little Sheepscot River, friendly and unpretentious and beautiful; and as a result, it's a very busy scene in summer.

The Five Islands district is historic, too. At Arrowsic an overgrown cemetery with slate markers dates back to 1729; and you can see the site of the old church which

Arnold mentioned in his account of his fabulous trek to Quebec. Nearby are the ruins of a house built in 1629, when the place was a thriving fishing settlement. It used to be on a point called Squirrel Point, but now it's on an island; which illustrates what we have just been talking about.

There are several small towns where accommodations may be had: Georgetown; Robinhood; Five Islands; and Bay Point, smack across the Kennebec from Popham Beach. At Georgetown is the Reid State Park, offering picnic facilities, surf bathing, and warmer and safer bathing in a salt pool. The place is apt to be crowded on pleasant Sundays, but on other days it is a nice spot for a picnic. Bridges and ferries make it possible to pass from island to island very easily, and the whole region is thoroughly charming.

In *Trending into Maine,* Kenneth Roberts suggests that you're not really in Maine, not actually Down-East, until you have crossed the Kennebec. That may or may not be true, depending entirely on the individual's feeling in the matter. It is true, however, that here at Five Islands the grand eastward sweep of the coast becomes pronounced, and the third great division, the Middle Coast, begins. That is the section we are now entering, and the section we shall explore next.

Piers standing on stilts at Port Clyde attest to the depth of the tides.

12 · The Middle Coast

Wiscasset, Edgecomb, The Boothbays
Monhegan Island, Newcastle, Damariscotta
The Pemaquids, Waldoboro, Muscongus Bay Area
Thomaston, Port Clyde, Martinsville

THE Middle Coast of Maine, extending from the west bank of the Kennebec to the east bank of the Penobscot, has been called the workaday part of the coast, the heart of maritime Maine.

This is because of the presence here of several deep tidal rivers, coming down from what was formerly a thickly forested country and providing good anchorages and harbors at every turn. The first of these, the Kennebec, we have already discussed, and we shall discuss the Penobscot in a later chapter. But between the two there are many other rivers, varying in size yet of a common nature: deep, sheltered, and navigable for a considerable part of their length. The four most important are the Sheepscot, the Damariscotta, the Medomac, and the St. George's, to all of which may be applied in a lesser degree, because they are lesser rivers, all that we have said about the Kennebec and its importance. These smaller streams, too, have floated down millions of feet of lumber, have seen the launching of a fleet of ships, and have provided safe haven for vessels returned from half a world away.

This is a land of ledges and pointed firs. There are few

beaches here, and those few are largely composed of shingle or cobble. The water is icy cold. The shoreline runs out to sea in ragged capes and peninsulas, and the ocean is strewn with countless islands of all sizes. The forests which even today come down to the high-tide mark in some places save it from bleakness and lend a softness to its austerity. Back from the sea, the land is fertile. Flowers here, whether wild or cultivated, are unusually large and bright, and gardens everywhere are riotous. It's a beautiful, busy section of the coast.

Part of this business is because of the climate and topography, but in addition the area is particularly well-endowed with natural resources. Besides the lumber and ice formerly available in all divisions of the coast, the Middle Coast possesses lime, granite, and brick clay, the handling, processing and exporting of which has required and still requires the services of armies of men and fleets of ships. This makes work for everybody and keeps the place humming. Then there's the farming and fishing, too; and it is here that the famous Maine lobster approaches its peak of succulence, tenderness, and flavor, and the lobsterman becomes a common figure.

A great deal of nonsense and some sense has been spoken and written on the subject of the lobster. Some people believe that a lobster is a lobster, so what; and others claim to be able at first taste to locate within a half mile the point of trapping. As one who has made a semi-lifework of eating lobsters, I would like to contribute my two cents' worth. There is a difference in lobsters, although I wouldn't go so far as to say that a mile or two of seaway in one direction or the other radically alters the quality of the meat. It's axiomatic, of course, that lobsters should be fresh and lively when prepared, and that they should be properly cooked. We will assume that these conditions have been met; but even so, lobsters do differ.

As far as I can find out, the quality of the lobster is determined by two things: the temperature and the depth of the water in which it has been living. Apparently the colder the water, the better; and the water of the Middle and Eastern coasts of Maine is about as cold as water can get and still support life. I speak from experience, having been in it for brief—very brief—periods, both accidentally and on purpose.

But in addition to being cold, the water here is comparatively shallow on a submerged shelf all along the coast. Maine lobstermen speak disparagingly of the Nova Scotia lobster, which has been caught in deep water. According to them, the added weight of the element serves to make the flesh both tough and soggy. This may be purest superstition, and the difference may be due to a different diet, a different strain, or some other factor of which I know nothing. It may even be as simple as this: that the turnover of lobsters along the Maine coast is so fast that they have usually come recently out of the sea and haven't been lingering around in pounds or shipping tanks, still alive but deteriorating under artificial conditions. Whatever the reason, Maine lobsters really are the best; and unless you are terrifically allergic to seafood, you owe it to yourself to sample at least one.

That's enough about that, for the time being. Let's get back to the Middle Coast.

I will always remember the first time I was ever in Wiscasset. I was driving through the town on the highway, which passes through the little shopping center, when I saw ahead of me a flock of white birds, feeding. Where I come from, pigeons in the street are not uncommon, so I gave the matter no thought. Suddenly the air was full of a wild and musical crying and all about me great wings, shining and strongly arched like the wings of angels, rustled and beat. The birds weren't pigeons, but gulls; and for the first time I realized what is meant by the term "a coastal town": a town where the things of the sea are as familiar and everyday as the things of the land.

Since then, Wiscasset—which means "Meeting of Three

Tides"—has always seemed to me to be a wonderful and beautiful place; but it's beautiful anyway, gulls in Main Street or no gulls in Main Street. Actually the town isn't right on the open ocean, but on the tidal Sheepscot River, which is crossed here by the longest wooden pile bridge in Maine. The place was first permanently settled in 1730, having previously been abandoned because of the Indian raids, and it is distinguished today by wide, tree-shaded streets and a great many perfectly lovely old houses.

In the early days, Wiscasset was a wealthy town and busy port, and that was when the old homes of the sea captains and shipping masters were built. At that time, it was a port of entry, but it isn't any longer. The place never really recovered from the Embargo Act of 1807 and the War of 1812. Some of the old homes are occupied still by the descendants of the original owners, but a great many have been bought by summer people and by writers and artists who have been attracted by the charm of the village. These houses have not been "improved" with turrets and gingerbread, so Wiscasset is really a Maine Williamsburg, which has never needed restoring.

The citizens have a very pleasant custom here. During August of most years they hold an Open House Day, when all the houses are opened to the public for a fee of two dollars, which goes into a fund for the town library. This is truly an opportunity. Not only are the houses themselves worth seeing, but they are full of furniture and articles of great interest and beauty, brought back from the ends of the earth in the days of Wiscasset's shipping glory.

This town library has been in continuous service since 1799, a remarkable record. On display there is an old piece of fire-fighting apparatus, hand-drawn and equipped not only with leather buckets but also with two big sacks for the collecting and carrying out of small articles from a burning building, and with a bed key.

In case you didn't know, the parts to the old four-poster beds are fastened in place and held rigid by means of a key that locks the pieces together. I have a friend who owns one, and when she wants to move the bed from one room to another, she always has to spend half the morning looking for the key. So it seems to me an excellent bit of foresight on the part of the old Wiscasset fire fighters to bring their own key with them for use in case the beds had to be removed from the house.

The Wiscasset Fire Society, organized in 1801, is still in existence. It's now a purely social club, but it maintains some of the old rules, including one that fines members ten cents for being absent from a meeting, and another that provides that the buckets, sacks, and the bed key must be kept handy.

Wiscasset is the place where Talleyrand and Louis Phillippe first trod American soil when they were forced to leave France; and later another Frenchman, General Lafayette, visited here in 1825. On this occasion, he was served the first ice cream ever made in America. I hate to keep harping on *firsts,* but in this instance I feel that I must, since ice cream is practically our national dish. Unfortunately I don't know what flavor was served Lafayette.

Daniel Webster once practiced law in Wiscasset, and the town has produced one governor and four congressmen.

From Fort Edgecomb in the harbor one has a good open view of the Sheepscot, a very pretty river. The fort itself has almost disappeared, although you can still see remains of the old earthworks and gun emplacements; but the octagonal blockhouse with its heavy overhang is in excellent condition, one of the few original and unchanged blockhouses in New England. The site is now a state memorial park, with a lobster pound and concession, picnic facilities, a rest room, and a play area. You often see seals frolicking in the river in front of the fort, and across the bay in Edgecomb stands the house that was prepared for Marie Antoinette.

That's a fascinating tale. It seems that Captain Samuel Clough, master of the merchantman *Sally,* in the following of his trade frequently found himself in France. He was a levelheaded, hardfisted, strait-laced Yankee skipper with no nonsense about him, so I find it a little odd that he should lend himself and his ship to so romantic an enterprise as the rescuing of the French queen from the guillotine. Something about her situation apparently appealed to his imagination and chivalrous instincts. Not only was he going to save Marie Antoinette, but he was also going to be sure that when she arrived in Maine she would be as comfortable and happy as possible under the circumstances.

To this end he loaded the *Sally,* as she lay in a French port, with luxurious furnishings and priceless bric-a-brac and even with rolls of fine wallpaper and heavy silk hangings and with some of the Queen's personal belongings and clothes, so that his plain Maine home would be a fitting background for Her Majesty. This must have been an extremely difficult and dangerous project. The Queen was under what today would be called house arrest, and the activities of anyone who had the slightest contact with her were subject to the closest scrutiny. Everything that Captain Clough accomplished had to be done indirectly, if he valued his head. I have no doubt that a great deal of hush money changed hands before the *Sally* was loaded and ready to sail.

I'm not sure how Mrs. Clough viewed this undertaking, but I can imagine. Undoubtedly she worried about her husband's safety, and I can imagine her slamming pots and pans around in her kitchen whenever she thought of Samuel's foolishness, because that is the way I would have acted in her position. Probably I would have worried too about what to feed the royal guest, wondering if, after a diet of fancy French cooking, she'd be satisfied with a good clam chowder and a slab of johnnycake. Possibly I would have resented my husband's news that he was refurnishing the house for this woman. Maybe these old chairs and tables weren't the best in the world, I would have thought; but they were mine and I liked them. I would certainly have felt serious qualms about my own qualifications to act as hostess to Marie Antoinette; and evidently Mrs. Clough experienced the same misgivings, because on one occasion her husband wrote her, apparently in answer to a letter expressing doubts, "Do not prepare to receive a queen, but only a very sad and broken-hearted lady."

Nobody knows how the rather unlikely situation would have worked out. After Captain Clough had waited and waited for the Queen to be smuggled aboard the *Sally*, there was a sudden and unexpected outbreak of violence. Marie Antoinette was seized, and eventually beheaded; and Captain Clough had to make sail with all haste to escape repercussions for his part in the attempted rescue. He had no time to unload the Queen's belongings, but perforce brought them back to Maine. For a long time he stored the possessions, unused, in a room of his home, either because—as some persons think—of his personal devotion to the Queen, or because—as seems more likely— his rigid Yankee sense of right and wrong wouldn't permit him to use or dispose of property that didn't belong to him.

In the end, however, when no one appeared to claim the things, they were gradually put into service in the big, plain, colonial house, and after the death of the Cloughs they were auctioned off. And that is how it happens that occasionally and in unexpected places there are still found in this area exquisite French court miniatures, delicate silhouettes, and priceless furniture richly inlaid with the fleur-de-lis. Some of the articles have made their way to the Metropolitan Museum of Art in New York, a few remain in the Clough House, and more are scattered around the countryside. The house, which has been moved from its original site to a spot opposite the North Edgecomb post office, may be visited by arrangement with and at the convenience of the present owner.

Captain Clough also introduced the coon cat to the Maine coast. This is a kind of cat very seldom seen anywhere else, a gentle and fragile breed with long frosty-gray hair and delicate ring markings, impossible to confuse with a gray Persian or Angora. There are a lot of rumors about the coon cat, most of them untrue. Those who should know better say that they are the result of interbreeding between an ordinary house cat and a wild raccoon, a biological impossibility, since animals of different genera do not hybridize. Coon cats are also supposed to die if moved to any other locality.

Actually the original coon cat was brought back from China by Captain Clough, and the present-day coon cats are its descendants, crossbred with common cats. They are rather difficult to raise, it's true, since they are susceptible to a number of diseases, especially to pneumonia; and they don't always breed true. However, quite a few people raise them for sale very profitably. They can be transplanted, in spite of rumor. I know, because I have an aunt who bought one in Maine, took it home to Ohio, and shuttled it back and forth between the two states for years, until it died of old age.

The Boothbays are beyond Edgecomb on a ragged peninsula which lies between the estuaries of the Sheepscot and the Damariscotta rivers and ends in a fair-sized bay, called Booth Bay. There are Boothbay, East Boothbay, Boothbay Harbor, and Ocean Point on the peninsula, and across Townshend Gut on a wooded island are Southport and Newagen. Boothbay, purchased from the Indians for twenty beaver skins (or their equivalent in trade goods), was settled as Newagen in 1630 and later renamed Townshend. Both names survive in other connections, as you see.

The town was abandoned during the Indian wars of 1668, but was later resettled when David Dunbar received a land grant from George II, in 1748. Dunbar brought to the peninsula a group of Scotch, Irish, and Scotch-Irish colonists, hand-picked for their industry and reliability, so the whole area flourished as a trading, fishing, farming,

Pleasure yachts abound at the docks and along the shores of Boothbay Harbor.

and shipbuilding center. Boothbay Harbor separated from Boothbay and was incorporated as a town in 1889.

With the decline of shipping, all these towns suffered a regression; but the rise of the tourist business certainly put them on their feet again. This whole locality is one of the most popular resort regions along the entire coast. Not only are there tourists by the drove here, but a great many artists and writers spend their summers in one or another of the Boothbays. Some of them like it so much that they live here all the year round.

Boothbay Harbor is a favorite port for small boat and pleasure sailors, and a regatta and water festival is held here annually. It is also the home port of MacMillan's yearly trips to Laborador and Greenland. In summer scheduled boats run daily to Squirrel and Monhegan Islands; you can take one of the regular sightseeing boats among the nearer islands; or you can charter a boat for deep-sea fishing.

If you don't like boating, there are a great many gift and craft shops ashore to browse through, and the art colony to visit; or you can go to McKnown's Point to inspect the U.S. fish hatchery and aquarium and to observe the life of the large colony of seals kept there near the wharf. There's no excuse for being bored in Boothbay Harbor.

Boothbay isn't quite as lively as the Harbor, but it's busy enough. For those who follow the straw-hat circuit, there is the Boothbay Playhouse, one of Maine's better-known summer theaters; and there are dozens of attractive shops. The narrow streets are always full of people who seem to be having a good time; and some of the oddest costumes for sea-town wear ever conceived by man or woman may be seen there.

In spite of the inevitable lunatic fringe that you always encounter at any popular resort, these places are surprisingly unspoiled and have retained a great deal of their old charm. One reason is that a number of the cottage owners take pride in preserving a native and weather-beaten effect in their dwellings, in keeping with the locale. Another is that boats are still built along here, and the boatyards lend a maritime grace. But perhaps the chief reason is that it is almost impossible for anyone to ruin as lovely a country as this is, no matter what modern wonders they try to perform. After all, there isn't too much man can do about the sea and the fogs and the gulls circling over. They remain as they have always been.

If you have the time and inclination to visit only one island of the Maine coast, Monhegan should be that island.

I'm not counting as islands places you can reach by car over bridges, although I suppose that technically they are. But it takes more than encirclement by water to make an island. There must also be inaccessibility except by boat. An island becomes a peninsula, to my mind, the minute it becomes available by bridge, no different from any other cape or promontory. Part of visiting an island is the change of means of transportation, with the accompanying change of pace and viewpoint. You haven't visited an island unless you have seen it rise from the sea, seen it change from a cloud on the horizon to a solid bastion of earth and rock, with houses small and clear in the sunlight. There's nothing very special about driving off the end of a bridge onto another piece of land, and nobody treats the occasion as anything special. But the docking of the boat from the mainland on any island is an event, and treated as such. Unless you've gone through that, you can't possibly absorb the island mood and atmosphere.

Monhegan is the best island to visit because of its remoteness and because of its small size. Both factors contribute to an evocation of the true island spirit. Measuring only one by two and a half miles, Monhegan lies twenty miles out to sea from Boothbay Harbor; or it may be reached from Port Clyde or Thomaston.

Monhegan was first described in 1569 as "a great island that was backed like a whale," and that description has not been bettered in as few words, although it would take a whole book to do it justice. The man who summed up this place so cleverly was David Ingram, whose word in some matters was not very reliable. Ingram was a sailor who had gone to Mexico on an expedition under the free-booter, Sir John Hawkins. There for some reason, probably disciplinary, he had been put ashore. Deciding to walk home to England, he did manage to walk from Mexico to Nova Scotia, where he thumbed a ride the rest of the way on a French trading vessel.

It's too bad he was such an awful liar, because a true account of his adventures on that incredibly long journey would be much more fascinating than any tall tale he could possibly have dreamed up. But we just don't know what really happened to him on the way, and we never will. In the matter of Monhegan, however, he was very accurate for a change. For this island really does have the humped, tapering appearance of a whale rising from the sea.

For such a small, isolated place, Monhegan has a long and colorful history. On the ledges of the adjacent islet of Manana there are marks which seem to indicate that the Vikings landed here as far back as the year 1000. We know that Basque, Breton, Spanish, and Portuguese fishermen were very familiar with the island before Columbus discovered America, and that Cabot visited it in 1498. Captain George Weymouth's *Archangel* put in here in 1605 for water, at which time he raised the first British flag and erected the first cross in New England; and later that same summer, Champlain sighted the island. John Smith landed here in 1614, and in 1625 the first deed of conveyance to be signed in New England was executed here by Abraham Shurt, a notary, who thereby won for himself the title "Father of Conveyances."

The first permanent settlement was probably around 1720, although the island had been used for years as a drying and repair base by European fishermen and had supported several temporary settlements of longer or shorter duration. It was just off Monhegan that the *Enterprise* fought the *Boxer* in 1813.

Monhegan has always been a fishing island, and it still is; but it's so much more than that. It's an isolated entity with the village on its lower side, near the tail of the whale, facing onto the little harbor, and great cliffs rising on the other side to drop straight into the sea from a height of 160 feet. The scenery is spectacular, with the surf, forever restless, breaking thunderously along the ledges and the sea spread out unhindered and unbroken to the far horizons.

There are flowers everywhere, and the little gardens of the island women, surrounded by picket fences, simply boil with prim, old-fashioned varieties. There's a forest of pine and spruce, called Cathedral Wood, traversed by little trails over which it is a delight to walk. It's shady and sheltered and aromatic; but you can still hear the gulls crying over and the distant trample of the surf above the singing of the wind in the treetops.

Monhegan is really a way of life. The islanders number less than a hundred, but they know how they want to live, and they live that way. There are no movies or hamburger joints or garish filling stations. There aren't even any concrete sidewalks, or any doctor, unless a visitor happens to be one. Life is quiet and paced by the tides and the seasons and the weather; and if you don't like it that way, you know what you can do about it. You can go somewhere else.

If you will take Monhegan as you find it, you are made to feel very welcome; and when you go home, you may well find yourself the recipient of bouquets of bright flowers, because it is the charming custom of the islanders to speed the departing guest in this fashion.

Monhegan has a few summer hotels and some of the homes will accommodate tourists. There are small shops, and a public library erected in memory of Jackie and Edward, two little children who were drowned while playing along the shore; so the visitor can find something to do on stormy days. There is an internationally known art colony, too, started by Rockwell Kent. Many serious and famous artists spend their summers on the island. It's a good place to work, not only because of its beauty but also because of the general atmosphere of quiet purpose.

Newcastle and Damariscotta, twin towns on opposite banks of the Damariscotta River, back on U.S. 1, seem almost urban after Monhegan. But they are really two pretty, tree-shaded villages containing some old houses and a great deal of charm. Newcastle has the distinction of having been the first Catholic parish in Maine, established in the latter part of the eighteenth century when Father Jean de Cheverus came to America from France to work among the coastal Indians.

His church, built in 1803, still stands and is the oldest Catholic church in Maine. The altar piece is older than that, having been made in France 250 years ago; and some of the paintings have come a long way, too, having been brought here from a Mexican convent during the Mexican War. Father de Cheverus became the first bishop of Maine, in 1808, and subsequently Cardinal de Cheverus, archbishop of Bordeaux.

Damariscotta is about the busiest place of its size I have ever seen. The name means "Meeting Place of the Alewives," because in the spring the alewives, a species of small herring, run up the Damariscotta River to spawn in the fresh water above. Before the coming of the white men, the Indians netted them by the bushel here, and today they are still netted. But more than alewives meet in Damariscotta. It's a shopping center for the area, a fair-sized resort town, the head of navigation in the river, the center of a lively clamming industry, and the take-off point for several nearby places. It also, like Wiscasset, sponsors Open House Days, which attract numbers of people.

Damariscotta's history is much like that of many other Maine coast towns. It was colonized early in the seventeenth century, abandoned because of the French and the

Indians, then rebuilt. After that it enjoyed a period of prosperity during the fishing and shipping era, and finally settled down to what it is today.

One of the most interesting things in this locality is the prehistoric shell heaps about half a mile up the river from the town. These are unusually good to study because they have been worked over to some extent, and you can see the various strata very easily. The top layer was deposited by the Abenakis, within history; but nobody really knows who is responsible for the bottom layers or how old they are. Inspecting these mounds is almost like seeing a blueprint of pre-European culture—a blueprint that you can almost, but not quite, read and fully interpret.

Seaward from Damariscotta near the end of the Bristol Peninsula is Pemaquid, and at the end of the peninsula, Pemaquid Point, one of the most photographed spots on the Maine coast. A heavy surf breaks almost constantly on the ledges here, and the firs and spruces grow to the high-tide line; so the character of the Maine coast is often, and fairly, illustrated by pictures of Pemaquid Point.

This area was about the earliest section of the coast to be settled. Champlain visited it in 1605, when he was charting the coast, and found a settlement already established here.

At Pemaquid Beach there are two hundred cellar holes and some segments of paved street that have never been satisfactorily accounted for. They date well before the Popham colony. Some people believe that the Vikings had a colony here; but the more widely accepted theory is that before the coast was opened up for permanent colonization, a group of English merchants maintained a fishing and trading base here. It was in existence in 1614, since John Smith then reported a port called Pemaquid "in the Maine" opposite Monhegan, and spent Christmas Day of 1614 in a cove across the bay from it, a place now called Christmas Cove because of that fact.

This land originally belonged to the Samoset who met the Pilgrims at Plymouth; or rather it belonged to his tribe, since Indians did not own real estate as individuals but controlled its use as groups. When the Pilgrims were near starvation in 1622, Samoset guided a party of them to Pemaquid, where he had a store of corn laid by. In recognition of this deed of charity, the English purchased this whole peninsula from Samoset for the equivalent of fifty beaver skins instead of simply appropriating it, as was their usual custom. Then in 1625, John Brown of Monhegan bought it in the transaction that won Abraham Shurt the title "Father of Conveyances," as we have mentioned before.

After that, Pemaquid had a stormy career. The first fort, built at Pemaquid Beach in 1630, was soon destroyed by the Indians. In 1677, a bigger and better fort was built by order of Governor Andros, but pirates burned that. Then Sir William Phipps raised an extensive and well-equipped fort on the same spot, supposedly impregnable. Shortly afterward, Baron de St. Castin, full of wrath over insults he considered he had sustained and breathing fire because some of his Indians had been tortured by the English, swept down on this indestructible fort and leveled it to the ground, killing all the garrison for good measure. In 1729, a fourth fort was built on the same site; and this establishes a record, not only for number of forts on the same foundation, but for optimism in continuing to build on a jinxed spot as well. This fort too was destroyed during the Revolution by patriots of the vicinity, to prevent its falling into British hands.

The fifth or present fort may have better luck. It really isn't a fort at all, but a reproduction of Phipp's Fort William Henry, and it houses a museum containing Indian relics, copies of old deeds, and ancient military equipment.

This peninsula and the adjacent islands, many of which may be reached over bridges, is a territory of outstanding coastal beauty. There are all sorts of accommodations for tourists, including an excellent camp site near Bristol and several picnic grounds. At Pemaquid Beach is one of the very few sandy beaches on this whole stretch of rocky coast. Boat trips may be taken to the farther islands, or, if you'd rather play golf, the Wewanock Golf Club between South Bristol and Walpole allows guest players.

The oldest schoolhouse in Maine, a rough granite structure now disused but kept in repair by a local organization, stands near the village of Round Pond. If you happen to have your children with you, and if they happen to attend one of our really luxurious modern schools, you'd better take them into this schoolhouse and make them sit on one of the rough plank seats nailed at right angles to the walls and accommodating three pupils each. Make them sit there a good long time, until their backs begin to ache. Then maybe you won't hear so much fussing about school when you arrive back home.

East of Pemaquid Neck is Muscongus Bay, into which flows the Medomac, one of the important smaller rivers of this coast. At the head of tidewater is Waldoboro, named for General Samuel Waldo, who held the Waldo patent covering this township and most of Waldo County as well.

In 1748 he encouraged a group of German immigrants to settle here, an unusual circumstance in a territory that was almost entirely English-occupied. I don't know exactly what inducements he offered them, but an inscription on one of the stones in the old German cemetery in the village reads: "This town was settled in 1748 by Germans who immigrated to this place with the promise and expectation of finding a prosperous city, instead of which they found nothing but wilderness."

This sounds a little bitter to me, and it's not surprising that the colony was a failure. Waldoboro is sometimes referred to as "Maine's Lost Colony," but it wasn't truly lost in the sense that Roanoke was, where all the inhabitants mysteriously disappeared. The settlers of Waldoboro merely became disgusted and moved away; although a few must have remained, since German names, borne by descendants of the original colonists, are still common here. The little old German meetinghouse still stands, too, and is open for services once a year. In it you can see a collection of old German books and other mementos of the early days. This was the first Lutheran church in Maine.

Waldoboro has another first—the first five-masted schooner, the *Governor Ames,* was launched here when Waldoboro, like most towns of the Middle Coast, was a shipbuilding town. Shipbuilding declined here as elsewhere, although some smaller vessels are still built in the boatyards. There is a seasonal industry of the catching and packing of alewives, and a pearl-button factory in the town.

But I imagine the largest source of income is from the tourists. The town offers a shopping and service center for the area and possesses hotels, restaurants, tourist homes, and gift shops. The boat-chartering business is lively here, as the deep-sea fishing is usually good. Here fly-fishing for pollock and mackerel has grown very popular, which should make some of my purist fishing friends exceedingly happy. When you charter a boat here or down the point at the little village of Friendship, you get the works. The captain furnishes himself, his boat, bait, and tackle; and in addition he will make your catch into as good a chowder as you ever ate, if you want him to.

If you would like to experience a clambake but don't quite know how to go about it, that can be arranged, too. At very reasonable rates, you can get someone to manage the whole thing: secure the clams and lobsters and crabs, the potatoes and green corn and coffee, build the driftwood fire between two granite boulders by the sea, steam the whole meal under a blanket of seaweed, show you how to deal with a lobster, and clean up the mess afterward.

This same service is offered in many places along the coast, and it's probably just as good elsewhere; but here in the Waldo-Friendship vicinity happens to be where I myself have attended the most clambakes, so I can speak from personal experience. If you are new to the Maine coast and have never been on a real clambake, I most earnestly advise you to try it. Clams and lobsters eaten outdoors within spitting distance of the ocean are *not* the same as those eaten at a white-clothed table where you have to mind your manners. Wear old clothes, though. They're going to require laundering immediately.

The little hamlet of Friendship, in addition to having such a delightful name, is a perfectly charming place. It's a true sea town. Almost all of the local inhabitants travel about, even on short errands, in boats, and almost every side street ends at a small wharf. They respect boats in Friendship, and take good care of them, keeping them trim and painted. The famous Friendship sloop, the carry-all and pioneer equivalent of the Ford pickup today, originated here; and while it was not the most famous and celebrated type of boat, it was probably the most generally useful to the largest number of people, in daily life along the coast.

In Muscongus Bay are many, many islands, two of which deserve special mention for different reasons. The first bears the unlovely name of Hog Island, probably because it was once used as a hog pasture. About fifty years ago, an Amherst professor and his wife, the David Todds, started spending their summers on Hog Island. After their death, their daughter, Dr. Millicent Todd Bingham, and Dr. James M. Todd acquired the whole island and in 1932 established the Todd Wild Life Sanctuary in memory of Mrs. Bingham's mother.

Most wild life sanctuaries confine their efforts simply to not molesting the birds and animals. This one is different. On thirty acres of the land you will find the Audubon Camp of Maine, conducted each summer by the National Audubon Society for adult education in nature and conservation. The sessions are especially planned for teachers, leaders of youth groups, and camp counselors, but anyone whose hobby is nature or who has a professional interest in nature may attend.

Plants and animals and birds are studied under their natural conditions on field trips about the island. The sessions are two weeks long, repeated throughout the summer; and friends of mine who have attended tell me that they had a wonderful time and made some lasting friendships, in addition to learning a lot. Some very fine books, photographs, and paintings of birds have come out of the Audubon Camp meetings, and the whole project seems to me to be an excellent and important one.

Loud's Island, which used to be called Muscongus Island and still is on government charts, is interesting for another reason. If you want to get over there today, you have to find someone in Round Pond, near Pemaquid, to row you. There isn't much to be seen after you get there. The population consists of a few families, and there is no village center: only a schoolhouse, a small store, and a post office in a room of one of the few homes scattered along a dirt road. There's a little church, too, which was moved piece by piece to Loud's from Malaga Island by the Maine Sea Coast Mission aboard the schooner *Abdon Keene,* and reassembled here by the entire population of the island. Aside from that, Loud's Island is just a quiet place that Progress has by-passed.

The interesting thing about it is its history. Although the island has been inhabited since 1650 and although it is three miles long and a mile wide, it was accidentally left off the Geodetic Survey map of the Maine coast. For a while the fact that they didn't officially exist failed to trouble the inhabitants of Loud's Island. They were accustomed to voting and paying taxes in Bristol, and they kept on doing so. Every year the tax collector would row over, chalk on the door of each house the amount due from the inhabitants thereof, and, as soon as it had been paid, rub his chalk marks off again—a very simple system that satisfied everyone until 1860.

That was the year when Lincoln came up for election.

In a practically solid Republican territory, the Loud's Islanders were, oddly enough, all Democrats; so when the votes were counted in Bristol, it was discovered to the horror of the authorities that the town had gone Democratic. This was a terrible thing. Then some genius remembered that Loud's Island was not on the map; was in fact a no-man's-land. So all the island votes were thrown out, and Bristol returned thankfully to the Republican fold.

Very understandably, the islanders were livid with rage. They notified Bristol that as of that minute they had seceded, and the next time the tax collector came they rubbed his marks off their doors and chased him from the island. Moreover, they set up their own government and became an independent republic, and by all accounts an excellent and successful one.

Bristol still ignored their secession. When the names of nine islanders were drawn for service during the Civil War, recruiting officers were sent over to collect the men. The entire male population of the island armed itself and met the officers with the news that if they tried to land, a state of open warfare would promptly ensue between the Republic of Muscongus and the Town of Bristol. When one officer returned later, he was subject to such a heavy bombardment of potatoes thrown by the women of the island that he fled in disorder. He reported back to his friends on the mainland that he'd undertake to capture Richmond itself, if only he could have one regiment of women from Loud's Island.

Then, having made it plain what was what, and since Loud's had no quarrel with the United States, but only with Bristol, the islanders held a meeting, conducted their own draft, and in addition sent the U.S. treasury nine hundred dollars—which was for them a very large sum indeed—to be used for war purposes. So if Loud's Island seems almost half asleep today, I think it may be forgiven in view of its spirited past.

Actually the people are as independent as they ever

were, in a quieter and less spectacular way. When the subject of public relief was broached to them during the depression, one man refused aid, saying, "Thunderation!
We ain't never had prosperity, so how'n tarnation can we
have a depression?" The citizens may not be rolling in
wealth, but they are self-supporting and self-respecting,
and they intend to remain that way.

In Maine, when anyone says, "If he don't watch snug,
he's goin' to land in Thomaston," it means just one thing:
if the individual in question isn't careful, he's due for a
stay in the state prison.

This is too bad, since Thomaston, incorporated in 1777
on the St. George's River, is really a pretty place, with
some nice old churches and trees and houses. One of these
houses is "Montpelier," open to the public for fifty cents.
It is a reproduction of the mansion built in 1793 by General Harry Knox, who first distinguished himself at the
Battle of Bunker Hill and then became the first Secretary
of War, under Washington. He married the daughter of
the Samuel Waldo who brought the Germans to Waldoboro. (One of the things I like about Maine coast history
is the neighborly way you keep meeting the same people
over and over, in different places and connections.)

Knox had some money of his own, and his in-laws had
land and money and influence, so after his Cabinet career
came to a close, he moved to Thomaston, built the beautiful "Montpelier," and went into business. Or businesses.
Thomaston was at the time a very active place with a
number of industries: shipbuilding, brickmaking, lime
burning, farming, lumbering, fishing, and trading. General
Knox tried them all and lost money at everything he tried.
He just wasn't a very good businessman, which is less of
a crime than a misfortune. He died in comparative
poverty.

Thomaston isn't as flourishing as it was in the days of
the General, but it is still a seaport, builds some boats,
has the usual hotels, services, and shopping facilities of a

town catering to a fairly large area, and is the location of one of the largest cement plants in New England.

Southward from Thomaston, a narrow, broken peninsula about fifteen miles long thrusts out to sea. It is wreathed with little islands and dotted with small fishing and lobstering communities: St. George, Long Cove, Tenant's Harbor, Martinsville and, near the end, Port Clyde. None of these is very large or very important as places go today, but they are all full of an unpretentious and unselfconscious appeal.

Probably Port Clyde is the best known. Life there centers around the wharves from which the boats to the islands and nearby coastal towns put out, and to which the fishing vessels return with their catches for the local packing plant. Sailors know its harbor as being exceptionally good and safe and ice free except during the severest winters. The business of the town revolves around the sea; and, while you might have a little trouble getting your car fixed, you can have your boat hauled out and repaired at a moment's notice.

It was near here that Weymouth seized the five Indians whom he later handed over to Gorges in the first hostile act by the English against the natives, an act which indirectly brought about the early development of Maine. But all that is ancient history and probably best forgotten.

What we've really come way out here to see is something else again: a simple country schoolhouse in the tiny town of Martinsville. This schoolhouse replaced another on the same site, in which Sarah Orne Jewett once taught, and in which she wrote *The Country of the Pointed Firs*, choosing to work here rather than at her boardinghouse because her landlady was so sociable that concentration was impossible. The book deals with this immediate locality—with the very same ledges and fields and views of the sea that you can see for yourself, standing almost anywhere in Martinsville. It's a simple book, more of an account of a summer spent on this cape than a plotted story;

but everything the author says is just as true today as it was back in the '90's, when the work was published.

Her characters are wonderful. I know an old lobsterman who is just *exactly* like Mrs. Todd's gentle brother William; and I recently spent an afternoon listening to the spit'n'image of Mrs. Fosdick, "the best hand in the world to make a visit." By this is meant that she made a career of paying visits of several days, not always at the convenience of her hostess. However she talked so entertainingly and continuously of old scandals and excitements during her stay that in the end nobody could help being glad she came.

But it's in descriptions of this peninsula that Miss Jewett really excelled. She was a native, remember, of the Eastern Coast, which is very different from the Middle Coast. Listen to this: "It had been growing gray and cloudy, like the first evening of autumn, and a shadow had fallen on the darkening shore. Suddenly, as we looked, a gleam of golden sunlight struck the outer islands, and one of them shone out clear in the light . . . like a sudden revelation of the world beyond this which some believe to be so near." Or to this: "A late golden robin, with the most joyful and eager of voices, was singing close by in a thicket of wild roses." Or this: "I watched the gulls agree and turn and sway together down the long slopes of air." All of this, and more, describes this region as accurately today as when it was written in the little schoolhouse of Martinsville.

Nobody could write like that without conviction; so I think there can be no doubt that Sarah Orne Jewett, at least, found her personal Down-East on the little tongue of land that separates Muscongus Bay from the eastern limit of the Middle Coast, the Penobscot River and Penobscot Bay.

Lobster shacks, traps, and buoys clutter the coastline at Port Clyde.

Tall masts tower above the docks at Rockland, formerly a great shipbuilding center.

13 · Penobscot Bay

Rockland, North Haven, Vinalhaven, Camden
Darkharbor, Islesboro, Belfast, Searsport, Bucksport
Castine, Deer Isle, Ellsworth, Blue Hill

OF THE hundreds of indentations in the coast of Maine, Penobscot Bay is the largest and most important. It measures over thirty miles across its entrance, and is about thirty miles long from the open ocean to the mouth of the Penobscot River. Passage for ships with a draft up to eighteen feet is possible and common for twenty-four miles more up the river to the city of Bangor, the tidehead and head of navigation. A chain of islands divides the bay laterally, and it is sheltered from the storms of the sea by other islands lying across the entrance.

The channels giving access to the bay have fascinating names: Eggemoggin Reach, Deer Island Thorofare and Merchant Row to the East Bay; and Muscle Ridge and Two Bush Channels to the West. It's a beautiful, beautiful bay! Spruce-covered headlands jut boldly from its shores, jewel-like islands float on its surface, and the gentle, glacier-rounded contours of the Camden Hills look down on its broad reaches.

All the early explorers knew Penobscot Bay: the English, the French, the Spanish, the Portuguese, and even the Dutch. They gave to some of the geographical features of the coast names which still survive: names like Ile au Haut and Verona and Owl's Head and Burnt Coat, which is a corruption of Champlain's Brûlecôte. A great many of these adventurers came in hopes of finding the fabulous city of Norumbega, supposed to be located somewhere on the Penobscot. In fact, that big liar David Ingram, who crossed the Penobscot during his jaunt from Mexico to Nova Scotia, actually claimed to have visited Norumbega. But no such misleading publicity was necessary, really. The advantages of the area were apparent to any experienced eye. It has been said that a great river is the equivalent of a great key unlocking the resources of a country; and nowhere has this been truer than in the case of the Penobscot.

The Penobscot was the old boundary between the French and the English possessions, the line between Acadia and New England. Since boundaries in those days were lively and disputed spots, the countryside saw a great deal of fighting between the French and the English, the Indians and the English or French, and on one occasion, the Dutch and the French. This was the Baron de St. Castin's home territory, and wherever that strange, proud Basque was, there was apt to be considerable activity.

Then later, during the Revolution, the bay saw Englishman pitched against Englishman, when the force under Lovell, Saltonstall, and Paul Revere disgraced themselves so thoroughly by abandoning their fleet to a small British force and walking home to Boston.

After the war was over and danger removed, the bay country was rapidly colonized and, along with the rest of the Maine coast, became a great and prosperous shipbuilding, lumber, granite, lime, fishing, farming, and ice region. It is still a thriving commercial area, with the tourist trade added to its other industries.

Rockland is the first and the largest town on the west shore of the bay. The Indians called the site Catawamkeag, the Great Landing Place, because of the excellent harbor and the location near the entrance of the bay. The city was originally a part of Thomaston, until it incorporated separately as East Thomaston in 1848. The name was later changed to Rockland in recognition of the importance of the limestone on which the city's prosperity depended at the time.

Unlike so many other Maine coast towns, Rockland is not particularly impressed with tourists and summer trade money. Oh, of course visitors are welcome and allowance is made for their entertainment and comfort, but they are not an obsession of Rockland. The city has other fish to fry. Due respect is paid the picturesque and historic past, but the present and future are the matters of most concern. As a result, Rockland is a busy, healthy modern port and community which has survived several acute crises.

For example, it was once a great shipbuilding and lumber town. Then the trees were all cut off, and ship-building everywhere declined; but Rockland didn't. It turned its energies to the burning of the local deposits of limestone into lime and became the largest producer in the United States and probably the world. Then increasing use of steel and Portland cement in construction seriously crippled the lime-burning industry, so that many of the old quarries and kilns had to be abandoned. Did Rockland dismay? Not at all. As much lime as is marketable is still burned in the locality, and the slack of manpower is taken up by other enterprises. Right now it so happens that Rockland is the largest distribution center for lobsters in the world; but if the lobster market suddenly collapses, I have no doubt at all that the city will find some other means of supporting itself. It seems to be a most adaptable place.

It's not a city that puts all its eggs in one basket, anyhow. Other aspects of the fishing industry besides the sale of lobsters occupy the citizens. A great fleet of trawlers operates out of Rockland, and several plants are kept busy processing and packing the fish. The shipyards haven't been entirely given up, any more than the lime kilns have.

Equipment has been modernized, so that steel boats as well as wooden ones still go down the ways in Rockland. Wrecking and salvage companies work from the port, hauling boats off reefs and towing disabled vessels into harbor. The Coast Guard maintains a section base there, as does the lighthouse service, and several ferries to the islands off the mouth of the bay berth in Rockland. In addition, just offshore is an arrangement of buoys in the water and towers ashore that mark an accurately measured mile. Often you can see naval and commercial ships out there, conducting speed trials. The Rockland waterfront is a very, very busy place.

Considering its present and past eminence as a seaport, which always connotes—perhaps unfairly—sailors celebrating shore leave by bending the festive elbow, I think it is a little odd that Rockland, over a hundred years ago, organized the first Total Abstinence Society in America. I'm not talking about temperance now, but complete abstinence, an unheard-of thing at the time. But on second thought, maybe it's not so odd. Maybe it's a clear case of cause and effect.

Rockland had her part in an almost notorious affair. Everybody has heard of the loss of the steamer *Portland* in a great storm just before Thanksgiving of 1898. She set out from Boston for Portland with about a hundred and seventy-five souls aboard, and was never seen or heard of again. Older people all along the New England coast still tell about the terrible night when the *Portland* went down. That same night a Rockland granite schooner, the *Addie E. Snow*, was lost too. Nobody knew exactly how or where, any more than they did in the case of the *Portland*.

The loss of the *Addie E. Snow* was a little more understandable, since granite schooners were rather unmanageable and could conceivably founder, while a great many people maintained that the *Portland* was too sound a ship and commanded by too experienced and able a captain to meet with any ordinary disaster. For half a century, the whole thing was one of the great mysteries of the sea.

Then in November of 1944, a Rockland scallop dragger brought up the *Portland*'s bell at a point just off the tip of Cape Cod. Now at least the place of her sinking had been determined. But Edward Rowe Snow, whose interest lies with the sea and ships, wanted to know *why* she sank. He hired a crew of divers to find out.

What they discovered seems almost unbelievable, when you think how big the ocean is and how small the chances are of two ships, neither of which is on her proper course in a used shipping lane, colliding with all that space in which to maneuver. Nevertheless the *Addie Snow*'s bow was found to be embedded in the side of the *Portland,* and both ships evidently sank almost at once, without the saving of a single person. It must have been horrible. But that happened a long time ago, and we can't hold Rockland responsible in any case.

As I have said before, Rockland is a city of today. It is a good shopping center, and available by both bus *and* by air. This fact is worth mentioning, because this far Down-East not every community has commercial air service.

There are some lovely scenic drives out of Rockland along the coast, especially to Owl's Head Light. The little lighthouse stands on a tall headland and is almost too picturesque to be true. It looks like something thought up to attract tourists; but it isn't. President John Quincy Adams commissioned its building in 1826, when nobody toured Maine.

One thing Rockland does sponsor for the tourists' benefit—and its own, of course—is the annual Lobster Festival. This usually takes place on the first week end in August, and it is really a gigantic clambake. There's a big parade in the morning, with bands from all over the state and floats and majorettes. Probably every state in the Union and a great many of the provinces of Canada are represented in the enormous crowd. The object of the occasion, as far as the visitor is concerned, is to eat the big shore dinner: lobster, clams, fish, green corn, potato chips, the works.

Over twenty thousand lobsters are served each year, along with a booklet instructing those from the prairie states how to dismember a lobster. It's a terrific undertaking on the part of the community. All the service clubs of the city cooperate to make the affair successful, and the profits are devoted to some project of civic benefit. If you're in the vicinity at the time, it's worth attending.

From Rockland it is possible to go by ferry to several of the offshore islands, like North Haven and Vinalhaven. Although separated only by a narrow channel called the Fox Island Thorofare, these two are very different in character. North Haven is a quiet and beautiful resort island, where several families of unostentatious wealth own summer estates, among them the Dwight Morrows. Anne Morrow Lindbergh speaks of the island with great affection in her book *North to the Orient*.

Vinalhaven is something else again. It is a fishing island, a working island, basically, although there are some hotels and resort facilities there. It was once a great granite-quarrying center; but, as we have said before, that industry declined with the extended use of other building materials. One of the odd old galumpuses which were used to haul the granite blocks to the ships now stands on Vinalhaven Green as a monument to bygone days. It looks like some sort of prehistoric monster.

The first settlers arrived on these islands around 1760, and there were enough of them by 1789 to justify incorporation as a town. The location of the islands in the open ocean off the mouth of the bay is such that the surveying of boundaries has always been a little vague and subject to revision. Therefore it is a fact that a man who was seventy-five years old in 1850, and who had resided all his life in North Haven, could truthfully say that he had lived in four counties, two towns, two states (Massachusetts and Maine), and two countries (the British Empire and the United States). He might possibly add with pride that, although he had been impressed by the British during the War of 1812 to work as forced labor on the fortifications at Castine, he had made such a nuisance of himself, breaking tools and malingering on the job, that they had returned him to the island in disgust. Islanders everywhere are apt to be pretty hard to force.

It would be impossible for me to say which of the towns along Penobscot Bay I like best, but I'd certainly hesitate a long time before passing by Camden. It's a perfectly lovely place. The location is naturally beautiful, on a high, wide tree-shaded bench of land with the blue, island-spangled waters of the bay spread out before it and the green Camden Hills rising abruptly behind. But a great many beautiful sites have been completely ruined by the hand of man.

Such is not the case in Camden. I used the town as a shopping center all one summer and, whenever I went there, I was enchanted all over again with the way the citizens kept house. The streets were always clean, and the trees arching over them always looked as though they'd been properly sprayed and trimmed. Everyone's lawn was green and recently mowed and edged, and all the ornamental shrubs were pruned enough to look neat but not tortured. The lamp posts along the streets had flower boxes ringing them at a point about ten feet from the ground, full of red geraniums and trailing green-and-white vinca, and the little parks were cared for and restful. In short, I just *loved* the looks of Camden.

Much of the credit for this state of affairs must be given to Mary Louise Bok, the daughter of Cyrus H. K. Curtis. Like so many other Maine coast towns that have become resorts, Camden used to be just another seaport and fishing town, with a few small local industries. Then the Maine coast was "discovered" by the wealthy and influential who took yacht trips along it or had artist friends who went to the wilds to paint. Among those who bought land and built summer places in Camden was Mrs. Bok. A sense of responsibility often goes hand in hand with great wealth, and such was the case of the Camden summer people. Under the leadership of Mrs. Bok, they set about improving the town.

Since they were people of taste and discrimination, their efforts were highly successful. The waterfront around the inner harbor, which used to have the cluttered look of most waterfronts, was landscaped into a lovely little park, where you can sit and watch the shipping in the bay. Between it and the public library is the outdoor amphitheater, planted with native trees and shrubs, which will seat fifteen hundred people; and for indoor entertainment, the old Camden Opera House has been remodeled into an excellent modern auditorium. In addition, annual contests are sponsored in which prizes are awarded for the best landscaping projects, which accounts for the well-groomed look of private property as well as public.

There are a lot of activities in Camden, but the one I liked best the summer I lived near there was the Dog Show. Usually dog shows fail to excite me. Sure, the dogs themselves are interesting and often beautiful; but it seems to me that a dog show places a wrong emphasis on the spending of care and time on animals that might better be applied to human subjects. However—

This Dog Show in Camden was different. It was conducted chiefly for children, and the regulations were so drawn up that anybody could enter his dog, and anybody's dog had a chance of winning something. Prizes were awarded not for the Best of Breed but to the dog with the longest ears, or the shortest tail, or the biggest feet. Any little old mongrel had a chance. There were prizes for obedience and for smartest tricks, too; and since mongrels are often—although not always, contrary to common belief —very intelligent indeed, any child's dog had a chance there, whether he was just a little mutt or a purebred, show-clipped French poodle. Both types appeared in the lists.

The big prize (a very nice camera) went to the Most Typical American Boy and Dog. The dog was a bright little thing of mixed—decidedly mixed—breed, in which Airedale and assorted terrier strains were apparent. His outstanding character trait was adoration of his master, coupled with a whole-souled desire to please him. The young man in question was about twelve years old, an engaging little devil with blue eyes, unruly hair, sunburned nose, rolled-up dungarees, and a clean, faded T-shirt. The dog's name was Gyp. The boy's name—in the best American tradition—was completely unspellable, if not unpronounceable.

But there's no end to the things you can do in and around Camden. There are frequent concerts, since a great number of musicians summer here, including the members of the Summer Harp Colony of America. In the winter there are winter sports at the Hosmer Pond Snow Bowl. There are wonderful walks in the hills in back of the village. From the top of Mt. Battie, which is really just an eight-hundred-foot hill, there is a fine view of the bay; or, if you feel up to a real climb, there is Mt. Megunticook, over thirteen hundred feet high, from the summit of which the view is truly superb.

Or you can sign up for one of the famous Windjammer Cruises which originate here in Camden. The Windjammer Cruises are aboard schooners, mostly two-masted, carrying a captain, a mate, and a cook. You and your fellow vacationists are the crew, hauling on the ropes, handling the sails and anchor—under supervision, I sincerely trust—and helping the cook occasionally. This sounds like the hard way to take a vacation; but the groups you see coming off the schooners at the end of one of the cruises look brown and healthy and in excellent physical condition, and they are always laughing their fool heads off. So I guess the rugged life has its compensations.

One of Maine's largest and best-equipped state parks is at Camden. This has not only picnic and camping facilities, but a trailer park as well. It's a wonderful place to spend a vacation on very little money, with the advantages of the seacoast, the forest, and the mountains all in one five-thousand-acre parcel. What's more, you can go there in winter for skiing, as there are shelters and trails for all classes of skiers. The Camden Hills State Park is one of Maine's better efforts along this line.

The summer that I did most of my shopping in Camden, I was living at Darkharbor on Long Island out in the middle of Penobscot Bay. This comes under my classification of a real island, since the only way you can get onto it is by ferry from Lincolnville. It isn't a very long boat ride—about half an hour—but it's long enough to make Long Island, or Islesboro as it is usually called, an island in atmosphere as well as fact. During that half hour you have a chance to readjust your thinking to island tempo as you watch the lighthouse by the island dock draw nearer and look for porpoises or seals playing in the water of the bay.

Every week I went through a period of soul searching, balancing the advantages and disadvantages of going over onto the mainland to shop. Was the tide right? If it wasn't, would I be able to get my car off the ferry without help? The tidal range here is about ten feet, and the gangplank isn't very long. If the tide is high, the gangplank lies level and everything is fine. But if it is low, the plank assumes the pitch of a roof, and whether you're going to get your jalopy up it becomes problematical, especially if it is wet with spray, fog, or rain.

There is a winch at the landing, and the boat crew will haul you up if necessary. This service is often, however, accompanied by comment, especially if you are a Woman Driver. The comment is delivered in a perfectly courteous manner and usually directed not to the driver but to the other members of the crew. Nevertheless, you wish you were somewhere else.

Then I'd ask myself if the money I'd save at the chain stores ashore (because on all islands prices are higher to take care of extra handling costs) would cover the ferry fare and the gas and oil consumed. And most of all, could I spare the time away from the island? I wasn't engaged in any project of any importance at all, aside from giving myself and my children a good time; but we liked the island and hated to waste a minute away from it.

Islesboro is about fourteen miles long and anywhere from a mile to a few feet wide, with three or four small hamlets on it. It's one of those islands that is largely given over to summer estates, where not too much allowance is made for the tourist trade. The one hotel hasn't been open for years. Most of the people own large houses and return year after year. However, there are some tourist homes, one restaurant, and some cottages for rent, so it is possible to stay there if you want to. There are no movies or other forms of commercial entertainment, but my children and I didn't feel any need for them. Everyone was so friendly, and we found so much else to do that we were never at loose ends.

What did we do? Oh, we dug clams and went fishing and built fires on the shingle beach to boil our own lobsters. We sun bathed and picked berries and explored the island and swam in the pool at Darkharbor. That was the only place north of Portland that I ever had comfortable ocean swimming. The pool is separated from the sea by a hinged gate across its narrow entrance, a type of tidal dam, so that it opens on an incoming tide and automatically closes when the tide turns. Thus the water is always at the same level, always calm, and always warmed by the sun. It's a great relief.

My son did a little caddying at the Tarrentine Golf Club and mowed the lawns of a list of clients he collected; and my daughter made friends with every child and dog on the island, and with the McCorrison's tame crow, which, although it had a large basin of water provided for the purpose, persisted in trying to bathe in a sardine tin. We sat for hours watching the shipping plying up and down in the bay: the oil tankers going up to Bangor and the lumber boats coming down, the shining yachts, and all the little sailboats. Every fair evening we saw the most beautiful sunsets of our lives over the faraway Camden Hills. We attended several entertainments by gifted summer residents, such as the monologist Ruth Draper, given for the benefit of the little island church.

We did a lot of walking, too. The southern tip of the island is covered with dense woods, and we followed an overgrown woods road down there and found an old cemetery among the trees with stones dating back to 1781. It was a wonderful, peaceful spot. Nearby, right in the middle of the woods, was one of the loveliest sights I ever saw, a great purple lilac bush that must have been fifteen feet tall and twenty-five feet in diameter, in full and prodigal bloom. You don't expect to see lilacs in the middle of the forest. We found the explanation. A few feet away was an abandoned cellar hole, so long disused that full-grown trees were rooted there. It must have been one of the original farm sites of the island, dating back to pre-Revolutionary days.

One thing we didn't see was a plaque marking the location from which the first scientific observation of an eclipse of the sun, by a group from Harvard, was made. We always meant to go and look at it, but we never got around to it. We didn't see the house in the tiny hamlet of Pripet, which had a hole shot in it by a British cannonball during the Revolution, either. There was always too much else to do.

And why do I go into all this detail about a place of relative unimportance and a summer of commonplace activity? Simply because I want you to know that staying on the Maine coast need not be a matter of running from one historic shrine or famous view to another. It's a good place just to fritter time away, too.

Sometimes, instead of going to Camden to shop, we went to Belfast. I always liked Belfast. It's a charming place, with a great many beautiful old houses and fine old trees.

If you leave U.S. 1, which goes directly through the center
of town, and drive along some of the back streets like
Church and High, you'll see some good examples of the
best architecture of the sailing era, which can be very
good indeed.

One of the reasons for Belfast's unusually tidy and well-
organized appearance may be the circumstances of its
settlement. Whereas most colonies just grew by the chance
increase of settlers, who really were nothing more nor less
than squatters, Belfast was carefully planned by a group
which secured a sound title to the land before they did
anything else at all. This group consisted of some families
of Londonderry, New Hampshire, who were dissatisfied
with that location. They sent out a surveyor named Stim-
son, who discovered and recommended the site at Belfast,
and in 1770 about thirty persons—carefully screened to
eliminate undesirables—arrived by ship.

They cleared the land as a joint project, laid out a city
plan, and then drew lots for their home plots so that there
would be no grudges or accusations of favoritism. Named
for Belfast, Ireland, since many of the settlers were of
Irish extraction, the town achieved a population of about
a hundred by the time of the Revolution. It was then so
harassed by the British stationed at Castine that it was
abandoned for five years; but after the war the same group
came back to stay.

During the shipping era, Belfast served as the home port
of a fleet of family-type schooners, the sturdy little carrier
built by a farmer in his barnyard with the aid of his sons,
and launched and manned by the men of the family. Few
of Belfast's ships were big traders to China and the Far
East. They operated along the coast, carrying fish, lumber,
lime, and ice on short, profitable hauls. Belfast never was
and isn't now a pretentious place. It just quietly and in-
dustriously minds its own business.

One example of its own business is the Belfast—Moosehead Lake Municipal Railroad. Originally this was intended to go clear to Moosehead Lake for the purpose of

bringing lumber and farm produce to Belfast for shipping away on the schooners. Actually it never got anywhere near Moosehead, but wound up forty miles from home at Burnham Junction, where it joins the tracks of the Maine Central. Nobody now has any notion that the road will ever get to Moosehead, but they keep the old name just the same.

Formerly the Maine Central leased this line for forty-thousand dollars a year. Since Belfast owns the railroad, this made it very nice for the taxpayers, who found the sum useful in balancing the town budget. In 1900, the Maine Central failed to renew the lease, so the town was left with a railroad on its hands. They could have voted to abandon it, I suppose, but they didn't. Instead, they floated a bond issue, which they are still paying off, for improvements and repairs on the line. They're still in the railroad business, running a line that shows a small profit at the end of most years. The board consists of townspeople who serve in most cases without pay, although the president does receive a hundred dollars a year and the treasurer twenty-five dollars. They have to take appreciable amounts of time from their normal means of earning a livelihood to attend to the affairs of the Belfast–Moosehead Lake.

The terminal of the railroad is down by the waterfront, and if you are a rail-road fan, you really should go down there and inspect the building and the rolling stock.

In 1893, Belfast—or most of its citizens—made a sally into that good old peculiarly American phenomenon, the patent-medicine business. This was a spectacularly profitable venture. The Dana Sarsaparilla Company started out with a capital of $25,000 and in a year paid 100 per cent in dividends. At the end of another year it was sold for $300,000 to outsiders, so that the original stockholders made more than 1300 per cent on their investment. Honestly, too; which must be some kind of a record. Naturally, this inspired a whole flock of imitators, one of which, King Solomon's Bitters, claimed to be a cure

for absolutely *anything*. There's a sucker born every
minute, I know, but even so, there weren't enough to
form a sufficiently large patronizing public. None of the
imitators did anywhere nearly as well as Dana's Sarsaparilla.

Today the people of Belfast engage in a number of small
industries, besides the shipping that is characteristic of all
sea towns. Shoes, clothing, hardware, and sashes and blinds
are manufactured there, and poultry and sardines are
processed. In August every year the city holds the Maine
Broiler Festival, which is like the Rockland Lobster Festival, except that this is a chicken dinner instead of a clambake.

The Belfast City Park, on the waterfront overlooking
the harbor, offers unusually good facilities for tourists.
It's a pretty location, to start with, and it has a camp site,
a trailer park, a small commissary, and free band concerts
on Sunday afternoons. Then there is swimming either in
a salt pool or on an open-water beach, *and* free swimming
lessons in summer. I don't know what more anyone could
expect. And even if you don't own a trailer and don't feel
like camping out, there are good hotels, tourist homes, and
restaurants in the town, so you can still use the park.

About six miles north of Belfast is the little village of
Searsport. This is one of the best examples of what the
decline of the sailing ship did to a flourishing and lively
community. There was a time when every port in the
world respected the name of Searsport and knew the faces
and business ethics of over a hundred and fifty shipmasters
hailing from this town near the head of Penobscot Bay.
In fact, during the '70's and '80's over 10 per cent of the
captains in the entire American merchant marine called
Searsport their home. Not only did Searsport men sail the
tall ships; they built them as well, and built them for
themselves. Not a single ship was ever constructed there
for outside registry. They were all owned in the town and
operated from the local wharves.

Searsport was home; but it was home not in the sense of being a permanent abiding place, but rather in the sense of being the one fixed point in lives which were lived all over the face of the globe. This applied not only to the head of the household, but to all the members of the family as well. The population of Searsport was truly cosmopolitan, even the toddler having cut his eye teeth on a shell he himself picked up on a beach of the Celebes, or having celebrated his third birthday off Formosa.

Women were no more surprised to encounter their next-door neighbors while shopping in Shanghai than they were to run into them on the main street of Searsport. Their taste was influenced by the beautiful things they saw all over the world, so that their big square houses in Searsport were built with a fine appreciation of line and form, and furnished with elegance and grace. Their mental horizons were as broad as the sea. They thought and talked about happenings in London and Calcutta as knowledgeably as they did about the goings-on of the town problem drinker. Even their cooking was cosmopolitan. They were as familiar with bouillabaisse and curry powder and guava jelly as they were with clam chowder and blueberry pie.

Then the times changed and, along with the times, the ships. The beaches of Searsport were found to be too shoal for the launching of the newer, larger types, and the prosperity of the town ebbed away. The whole fine, gracious way of life had to be abandoned, and Searsport slipped into the sleepiness of old age. Only the big houses remain with their back doors facing the street and their front windows looking out over the harbor that was once, but is no longer, the open gateway to the wide world.

One of these houses contains the Penobscot Marine Museum, an unusually fine collection of relics of the great days of the sailing ships. It's on a little green in a quiet backwater off the main thoroughfare. The big brick house is one of the best examples I have ever seen of the colonial feeling for space and line and simplicity of design. Among other things, this museum contains a fascinating display of old photographs. One I remember especially shows the families of several Searsport captains who happened to run into each other in Singapore Harbor. There they are, shipmasters, wives and assorted children, grouped on the deck of one of the ships for the souvenir picture. The men's faces are stiff above their formal white collars, the children's hair has been slicked back unnaturally, and the ladies are primly elegant in little hats, big bustles, and long lace mitts. I can just imagine them poring over the pictures when they all met again in Searsport, half a world away:— "Just *look* at me! Why didn't somebody *tell* me— But I never *was* satisfied with that dress. You simply can't depend on an Egyptian tailor, that's all there is to it."

The Waldo-Hancock suspension bridge crosses the Penobscot to the island of Verona in midstream, and the Verona bridge carries the highway over to Bucksport on the east bank. Verona used to be a shipbuilding town, but it isn't any longer. The last vessel launched there was Commander Peary's *Roosevelt*, on which he took his final expedition to the Arctic, when he discovered the North Pole.

My father-in-law was born and brought up in Bucksport. Like so many Maine boys of a hundred years ago, he ran away from home at an early age; only he didn't run away to sea but joined a little moth-eating traveling circus as general handy boy. The idea was the usual one, though. He was going to see the world and make his fortune. You can't defeat the old Maine Yankee on sea *or* land. He eventually owned that circus and several others and finally went into the theatrical management business as being more profitable and genteel, as well as easier. On the last count he changed his mind, I guess, since he is reported to have said on a great many occasions that he'd rather deal with a whole cageful of wild lionesses than with one well-known and temperamental actress who shall remain nameless. That is beside the point, however.

His fortune (such as it was) having been made, he decided that it would be fitting and proper to do something for his home town. So he gave Bucksport a granite watering trough for horses, which was placed in front of the Jed Prouty Tavern, one of the most famous old inns in Maine, whose register has been signed by such people as Martin Van Buren, William Henry Harrison, and John Tyler. Mr. Rich's gesture was made in the horse-and-buggy days, so it wasn't as silly a gift as it sounds now.

A few years ago I made a special trip to Bucksport to show my children their grandfather's drinking trough, now full of pink geraniums. They were not in the least interested, so I had to find something else to amuse them. I told them that the town was the birthplace of William and Dustin Farnum, actors with whom their grandfather had had some dealings; but they'd never heard of the Farnums and couldn't have been less impressed.

Then I thought of Buck's Curse and told them that story—or one version of it, since there are many. That really fascinated them, so that I ended by having to take them out to the cemetery to see the obelisk in question.

This is the story. Colonel Jonathan Buck, who founded Bucksport in 1762, was also the local judge. One day the dismembered body of a murdered woman was found; or all of it was found except one leg, which had somehow been lost in the shambles. The crime was pinned on a harmless natural, as the mentally deficient were called in those days. The poorman went to his hanging protesting his innocence, and cursing the judge, Jonathan Buck, who was causing him wrongfully to be put to death.

In time the judge also died and was buried in the cemetery near the end of the Verona bridge. A fine granite shaft was erected to mark his grave. Very shortly afterward, to the horror of the superstitious, the faint outline of the leg of a woman (presumably of the murdered woman) appeared on one face of the monument. It grew darker and darker; and, when any effort was made to obliterate it, it came right back again in a little while. It can be seen on the stone today. While not a perfect diagram of a leg, it is near enough for purposes of folklore. Naturally this is supposed to prove something, probably the innocence of the condemned man.

The real cause must be an imperfection in the stone, as I have carefully explained to my children. I could better have saved my breath. They prefer to believe the macabre old story. Of recent years the outline of a heart has begun to emerge above the leg. What this is supposed to mean I don't pretend to know. This I do know, however—that it won't be long now before we have an amended version of the legend to explain it.

There are very few towns in all Maine with as hectic a history behind them as Castine, on the eastern shore of Penobscot Bay, and very few that are now any more decorous and peaceful. The Indian name of the site was Passageewakeag, the Place of the Spirits, and it is a very good name for so beautiful a location.

Castine was founded as the trading post of Bagaduce by the Plymouth Pilgrims in 1629, when they were raising money to pay for the *Mayflower*. Very soon afterward it was captured by the French and remained in their hands for a considerable period. It was on their side of the river anyhow, so no great effort was made for some time to take it back. Then when the Baron de St. Castin appeared on the American scene, he chose the site, then called Pentagoet, as his headquarters and trading center. As we know, he married the daughter of a powerful Indian chief and rose to a position that combined all the best features of feudal lordship and minor godhood, so that his influence in the area was tremendous and his activities pretty nearly unhampered.

In the late 1660's the British again briefly acquired possession of Pentagoet, but it was again returned to France in 1667. In 1673, a force of Dutchmen under Jurriaen Aernouts arrived in the *Flying Horse* and captured the fort and post from St. Castin. They were not a part of the Dutch navy, but more like a band of Flemish pirates. Whatever their status, they pulled down the French flag and raised the Dutch. St. Castin, who had been up-country at the time of the capture, was not a man to let this act go unchallenged. As soon as he could rally a strong enough war party, he took the place right straight back again; and what was more, he expelled any Frenchmen who were suspected of having collaborated with the Dutch occupiers and confiscated their property.

Then in 1688, again while St. Castin was absent, Sir Edmund Andros seized Pentagoet for the British. He made the mistake of sending taunting messages to St. Castin. That fire-hearted gentleman retaliated by organizing raiding parties and terrorizing the entire western coast of Maine with his burning and plundering. He made himself a holy terror to the English, and finally recovered Pentagoet in 1693.

When the French and Indian Wars finally ended in 1763, with the Peace of Paris, all of New France was ceded to the British, and Castine—so named in 1796—remained under British rule until the Revolution, when of course it became American. Except for a brief British occupation during the War of 1812, it has belonged to us ever since.

So this quiet little village, so pretty in the sun with its old trees and houses and shady streets leading down to the wharves, has been possessed by four different nations and changed hands among them no less than nine times. No other place in Maine can claim such a record.

Because of the very storminess of Castine's career, there aren't as many old buildings and historic landmarks as you might expect. It's been through so many burnings and pillagings that many of them have been destroyed. However, the scenes of more than a hundred important events are plainly marked with explanatory signs, so that if you wish to reconstruct history, it isn't hard to do so. These

A battleground in colonial days, Castine now faces peace-fully on the village green.

historical plaques are exceptionally informative and detailed. There is one marking the spot where the Second
Miracle of New France took place, quoting the *Jesuit Re-
lation* on the subject. I'm not going to tell you what the
Second Miracle of New France was, because I don't want
to rob you of the pleasure of finding out for yourself what
it is.

Among the buildings that remain today are Fort Madison, which was built by the colonists in 1811, but taken
over by the British during the War of 1812; and Fort
George, built by the British in 1779, at the same time
that they dug a canal across the peninsula, which can still
be seen, as a part of their defense system. The Maine
Maritime Academy stands today on the site of the old
British barracks, and above it are the ruins of the old
British Fort George. It hasn't been restored, but the outlines and the four corner bastions can be seen plainly.
When this fort was being built, Americans were taken
from the vicinity to be used as forced labor; only in many
cases they didn't force very well.

The Wilson Museum on Perkins Street contains some
good collections of colonial and Revolutionary pieces, as
well as anthropological and geological exhibits, and the
Old Meetinghouse, built in 1790, is one of the oldest
churches in Maine. It has a Bulfinch steeple and a Paul
Revere bell, and is about the best example I know of
old New England church architecture. Some of the lovely
old houses are open to the public and others may be seen
by special arrangement with the owners.

One of the things I like best in Castine, though, isn't
a building at all, but the town's little village green. It's
perfectly lovely, shaded by huge old trees and surrounded
by ancient buildings. It looks exactly like a stage setting
for a play about old New England.

Castine is a resort town today, of the quieter, more
restrained type. That's its appeal. There are golf and boating and good accommodations and shopping facilities; but

it's not noisy or bustling or too populous. It's just an awfully nice place to stay.

Deer Isle, down at the end of East Penobscot Bay, hasn't been very much developed, and therefore I find it an area of particular charm. It's composed of a whole mess of islands, some of them fairly large, many of them very small. Causeways and bridges connect the more important, so accessibility isn't any particular problem. There are limited accommodations for tourists. They aren't what you might call overelaborate, but you can find something to eat and a place to lay your head. The soil isn't very good, so there isn't much farming. All the little towns—*all* being about four hamlets, of which Stonington is the largest—depend largely on the sea for livelihood: on the lobster and the fish. Deer Islanders have always been famous for their seamanship, and both the *Defender* and the *Columbia* were manned almost exclusively by Deer Isle crews when they won their international yacht trophies.

The houses of these little villages are small and unpretentious, and they cling to the ledges, which are pink here. There aren't very many trees because the soil is so shallow and the land so exposed to winds from the sea; but oh, the flower gardens! They're small and irregular and informal, because there's more rock than there is earth, and they look like scraps of brilliant brocade blowing over the granite slopes. They bloom clear into October, and there can't possibly be a prettier sight than Stonington on a clear autumn day, with the sea deep blue, the land a soft pink, and the flowers every gorgeous color you ever imagined, rooted heaven knows how in the crevices and saved from frost by the fogs and the stored warmth of the sun on the rocks.

The rocks are useful too for something besides warming flower beds. The granite here is of superior quality as well as unusual color, so it is quarried for building purposes. The stone used in New York's Triborough Bridge came from Deer Isle. It took two hundred men two years, even using what is said to be the largest gang-saw in the world, to cut the rock into blocks. The other industry of Stonington is sardine packing, which is a seasonal occupation, extending from August to December.

The tourist trade does not count as a major enterprise in the Deer Isle locality, which is a refreshing change. That's why I think it's a good place to go if you want to see the real coast; only I hope too many people don't follow this suggestion.

The land along here begins to take on the nature of the Eastern Coast, the last great coastal division. Great shade trees are not quite so common, and the whole countryside looks harder and less lush. It would be difficult to say just where the line of demarcation comes, but I myself have always considered that I have left the Middle Coast behind me *after* I have passed through Ellsworth. Ellsworth is on the Union River, which flows into Blue Hill Bay, and so shouldn't really, I suppose, be included as a Penobscot town. But its character is that of the Middle Coast, and it seems to fall very definitely into that category. For one thing, its streets are always full of tourists from Mt. Desert, which is only a few miles away; and it seems a sort of gateway to *Way* Down-East.

Ellsworth is the county seat and the only city in Hancock County, the shopping center for a large rural and coastal area, and the home of several small industries. It was settled in 1763, the site having been chosen, without doubt, because of a sixty-foot falls in the Union River, a good source of power. The falls may be seen from the bridge over the river in the center of the little city—a very pretty sight. Ellsworth was at one time the second largest lumber-shipping port in the world; but of course the lumber industry has gone the way of the shipbuilding industry here.

The town is now a busy commercial and tourist center,

and I myself have always liked it very much. I've shopped there during summers when I've been farther Down-East, and it has always seemed to me that the choice of goods was unusually wide and the services unusually efficient. I know I have never had dealings with a tourist information bureau that was anywhere nearly as helpful as the one in Ellsworth. They tell you not only the things they are supposed to know about, like the route number to Bangor or how to get to the Black Mansion; but they'll recommend a good dentist or call up to verify a bus schedule for you— things you really ought to tend to yourself. They are just plain neighborly.

The town is pretty. It has lovely trees and some fine old houses and buildings. A large part of the center was destroyed by fire in 1933, so there are many new and modern buildings, too; and they don't fight with the old at all. The graceful old Congregational Church with its delicately fluted columns and slim white spire seems perfectly at home with the new city hall, which is of modern Scandinavian design. Today's best-sellers don't look at all out of place on the shelves of the public library, which occupies a house built in 1820 and still retains its open fireplaces. Ellsworth is a happy combination of the past and the present, and proof—if proof is needed—that good taste carries over easily from period to period.

One of the old houses that is open to tourists (for fifty cents) is the Black Mansion. This was the home of Colonel John Black, whose father was an aide-de-camp of General Washington. It's a fine brick house of Georgian design, with an especially beautiful staircase in the front hall. There are a great many lovely old things in this house, and it is really worth visiting.

South of Ellsworth on the west shore of Blue Hill Bay lies the very lovely town of Blue Hill, settled in 1762. There is a lively shopping center with good gift shops, and Rowantrees pottery is made here. In summer, Kniesel Hall, a chamber music school, gives concerts twice a week;

and in late summer, the Blue Hill Fair takes place. Mary Ellen Chase is perhaps Blue Hill's most famous daughter.

When I am leaving Ellsworth I always feel as though I were leaving the last outpost of civilization behind me. This is entirely unwarranted, I'll admit freely. There is actually no danger of being ambushed and scalped by hostile Indians on the road to the Canadian border; but on the Eastern Coast the towns are fewer and smaller and farther apart, and the works of man much less in evidence. It's a land that—

But before we go into that, we'll have to take a look at Mt. Desert, which has been called, and I think with good reason, the most famous island of the Maine coast.

14 · Mt. Desert Island

Mt. Desert Island, Cadillac Mountain
Somes Sound, Bar Harbor, Seal Harbor
Northeast Harbor, Cranberry Isles

THERE'S no getting away from the fact—Mt. Desert Island really is a fabulous place. Those who love it claim that it is one of the most dramatically beautiful spots in the world; and I'm forced to admit that they could be right. It's a big island, sixteen miles long and about twelve miles wide, connected with the mainland by a bridge. It is cut almost in two by Somes Sound, the only true fjord on the Atlantic coast—a deep, narrow, seven-mile stretch of water between high cliffs, penetrating to the very heart of the island. In addition, Mt. Desert has perhaps a score or so of lakes and ponds, and I don't know how many salt-water coves and harbors.

Cadillac Mountain, the highest mountain on the whole Atlantic coast, rises fifteen-hundred and thirty-two feet from the eastern half of the island; and there are several other hills which the inhabitants call mountains as well. All around the shore are scores of smaller islands in the waters of Blue Hill Bay and Frenchman Bay. Although the name of the island, and especially of the town of Bar Harbor, has for decades been a household word connoting a playground for the very wealthy, actually by far the larger part of it is wild land, covered by unspoiled forest

*Discovered and named by Champlain, Mt. Desert Island
is a paradise of mountains, forests, and migrating birds.*

and open to anybody to enjoy. There are excellent roads all over the island, and you can drive scarcely a hundred feet without having a new and stunning view revealed to you.

And that's not all. Mt. Desert happens to mark the ornithological and botanical boundary line between two zones, so that there are found here both temperate and sub-Arctic birds and vegetation, together with coastal, inland, and alpine types of plants; and it lies on one of the great migration lanes, so that all except true tropical birds pass over it at one time or another. Naturalists go crazy here, and you can see why. Rare specimens of a great variety of natural objects can be found within a very small area. Two of America's pioneers in this field, John James Audubon and Louis Agassiz, both spent a great deal of time on Mt. Desert.

Undoubtedly all the early explorers of whatever nationality knew about the island. They couldn't very well miss it, since Cadillac Mountain is by far the most conspicuous feature of the coast for many, many miles. But the first written account of it was by Champlain, who discovered the place on September 5, 1605, and described it with his usual accuracy. He it was who named it L'Isle des Monts Deserts, because of its bleak and forbidding aspect. The first settlement was the Jesuit Mission de St. Sauveur. It was established in 1613 when Father Biard and Father Massé were fogbound on their way to the Penobscot, you remember, where they intended to convert the Indians to the greater glory of the wealthy and pious Marquise de Guercheville. You may also remember that this mission was destroyed by Samuel Argall of the Virginia Company in the first conflict between the French and the English in the New World.

After that there were various attempts to settle Mt. Desert. The Plymouth Pilgrims claimed it rather half-heartedly and established temporary fur-trading posts on it from time to time; but it was too remote and rugged and too near the French strongholds to be anything but an uneasy possession. In fact, the island was owned or claimed at various periods by a great many different people, but that is much too complicated to go into here.

One owner whom I feel we should mention was the Sieur Antoine de la Mothe Cadillac, who received a grant of the island from Louis XIV in 1688. It was his idea to set up a feudal fief or domain over the Indians; and with that end in mind, he and his wife came to Mt. Desert and lived there for a while. But things didn't work out as he had hoped, so he went West to Detroit, where he succeeded in his plan for a feudal lordship, as everyone knows. It is for him that Cadillac Mountain is named, of course, and *not* because a Cadillac was the first car to reach the summit, as I was once told in all seriousness.

In 1713, when France ceded to England a large part of Maine by the Treaty of Utrecht, Cadillac lost the island; and it was subsequently given to Sir Richard Bernard, the Royal Governor of Massachusetts, for "his extraordinary services." He lost it by confiscation at the time of the Revolution; but his son raised such a howl that he later succeeded in having half the island restored to the family.

At the same time, someone persuaded Cadillac's granddaughter, Marie Therese de la Mothe Cadillac de Gregoire, that she had a legitimate claim to Mt. Desert. She believed them and came to this country from France to take over her domain. Poor puzzled lady, she didn't understand about legal matters and spent a long time and most of her money trying to get the question straightened out. Finally, perhaps because he was sorry for her and because Mt. Desert wasn't worth much anyhow, Thomas Jefferson gave her a clear title to the other half of the island. She went there to live on her very much diminished means and eventually died and was buried there. And that is why a large number of real-estate titles today can be traced way back to Cadillac ownership.

In the meantime, in 1761, a man named Somes had come to the island by boat from Gloucester to cut a load of barrel staves. He liked the place so much that he went home and got his family, and they returned to settle on Somes Sound, living on their boat until they had built a house. So Somes is generally accepted as having been the first permanent settler. He was soon followed by a few others, and during the Revolution a small community existed there under a form of plantation government, which was really the classic New England self-government by town meeting.

The first such meeting on record was held at the home of a Stephen Richardson on March 30, 1776. At that time the handful of citizens voted to contribute their individual services toward the building of some "rodes" in accordance with a New England practice, still in existence today in some places, which allows you to work out your taxes on the highways. The citizens also elected a committee to prevent anyone's taking hay off the island, since they needed for their own livestock all they could raise on their few cleared acres.

I don't know who was supposed to be taking the hay where, as the territory on the mainland wasn't inhabited to any great extent, and the few settlers there should have had plenty of hay of their own; and as for selling it to Massachusetts interests, it would seem to me that they must have had nearer, more convenient, and less expensive sources of supply. However, as of March 30, 1776, no one was allowed to take hay off Mt. Desert Island.

All the other towns that we have visited along the coast played important parts in the Revolution and cherish records of their participation. Let me tell you about how the war came to Mt. Desert. In the first place, one or two of the citizens did fight with Saltonstall's fleet at Castine. They were so disgusted with that fiasco, however, that they went home and stayed there, washing their hands of the whole business. Then, on the night of February 24, 1781—a little late in the war—H.M.S. *Allegiance* came sailing into Frenchman Bay and anchored. A landing party rowed ashore and took several citizens into custody, escorting them out to the *Allegiance* for questioning. It was soon obvious that these particular colonials hadn't been anywhere, seen anybody, or done anything; so they were returned to the beach and released in time to go home and get a good night's sleep. And that was the full extent of the Revolution on Mt. Desert.

For over half a century after that big excitement, nothing much happened on the island. The inhabitants pursued a policy of live and let live. They'd mind their own business, if others would do the same. This was not too difficult a program to carry out, since access to the island was by ferry, and few people could be bothered making the inconvenient trip. The islanders fished and cut lumber, which they worked up into planks and boards at their own sawmill, and shipped the results of their labor away on their own ships. There was very little farming done, as the soil and climate were not suitable; but the population managed to eke out a living from the other sources.

In 1836, a bridge to the mainland was built by a group of citizens calling themselves the Mt. Desert Bridge Corporation, and this innovation spelled the end of one way of life and the beginning of another. The corporation continued to own the bridge until it was taken over by the county in 1917, but long before that its influence had revolutionized island life.

September 4, 1844, just eight years after the bridge was built, has been isolated as the date of the discovery of Bar Harbor. That was the day when the painter Thomas Cole arrived on the island. He was the founder of what is commonly known as the Hudson River School of painting, a type of painting devoted to the accurate transferring of Nature to canvas and so-called because Cole and like-minded artists began their work on the Hudson River and in the Catskills.

In general, the Hudson River School suffered from a passion for the picturesque, so that many of their paintings are oversentimental and declamatory. It was the literary vogue of the time to preach that Nature was Simply

Grand (see Emerson, Thoreau, William Cullen Bryant and others of their ilk), and the artists took the preaching to heart. Having exhausted the possibilities of the Hudson, they went looking for further proof of their doctrine; and that is how Cole happened to land on Mt. Desert. He was looking for something to paint.

He certainly found it. As it happened, he was not only a pretty good painter, but a vocal and enthusiastic personality, with a tremendous circle of friends among the wealthy as well as in the world of Art. He talked so much and so rapturously about the glories of Mt. Desert that it became The Thing to go to this place that Cole had discovered, and before long regular steamers were running there and hotels were built, to be followed a little later by the great estates of such people as the Morgans, the Tracys, and the Rockefellers. By 1890 the town of Bar Harbor had become the summer social capital of the United States.

Those were the days! The wealthy had come there for peace and quiet, and they intended to have it. In spite of the fact that they built enormously costly summer "cottages" furnished luxuriously, they lived lives of great simplicity—the very special simplicity of the extremely wealthy, which I find a little touching. There seems to me to be something almost childlike about it; and I suppose the reason is that the rich, like children, are shielded by their money. Like children, too, they were averse to any change on the island, and they went to great lengths to insure that there would be none. The town elected, for example, both a fence viewer and a hog reeve at Bar Harbor until about 1930, decades after these offices had any meaning or the officers any duties at all.

One of the great houses had a dining table that sank through the floor into the kitchen below between courses, to rise again with the next course beautifully served; but often there was no fresh meat to fill the Limoges plates, because of primitive refrigeration and lack of adequate transportation, and the water in the lovely crystal goblets was pumped from a well of questionable purity. All this seems to me to be as lacking in realism as children's elaborate games and rituals.

And then the summer people entertained themselves in such self-consciously simple ways. They went on long walks and collected flowers and shells, and even the emptiest-headed debutante knew the proper Latin names. They espoused Nature and observed the stars and kept records of the flight of birds. They gave elaborate dinner parties to the same people they entertained back in New York or Boston or Philadelphia; and then they built little cabins hidden deep in the woods, where they could retire to escape their social obligations, and to think about Life and write their memoirs. They were rather sweet.

The sweetest of all were Dr. Robert Derby of New York and Colonel Albert Stickney of Boston. Every year, starting in 1871, they used to row a little wherry or light skiff from the Union Boat Club in Boston to Roberts Wharf in Bar Harbor. This expedition took *weeks*. It's a *long* way, hundreds of miles. During the early laps of their journey, they could go ashore at fashionable resorts and stay at good hotels over night; but as they progressed farther and farther up the coast, they had to stop at farmhouses and lobster shacks and lighthouses. Can't you just see them in their little rowboat, two dignified gentlemen battling their way up the long, long coast of Maine, landing on a lonesome shingle beach and trying to explain to a bewildered fisherman who they were, where they were going, and *why?* That last must have taken some explaining.

I'll bet they had a wonderful time, at that, and the trips probably did them a lot of good.

No one knew exactly when they would arrive, of course, but the local grapevine carried word of their slow approach. As soon as the bulletin came that they had passed the little island of Thrumcap, the entire summer population went down to Roberts Wharf and gave them a big welcome. It was one of the Events of the Season. See what

I mean about the simplicity of the wealthy? Poor men couldn't leave their jobs to row from Boston to Bar Harbor, and wouldn't want to if they could. It would be too much like work. Only the rich had the time and the inclination.

Another phase of the antipathy to change was the Great Automobile War. The automobile represented speed and noise and restlessness, and the summer people had come to Bar Harbor in the first place to escape all this. They were not going to have their peace and leisure destroyed without a struggle. Therefore they passed a law forbidding the introduction of cars to the island. It wasn't easy. Some of the native islanders and some of the younger summer people took a more progressive view. But the islanders depended on the summer people for a prosperity the like of which they'd never had before, and the scions of the rich had been brought up to respect the wishes of their elders; so long after cars were common on the mainland, Mt. Desert was still horse-drawn.

Finally, however, a patient died because his doctor, who could have saved him had he owned a car, was unable to reach him in time to administer aid. This affair aroused so much feeling that the law banning automobiles was revoked in 1913, and now there are hundreds of cars all over Mt. Desert.

The acceptance of the automobile started the great change in the whole atmosphere of Mt. Desert, as it has done almost universally, but there were many contributory causes as well. One of them was probably the establishment of the Acadia National Park, the first National Park east of the Mississippi and the only such park in America to be purchased with private funds and given to the people by individuals. It covers thirty thousand acres or two-fifths of the island and within its bounds are two hundred miles of foot trails, motoring roads and bridle paths, passing through country that seems to be as wild and untouched as it was when the first explorers sighted Cadillac Mountain from the sea.

That this beautiful tract has been preserved and is open to all the people is due largely to the efforts of George Bucknam Dorr and Dr. Charles Eliot of Harvard. They were very much disturbed when lumbering operations were started on the island, fearing that all the timber would be cut off and the island scenery ruined. Therefore they went about among their wealthy friends and raised enough money to buy the endangered land. After they got it, they didn't quite know what to do with it. Then they had the happy and generous idea of giving the land to everybody, and the federal government finally accepted it in 1916.

Since then the place has been developed and improved a great deal, and is responsible for attracting thousands of tourists who probably wouldn't be at all interested in the old Mt. Desert. The whole area of the park is now 35,000 acres, two portions of which do not lie on Mt. Desert but on Schoodic Point, near Winter Harbor on the mainland, and on Isle au Haut. Right now we are discussing only the Mt. Desert section. There is a large free public campground with barracks, running water, modern sanitary conveniences, outdoor fireplaces, electric lights, and even facilities for doing your own laundry. It and the rest of the park is under close supervision, so that you are perfectly safe in this wilderness and free from any form of annoyance from anybody. The park is so large and has so many beautiful trails and roads that it would be possible to spend a whole summer there without exhausting its possibilities.

There is a park naturalist, for instance, with a corps of assistants who give free nature-guide instruction and assistance. And there's an archeological museum, the Abbé Museum, with an archeologist in charge who will explain the exhibits and relics of Stone Age Indian culture in this locality. There's boating and swimming and fishing and cycling and golf and, in the winter, all kinds of winter sports. The footpaths are so laid out that it doesn't make any difference what kind of a walker you are, you are certain to find a trail that will suit you. You can do some real mountain climbing, or you can take a ladylike stroll on the level. You can't get lost, either; or at least, not very easily. Then there's about fifty miles of bridle path, the personal gift of John D. Rockefeller, Jr., and stables where you can rent horses. The bridle paths are so laid out that they are entirely separate from the motor roads, and you can ride for hours without ever seeing a car.

The most spectacular thing you can see is the view from the top of Cadillac. The road that goes up there is said to be the best-engineered and best-constructed mountain road in the world, and I can believe it. The grade never exceeds seven per cent, and any potentially dangerous spots are well protected by buttresses. If you want to stop your car on the way up and admire the view that keeps unfolding and changing from minute to minute, you can. The engineers apparently had an eye for beauty, too. They provided parking areas all along the way, where you can pull off the road and sit and stare and stare. I'm not going to try to describe the view from the summit. You'll have to go up and see for yourself. It's—well—unbelievable.

There are a lot of other things to be seen in the park, but since there is also a good information service, you can find out about them when you get there. I would suggest, though, that you drive along Ocean Drive, a six-mile loop of highway that follows the shore south of Bar Harbor. Every bend in the road reveals new and enchanting vistas. A rock formation called Thunder Hole is out there, too, a fascinating place where the waves rush into a deep crevice in the rocks with a terrific roar, sending up spouts of water and spray forty feet into the air.

Along this drive, you will come to Otter Cliff, a narrow point from which you get a most marvelous and unobstructed view across Frenchman Bay. Near here is Otter Creek. During the First World War, when radio and other means of communication were less developed than they are now, there was a great deal of difficulty in keeping touch with Europe. Periods of blackout would occur at the best and most powerful stations.

A man named Allesandro Fabbri discovered that good clear reception was *always* possible here at Otter Creek, so a twenty-four-hour-a-day contact with Europe could be maintained. It was the only place in the Western Hemisphere, as a matter of fact, that this was possible. So the Navy awarded Fabbri the Navy Cross for his services and took over Otter Creek for the establishment of a station which proved to be of tremendous value. The station has now been moved to Schoodic Point on the other side of Frenchman Bay, where I suppose it serves just as efficiently, with improved modern facilities.

Beyond Otter Creek on the shore drive are Seal Harbor and Northeast Harbor, summer-residential towns of outstanding beauty. Well-known people like the Rockefellers and Gary Moore summer here. Thuya Lodge is in Northeast Harbor. This used to be the summer home of Joseph H. Curtis, the landscape architect, but now it is open to the public. It shelters a small museum and a reading room where many books of especial interest to the naturalist are available. The grounds—as might be expected, considering the occupation of the former owner—are beautifully landscaped, with a great variety of odd and rare trees and shrubs.

Northeast Harbor, too, is a village of great and lovely estates, but it is known chiefly as a yachting center. During August the Northeast Harbor Fleet, which consists of about a hundred and twenty-five or so small craft of the various pleasure types and classes, holds a regatta, with daily races and cruising events. Even if you yourself don't sail, the affair is pretty to watch.

Another contributory cause of the change in Mt. Desert is almost certainly the great fire of October 1947. I have no doubt that the change would have come about anyhow, in time—it was, in fact, well under way. The whole

way of life represented by the great estates was doomed
to be modified in any case. In these days of high taxes
and no real servant class in the old sense, nobody, no
matter how much money they have, can live according to
the old pattern. Maybe they don't want to. I think it is
very possible that that way of life is emotionally and
intellectually as well as socially and economically out-
moded. But be that as it may, the physical destruction of so
many of the great and beautiful estates by fire abruptly
terminated much that was essentially Bar Harbor.

It was one of those dreadfully dry autumns, when there
were forest fires all over the parched state of Maine. The
woods were so tindery that fire could break out spontaneously anywhere, and the wardens prayed for rain that
didn't come and didn't come. The fire on Mt. Desert broke
out near the dump, although the dump isn't blamed, and
spread with horrifying speed over a large part of the island.
It was completely out of control on a brisk wind for four
days, and only lightly controlled for four more. Crews of
men from all over the state and farther away were rushed
in to help fight the blaze, and the village of Bar Harbor
itself had to be evacuated. Nobody who hasn't been in a
forest fire can know how terrible a thing it is; and this
one wasn't over until scores of estates and smaller homes
and a great area of woodland had been destroyed.

So great was the fame and glamor of Bar Harbor that
the fire was reported all over the world. I think that's
remarkable, when you consider that the place was really
only the summer resort of a comparatively few people. I
particularly like the report of *Le Figaro* of Paris. According to it, the city of Bar Harbor was wiped out by fires
set by the peasants of Maine in an uprising in protest
against the existence of big feudal domains. The editors
of *Le Figaro* ought to hear what some of my peasant
friends said about their reporting. That would larn 'em
whom to call a peasant!

But this fame was an advantage, too. Money for reconstruction poured in from private sources everywhere, as

well as from such organizations as the Red Cross, the Damon Runyon Fund and others. Believe it or not, even the natives of New Guinea sent in a contribution. As a result, Mt. Desert has been rebuilt and is still being rebuilt into a better place than ever.

Let me explain quickly that neither the Damon Runyon Fund nor the natives of New Guinea were donating money for the rehabilitation of the estates of the wealthy. Obviously that wasn't necessary. Mt. Desert Island has, however, some institutions that are justly famous all over the world, which could use help. One of these is the Roscoe B. Jackson Memorial Laboratory, probably the world's outstanding laboratory for cancer research.

This project was located on the island because the conditions there are ideal. For one thing, there are no earth tremors whatsoever to disturb delicate instruments. For another, the whole atmosphere of the place is remotely quiet and serene, so that technicians suffer few distractions and little pressure and can give their undivided attention to their work. A large per cent of the staff is local, the sons and daughters of the Maine fishermen and farmers. Probably they were hired at first because they were available, but they were found to be unusually good at the job. Apparently they are natural-born observers, patient and thorough, who can be trusted to be accurate and painstaking. I know a few of these native technicians, and they are almost fanatically devoted to the laboratory and proud of the work it is doing.

One of the tragedies of the fire was the loss of a hundred thousand mice whose complete cancer history for many generations was on record. It was to replace these and to repeat the work thus undone that the Damon Runyon Fund and New Guinea gave their money.

Another wonderful institution which has its headquarters in Bar Harbor is the Maine Sea Coast Mission. This is an independent philanthropy, supported by gifts from individuals, which has been doing remarkable work all along the coast for half a century. The purpose of the mission is to render services to those who are isolated on small islands or inaccessible capes, or at lighthouses or Coast Guard stations, or on lightships. These services may be of a religious nature, but they may equally well be medical or social. Nurses, dentists, doctors, and social workers, as well as clergymen, go from island to island on the mission boat, which is always named the *Sunbeam*. I think the present one is *Sunbeam III,* although it is sometimes referred to as "God's Tugboat."

Besides the more obvious services, the boat distributes reading matter to shut-ins or those whose jobs isolate them, collecting tons and tons of magazines each year for redistribution. An attempt is made to satisfy all preferences, but usually the supply of Westerns is insufficient. Lighthouse keepers love that type of reading, for some reason. I suppose it's a form of escape from all that salt water.

Then each year twenty-five hundred Christmas boxes are distributed, mostly, although not exclusively, to children. Each child gets three things—something useful, like a sweater or blouse; something useless, like a doll or toy truck; and something to eat, like ribbon candy. Often a projector is carried along and set up in a church or hall, and the people of a remote island see their first movie in months and their last one until the *Sunbeam* comes again.

I can't begin to tell you all the things the Sea Coast Mission does. It isn't too well known outside of coastal Maine, but there it is a part of the scheme of things. When any emergency—birth or death, fire or famine—occurs in the huge, scattered parish of sea and rock, someone puts up a holler for the *Sunbeam* and she heads out to sea to save a life or to make a life saved a more joyful and rewarding thing. The biggest wonder of all is how she does so much on so very little money. In the year 1954-55 it cost only $14,647.81 to operate the *Sunbeam*.

One of the lighthouses she visits is Mt. Desert Rock Light, which is one of the most important lights on the Maine coast. It rates with Hatteras and Key West as a notorious scene of disaster. The light is on a rock twenty-seven miles out to sea, which is a long way. It has an area of only half an acre and the highest point is just seventeen feet above the water. So you can see that some sort of warning to ships is necessary here, especially in winter when, for long periods, the seas break entirely over the rock. The light is now what is called a "stag" light, which means that there are only men there; but it used to be a "family" light and the keeper had his wife and children with him.

In those days there was a custom that I keep thinking about with pleasure. First you have to imagine what life for any woman would be like out there: nothing but ocean to see; nothing but housework to do; no one but your family to talk to; no place to go except the half-acre of bare rock, without even a spear of grass on it. You couldn't get away for even a half-hour of privacy. You couldn't take a respite from your troubles in any other environment except the world of books, and nobody can read all the time. A woman out there could be little better than a prisoner.

But every spring each fishing boat that passed the rock brought with it a grain sack or bushel basket full of good rich garden soil. This was packed into the crevices of the rock, and the keeper's wife started a flower garden. The rock simply frothed with gorgeous bloom as the lonely woman worked out all her repressions in the sun and salty air. You can call it some cold name like occupational therapy if you want to, but it was more than that. It was a labor of love. So beautiful were the gardens that people took special trips out to see them, and the woman made lasting friendships and stored up things to think about all winter long when the cold gray seas rose to break over the rock and carry away every grain of the soil. By spring there was never a teaspoonful left.

She didn't have to worry though. She could pore over seed catalogues during the bitter months, making out her lists of annuals and planning new color combinations, fully confident that as soon as the sun was high again and the seas subsided, the lobster boats and the sardiners would be stopping by with their gifts of earth.

If you'd like to visit an island off Mt. Desert, the Cranberrys are easy to reach. Take the mailboat from lively little Southwest Harbor, near the entrance to Somes Sound. (The famous yacht basin of Northeast Harbor is across the bay.) The islands were named for the wild cranberries on Big Cranberry, of particular interest to bird lovers. Herring gulls and terns breed here in great numbers; and so do rarer species like Leach's petrel, which is seldom seen except far out at sea. The Sawtelle Museum of local relics and documents is on Little Cranberry; and Sutton Island was the scene of Rachel Field's *Time Out of Mind*, and her summer home.

Near Southwest Harbor at Seawall is a big National Park campground, and farther along at McKinley, Ruth Moore and Eleanor Mayo live and write good books about Maine. Up at the head of Somes Sound is Somesville, which is, I think, without exception the very prettiest village I ever saw, bar none.

There are accommodations now on Mt. Desert Island to suit anybody's purse, from expensive-luxurious to good-inexpensive to overnight cabins to the cheapest of all, pitching your own tent in the park and cooking your own hot dogs. There is entertainment of every sort—movies, concerts, summer theater, and all the outdoor activities. There are gift shops and branches of many famous New York stores. It is, as I said before, a fabulous place; and I'd better warn you now that you aren't going to run into another like it between here and the Canadian border. Or almost anywhere else, for that matter.

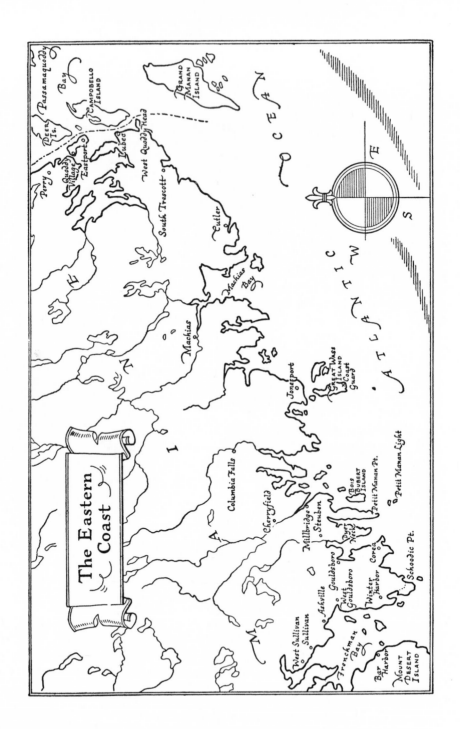

The Eastern Coast

15 · The Eastern Coast

The Sullivans, Winter Harbor, Steuben
Petit Manan Point, Milbridge, Columbia Falls, Jonesport
Machias, West Quoddy Head, Lubec, Perry
Quoddy Village, Eastport, Hancock

THE EASTERN COAST, between Frenchman and Passamaquoddy bays, is the largest single division of the Maine
coast. It is also the most remote, the most forbidding, and
the most thinly peopled. Milbridge, Jonesport, Machias,
Lubec, and Eastport are the only towns of any size at all,
the shopping centers for large, sparsely populated areas.
All the rest are small communities of a few hundred or
less, separated by long stretches of nearly uninhabited
countryside.

The territory is amost devoid of historic interest or
cultural achievements. The trees are scrubby and much of
the terrain has a tundra-like appearance. Dense fogs are
frequent. The soil is light and shallow and the climate
difficult, so that farming is not a particularly rewarding
occupation. The two profitable crops are blueberries and
Christmas trees. Both of these are grown with a minimum
of attention from man. The blueberry barrens are burned
over every few years to insure a better crop, but otherwise
left mostly alone.

Until recently, even the summer trade was not especially

good here. It was so far away from everywhere, and the water was—and still is—impossibly cold for swimming and dangerous for boating. Better roads and better cars, however, have opened up this previously almost inaccessible coastline, and things are beginning to pick up a mite, as they say around here. It is, after all, about the only place left to go, the supply of available shore property to the south and west having been pretty well exhausted.

This is really wonderful country! Those who have found their own Down-East among its towering headlands and ragged capes and deep, still bays—and I had better say right now that I am among them—speak of the Eastern Coast with an almost religious fervor. They are like a small secret fraternity, whose members have been through a demanding initiation and now share a special knowledge and experience unavailable to others. They have eaten goose-grass greens and seen thirty-foot tides and been out with the lobster fleet at four o'clock in the morning, and the world will never be the same for them again.

I am going to indulge myself later by going into trivial and personal detail about my own insignificant claim on this Down-East. I tell myself that this is justified by the fact that my corner is not unique, that it is typical and representative of dozens of tiny hamlets hidden among the great escarpments of the Eastern Coast, and that what I have to say about it, what I feel about it, can be applied to any one of them. For once I am telling myself the truth. The Eastern Coast is basically all-of-a-piece, and if you like it at all—and some people hate it—it doesn't make too much difference which part of it you choose for yours. But before we go into that, I think we'd better take a look at the whole coastline. Then we can come back and settle down in one spot.

The road east from Ellsworth isn't particularly interesting for several miles. Not until you approach the Sullivans does the country begin to take on its special character.

There's a place there where the highway follows a ridge
along an arm of Frenchman Bay, and that is the point
that marks for me the beginning of Down-East. If you
are very lucky, you will arrive at that spot latish in the
afternoon of a clear day, when the sun is still well up,
but definitely westering. A benign light falls from behind
you onto Mt. Desert Island, ten miles away across the bay.
Everything is clear and soft in the luminous air—the small
islands below you, the bright sails of all the boats, and the
soaring pink granite mass of Cadillac Mountain across the
dark blue water. It's all diminished with distance, and yet
it looks near enough to touch. It's beautiful.

There's an interesting geological oddity here near the
Sullivan bridge. It's a reversible waterfall. There's a
natural rock dam across a narrows at the head of Frenchman Bay, separating it from Hog Bay, a fourteen-mile
basin reaching inland to the town of Franklin. When the
tide is coming in, the constricted water tumbles over the
ledge with a roar that can sometimes be heard for more
than a mile; and after a brief period of calm, when the
tide is at the full, it turns around and falls back in the
opposite direction.

Before reaching the bridge, you pass through Hancock,
the summer home of Pierre Monteux and the location
of his summer school for orchestra conductors. After
his death, Madame Monteux established a music school
and foundation here. During the summer, the school
gives concerts on Sundays, often with illustrious guest
artists.

All the towns along there—the Sullivans, Ashville, the
Gouldsboros—are tiny and unpretentious, but indescribably appealing. There are no houses of outstanding size
and architecture. They are small—and look smaller in the
immensity—and neat and white, with little gardens and,
more often than not, piles of lobster traps in the barnyard
and freshly painted lobster buoys hung on the buildings
to dry. The odd part of this is that they don't look self-
consciously picturesque, as the same things did back along

the coast where we have been, but simply businesslike and matter-of-course. You know that the bright buoys were hung out there for convenience only, and that they will be taken down and put to their proper use as soon as the paint stops tacking. If tourists think they are quaint, that's unimportant; and any picture-taking had better be done now, because tomorrow will be too late.

These are the towns that Margaret Henrichsen describes in her book, *Seven Steeples,* so named because she was the minister of the seven churches in the district, holding seven services each Sunday.

Winter Harbor is the largest town on the Gouldsboro Peninsula and the only one not incorporated into the Town of Gouldsboro. It is not typical of the area. It has a colony of wealthy out-of-staters on Grindstone Neck and two large Navy housing developments occupied by Navy personnel from the radio station on nearby Schoodic Point. There is a good supermarket in Winter Harbor, a five-and-ten-cent store, and several gift shops and restaurants. There are overnight accommodations to be had, too. The harbor is sheltered and safe, so it is often used by small pleasure craft cruising the coast. Each summer the town, in conjunction with the Navy, sponsors a gigantic lobster and blueberry pie dinner out on Fraser Point, featuring lobster-boat races.

Just outside Winter Harbor is that part of the Acadia National Park called Schoodic Point. There are no camp grounds here, but there are picnic grounds; and, if you want to stay in the locality for a while, there are plenty of accommodations around Winter Harbor, as I have said. Schoodic is a lovely spot, a long wooded tongue of land thrust out to sea and ending in a great terraced ledge, where the surf is always spectacular. A parking area has been laid out on the benches of rock so skillfully that the natural beauty has not been marred at all. In fact, the whole charm of Schoodic is that so much has been done to improve it without ruining it.

The park is best before it officially opens in mid-June

and after it closes in September. There aren't any people around then to block the view, except the wardens and the naval personnel, all of whom are too preoccupied with their own affairs to bother you. The roads are surfaced with crushed pink granite, and in the spring they are bordered solidly with sheets of daisies, all gold and white. You can't imagine how fairy-tale-like it is. In the fall the roads are still pink, but the trees overhead blaze orange and scarlet, and everywhere the low blueberry bushes are a brilliant dark crimson. The sea has taken on a hard, deep blue, laced with whitecaps. You see it and you know it is so, but you still can't believe it.

Another advantage of the off-season is that the wild life is full of confidence then, so that you often see deer and foxes and all manner of birds, which are frightened into hiding in the wilder parts during the summer. The gulls get back their manners, too, if they ever had any. In the summer, they spend their time swooping around, begging for handouts of bread crusts and ripe olives from picnickers. In the spring and fall they revert to their normal habits.

They're very entertaining birds, when they're acting natural. My young daughter and I spent a whole morning once watching them playing with an up-draft of air. There is out at the end of Schoodic a Thunder Hole like the one over on Mt. Desert, only smaller, where the sea rushes into a deep cleft in the rock. This sends up a fountain of spray and also, apparently, a strong current of air. The gulls hovered around the edge of it, getting up their courage like swimmers on the edge of a rapid. Then they plunged into it and allowed themselves to be tossed helplessly upward, squawking like mad all the while.

When they were high enough so that the blast lost its force, they slipped out, coasted back down to earth, and did it all over again. There was a line of about fifty of them, waiting their turns to take the ride; and once in a while a smart-aleck would shove an unsuspecting friend into the current before he was ready. Then the screaming and mewing was deafening. My daughter and I laughed ourselves sick and wished we were gulls.

I intend to come back to the Gouldsboro Peninsula later, so now let's go along the coast to Steuben, at the head of Gouldsboro Bay. The town was named for Baron von Steuben, inspector general of the Continental Army during the Revolution, and pronounced Stew-BEN. Although it is a very small hamlet, it has one of the prettiest village greens, flanked by a lovely little church and some old houses, anywhere along this coast. From Steuben you go down to Dyer Neck and Petit Manan Point, dramatically beautiful and completely unspoiled capes which a few summer people have found. Mary Ellen Chase lived on Petit Manan Point, too, and has written about it. The roads out there aren't very good, and I don't think that the inhabitants want them to be very good. I wouldn't, if I lived there myself.

There's an island off Petit Manan Point to the east which I called Bwubba all one summer, because that's what all my friends among the permanent residents called it. Finally I got around to looking at a map and found that the cartographers call it Bois Bubert Island. Well, maybe so. It's still Bwubba to me. No one's going to accuse *me* of putting on airs; and besides, no one would know what I was talking about if I started bois-buberting around.

Off the end of Petit Manan Point (pronounced Titm'-nan locally), and connected with it by a long, deadly, submerged reef, is Petit Manan (Titm'nan) Light. It is a tall tower on a low, bare ledge, one of the important lights of the coast. This is an extremely dangerous area for all shipping, and its perils were described very vividly by Champlain and subsequently by many others. (Champlain named Petit Manan Point, too, because the cape reminded him of the island of Grand Manan, farther east.) Titm'nan Light is a lonely station, since the Coast Guard cutter which serves it is often unable to land for long periods on account of the tremendous surf and lack of lee. It was therefore until recently a stag light.

A Maine friend of mine went to Florida one winter, and one day while he was sitting in the park at St. Petersburg, he fell into conversation with another man who, it developed, also hailed from Maine. My friend asked how his new acquaintance liked Florida, and it seemed that he didn't like it at all. Too damn lonely. So my friend asked where the other's home was, and it turned out that he had been born and brought up in Steuben.

"Funny I've never seen you around," said my friend. "I've been going to Steuben summers for the last fifteen years. Thought I knew everyone in town."

"Wal," said the Steuben man, "I ain't been in town much during the last twenty years. Been keepin' light out to Titm'nan. Be glad to get back, too. Too damn lonely here in Florida."

On Titm'nan he knew where he was and why; so he wasn't lonely, but only isolated. There's a difference. Titm'nan is automated, so that state no longer exists.

Starting at Cherryfield on the Narraguagus River and ending about sixty miles east at Dennysville on the Dennys River are a number of small streams in which there is very good and not very highly publicized fly fishing for Atlantic salmon. Most fishermen go to more widely advertised spots for this sport, but I don't think they get any better fishing. The salmon in these little rivers, most of which can be waded and some of which can be fished from the banks, frequently run up to fifteen pounds and sometimes almost to twenty. The season starts the first of May, legally, but the fishing doesn't get really good until almost the first of June. I'm not going to start giving you a lot of advice on how to fish these streams, or what ties to use. You'll have to work that out for yourself; and if you can't, there are local fly-tiers in such places as Cherryfield

*The prosperity of the shipbuilding era is preserved in the
Ruggles House in Columbia Falls.*

and Harrington who will gladly tell you all about it in great detail.

This is also the area of the great blueberry barrens. Blueberries always grew here abundantly, but now they have been even more encouraged, so that a whole seasonal industry rests on them. Blueberries are about the only profitable crop along this desolate coast; the great potato county is Aroostook, north and quite a way inland. Here there are just the wild blueberries. In order to increase production, many old marginal farms, which never really supported themselves, have been bought by packing companies and burned over, so that the berry bushes flourish and produce plentifully. The burning has to be repeated about every three years. Canning and freezing plants have been built in many of the towns like Milbridge and Columbia Falls and Jonesboro, where there are also sardine-packing plants. These are both small seasonal industries, but they do provide supplementary employment to the fishing and lobstering.

Originally many of these towns were shipbuilding centers. A type of small and very seaworthy boat called the pinky, which was once common all along the coast and is still seen in Nova Scotia, originated in Milbridge. ("Pinky" was old English slang for "small.") The building of these boats was revived in Milbridge in 1927 by a naval architect named Howard Chapelle, but the revival was short-lived.

Another town that once built a great many ships is Columbia Falls, and here the evidence of a former prosperity is apparent. Some of the few fine houses along this coast are located here, among them the Ruggles House, open to the public. This house was used by Arthur Train as a setting for his short story "The House That Tutt Built." The interior woodwork is simply beautiful, and it was all done by some unknown whittler with only a penknife for tools. It seems impossible that anyone could have the patience and muscular control to carve this delicate and exact work. There is a legend that an angel appeared to guide and steady the hand of the artisan, and it's easy to see how such an idea was born.

At Columbia Falls the road to Jonesport branches to the right off U.S. 1. For years I thought that Jonesport was a make-believe place, conceived for the purpose of providing a background for the radio program, "Sunday Night at Seth Parker's." It was the background for the program, all right; but it is also a real place.

It is, incidentally, 120 miles nearer Europe than Portland is, which gives you an idea of the eastward sweep of this coast. Comparatively speaking, there are quite a few summer people here, many of them attracted by the excellent deep-sea fishing, the way of life, and the fact that there is a good harbor for those foolish enough to sail small boats on this shore. Across a strait is Great Wass Island, on which stands the Coast Guard station that reported the hundred-eighty-odd days of fog in one year. That tells you all you need to know about the climate.

I mentioned once before, in connection with the Siege of Louisbourg, the fact that the hardheaded, down-to-earth, sensible Yankee is prone to unpredictable fits of completely haywire and unrealistic behavior, to spells of being carried away by a crazy enthusiasm. This happened in Jonesport and the neighboring towns of Addison, Beal's Island, and Jonesboro just at the close of the Civil War.

In 1865, a discredited Mormon elder by the name of George Washington Adams journeyed up and down the coast preaching his own brand of religion. He had formerly been an actor, and knew how to speak effectively and to play upon the emotions of his audience, which probably accounts for his success in persuading these ordinarily sensible, if unworldly, people to a course that was foolhardy, to say the least.

At any rate, 156 of them—men, women, and children—sold all their possessions, gave the proceeds to Adams' organization, which was called the Palestine Emigration

Association, and left their homes to sail to the Holy Land on the barkentine *Nellie Chapin*. They planned to establish a colony near Jaffa "to commence the great work of restoration foretold by the old prophets, patriarchs and apostles as well as by our Lord himself." Adams must have been a spellbinder to put that one over. The expedition sailed from Jonesport in August of 1866 and actually did arrive in Palestine and found a colony.

Then everything bad that could happen to them promptly happened. George Washington Adams embraced the bottle and was of no use whatsoever. He finally disappeared, to reappear inexplicably some years later in California. When he did his disappearance act from California, he took with him a large sum of money that did not belong to him and is—so far as I know—still missing. This has nothing to do with the Palestine colony, but it shows you what kind of a man the citizens of Jonesport fell victim to. To get back—

No one could speak the language of the land, so the colonists were cheated unmercifully and soon ran out of funds. They weren't used to the climate or immune to the diseases of the country, so most of them fell ill and many of them died. At the end of the first year, those who still had the price went home; but seventy-six remained stranded in this place so far away from Jonesport and so dismayingly different.

Finally a reporter of the New York *Sun* who happened to be in the Holy Land heard about their plight and loaned them enough money to get back to America. Most of them never did return to Jonesport. They didn't want to listen to "I told you so!" Instead, they scattered to different parts of the country, where many of them prospered. They had to, I suppose, so that if they ever did want to go home, they could do so in style.

Two members of the party chose to remain in Palestine for reasons which are both typically Maine Yankee, although they are about as diverse as can be. One of them, a youngish man, thought that what the Holy Land really needed was a stage line running between Jaffa and Jerusalem, so he stayed to establish one. It did very well indeed, and he died a well-fixed man, as we say in Maine. This is an almost classic example of Yankee enterprise in odd places.

The other member was an old lady, and she stayed in order to spite herself for having been such a fool as to come in the first place. This is a very common reason in New England for doing something that you don't want to do. I know a woman who went around all one winter with wet feet, to punish herself for carelessly losing her rubbers, although she could well afford to buy a dozen pair; and a man who— But who am I to talk? I often subject myself to discomfort to get even with myself for having done something unusually stupid. This pot is in no position to be calling other kettles black.

Machias, which means "Little Bad River," lies near a gorge of the Machias River, where the water roars down to empty into Machias Bay. It's an excellent site, sheltered, easily available from the sea, and—in the days when seclusion was important—hidden from the open ocean. For that reason, the Plymouth Pilgrims, about the time that their fur-trading post at Pentagoet was destroyed by the French in the 1630's, established another here. The French, however, found them almost at once and put them out of business. Then, since the French had no particular need for a foothold at this point, they simply abandoned the place, and Machias and the territory around it remained undisturbed and unsettled for several decades.

During this period, piracy rose to be a fairly common means of livelihood. This was a natural development of privateering, which was, when you come right down to it, only a form of government-approved piracy. After holding up the ships of foreign powers and robbing them for the government, unscrupulous minds quickly turned to doing the same thing for private benefit. Cotton Mather, in one of his "hanging sermons," warned that this would happen, and it did.

However, the pirate had one disadvantage—everyone, including his own government, was against him. The recognized pirate was not welcome in any port or shipyard anywhere. Since even pirate ships have to be repaired occasionally, and even pirates like to get ashore and stretch their legs once in a while, it was necessary for the pirate captain to find some place that he could use as a headquarters, for careening his ships, storing his loot, and providing his men with diversion. This base had to be secluded, and it had to have a supply of fresh water and good beaches for repair work. Machias filled all the requirements. It was discovered and first used for this purpose by the pirate Rhodes; and then the notorious Samuel Bellamy took it over in the early 1700's.

Bellamy was more ambitious than most pirates. He didn't want to spend the rest of his life skittering around a sea where every man's hand was against him. His aim was to form somewhere a sort of independent little kingdom of his own, where he could be boss and live a life of ease on the profits of the expeditions he would send forth from time to time to prey on the shipping. The pirate Mission had done this in Madagascar, and Bellamy saw no reason why he shouldn't do it in New England. Machias struck him as being the ideal location, so he landed there and built a fort and some barracks, the nucleus of his proposed monarchy.

Obviously he couldn't have much of a kingdom unless he had some women in it, so he went out looking for some—along with loot and more recruits for his band— in his ship, the *Whidaw*. He almost immediately made a bad mistake, which is a little difficult to understand, since he had been pirating for years with great success. He sighted a French corvette of thirty-six guns, carrying troops to Quebec. Instead of turning tail and slipping modestly over the horizon as he should have done, since he was badly overmatched, he attacked her. After a terrific fight, he barely escaped under cover of darkness, in a ship that was badly damaged, with a crew of greatly reduced numbers.

It occurred to him then that, if he lost the *Whidaw,* he'd be in a very bad way indeed; so instead of going home to Machias, he went south to the more frequented trade lanes along the Massachusetts coast. Off Nantucket Shoals he encountered the New Bedford whaler, the *Mary Anne,* which he had no difficulty in capturing, since whalers did not customarily carry heavy armament.

It was a part of Bellamy's policy to give the men of the crews he captured an opportunity to join his band, if they chose to do so. And apparently he went to some trouble to convince them that there was nothing reprehensible about piracy; that it was, in fact, simply a means of fairly distributing the wealth of the world. I guess he was a type of eighteenth-century Communist. Anyhow, he went into his usual spiel to the New Bedford captain of the *Mary Anne,* who decided that Bellamy was clearly crazy and had better be humored for the time being.

Bellamy, convinced that his golden oratory had won a valuable recruit, then made his last and biggest mistake. He was in waters that were dangerous and unfamiliar to him, so he asked the New Bedford whaler to hang a lantern on the stern of the *Mary Anne* and guide the *Whidaw* through the shoals off Eastham, Massachusetts.

The skipper of the *Mary Anne* deliberately wrecked his ship, and the *Whidaw* piled up on the bars beside her. The pirates were captured by the Cape Codders ashore, tried, and hanged. The installations at Machias rotted away and were engulfed by the encroaching bushes and trees, and that was the end of Bellamy's kingdom. The ridges and hollows that were breastworks and moats may still be seen, though, near where the bridge crosses the Machias River.

The first permanent English colony at Machias was established there in 1762 when settlers moved east from Scarboro. The town became a thriving shipbuilding and lumbering center. It was the last place in Maine where long logs were driven before the practice was outlawed.

Machias has been called "the Birthplace of the American Navy," because it was here that citizens, early in the Revolution, captured the armed British *Margaretta*, the first successful naval engagement by the colonists against the Crown. If you want to call it a naval engagement. It was really just a fight between two small schooners. However, its importance was all out of proportion to its size. It gave those in Philadelphia who were urging the commissioning of an American navy an excellent talking point, with the result that such a navy was established.

Machias has a remarkable history for fiery patriotism. There is near the center of the town, for instance, a brook called Foster's Rubicon. In June of 1775, very early in the Revolution, before the issues were clearly cut or the sides definitely drawn, the British in Boston sent to Machias for some lumber they needed to build barracks for their troops. The townsmen of Machias met on the bank of the brook to talk the matter over. I have an idea it wasn't a formal town meeting, but just one of those gatherings that occur spontaneously in any small town when there is an important problem to be discussed. Sometimes they occur in the general store or after church or down to the stage stop. This one happened to take place by the brook.

Machias was remote from sources of news, and the whole affair of the Revolution was a bit vague and unreal to the citizens. Some wanted to send the lumber as usual, and some wanted at least to make a gesture by refusing. Finally Benjamin Foster got tired of the arguing and jumped across the brook, inviting everyone to follow who agreed with him that they should have no dealings with the British oppressors. Some leaped at once and some were a little slower, but in the end everyone was on Foster's side of the brook, and then the little settlement was committed to the course of rebellion.

In those days the meeting place for discussion of affairs

*Only a few miles from Canada, the little town of Lubec
was a smuggling center during the Revolution.*

was Burnham Tavern, which still stands today and is open on Saturday afternoons for a small fee. Built by Joe Burnham in 1770, it is a plain, gambrel-roofed structure of simple charm. Burnham must have been a rather nice man with a fine feeling for the appropriate. Underneath each of the four cornerstones he placed a little box containing a slip of paper on which were written "Hospitality," "Hope," "Cheer," and "Courage" respectively. His original sign still swings over the door. It reads, "Drink for the thirsty, food for the hungry, lodging for the weary, and good keeping for horses."

All this area is forested and sparsely settled with rather scrubby-looking farms, and yet the little villages off the main highway, down on the shore—villages like Indian River and South Trescott and Little Machias—are perfectly delightful and completely unspoiled. Probably as nearly unknown as it is possible for a place to be in these days of easy transportation these almost lost little hamlets depend on the sea for a livelihood and they are protected by the great granite bastions and the silent fogs and the thunderous breakers of this exposed coastline. For those who like their pleasures simple, who can easily entertain themselves, I don't know of any finer places to go.

Between South Trescott and Lubec is West Quoddy Head, where there is a lighthouse and a Coast Guard station—and believe me, they need both along this stretch of the coast; but West Quoddy is particularly distinguished as being the most easterly point of the whole United States. You can stand there on the rocks between the sea and the forest of spruce and fir and feel, backing you up, the whole expanse and power of this country, reaching away behind you to the Pacific and the Gulf of Mexico. It's quite a sensation.

Lubec and Eastport are on opposite sides of the entrance to Cobscook Bay, with less than three miles of water between them. The distance by road is over forty miles.

Out in front is Campobello Island, which is in Canada, is reachable by bridge, and is famous as having been the summer home of Franklin Roosevelt. Eastport is on Moose Island, to the northeast of which is Passamaquoddy Bay and the province of New Brunswick. Because this country is so broken and so near to Canada, it has since earliest times been a wonderful place for smuggling, when there was anything to be gained by that activity. I don't know what, if anything, is being smuggled right now. I do know that during prohibition, a large percentage of the boat-owning population made a great deal of money slipping in and out among the islands and capes with their vessels loaded to the gunwales with contraband.

But long before that, during the Revolution and during the War of 1812, all manner of goods was smuggled into or out of the country at this point: sugar, molasses, rum, flour, fabrics, almost anything. Vessels hailing from East-port and Lubec took out sailing papers for Spain and Portugal and France and made some of the quickest trips in history. Two or three days later they would be back with full holds. Of course, they really went no farther than the nearest Canadian port, where they could buy a barrel of flour, worth eight or ten dollars in this country, for four dollars.

Two inns still standing in Lubec—Chaloner Tavern and the Golden Ball, now called the Comstock House—acted as receiving points and hiding places for this illegal goods; and the Golden Ball had a secret room where the proprietor hid deserting British sailors until they could move along. He usually had to dry them out, too, as most of them had swum ashore from their ships. This was a very profitable sideline; and, besides that, one of them married his daughter.

If you drive around Cobscook Bay from Lubec to East-port, you will be nearly halfway between the Equator and the North Pole when you get to Perry. If you'd like to stand *exactly* halfway between the two points, you can drive out of Perry toward North Perry, and you will find a granite marker placed near the road by the National Geographic Society to mark the forty-fifth parallel of north latitude.

At a little less than a mile out of Perry on the Eastport road, there is a dirt thoroughfare to the left which goes to Pleasant Point, the Passamaquoddy Indian Reservation. These Indians are self-governing, although they have a state agent to supervise their business affairs, and may, if they wish, elect a member of the tribe to represent them at the State Legislature. They do a little farming, but they derive most of their living from fishing. They are marvelous fishermen and seamen, and always have been. They have an extremely distinguished record for bravery under fire in various wars that the United States has conducted against other countries. One, Charles Nola, was posthumously awarded the Croix de guerre for his remarkable courage and tenacity during the First World War, in which he lost his life. The Passamaquoddies are mostly Catholics, and devout ones, too; but they sometimes celebrate such occasions as weddings with tribal as well as church ceremonies. They dress and paint their faces in the traditional manner and perform the ancient rituals. Visitors are welcome at these affairs, whenever they happen to occur.

After you cross the bridge from the mainland onto Moose Island, you come into Quoddy Village. I'm not going into a long dissertation on the whole sad business of the Passamaquoddy Tidal Power Development Project here. It's too complicated and too controversial. The idea, as I suppose everyone knows, was to build a great dam, or series of dams, linking several islands and the mainland, so that the tremendous tide range of this region could be used to generate power. This was not a new idea at all. Way back in colonial days, if you remember, there were small tidal dams all along the coast and they worked very well. Passamaquoddy was going to be the same thing on a gigantic scale, and this is one of the very few possible sites in the world for such an undertaking. There was no reason why the plan wouldn't have worked, and if the project had been completed, all the farms and industries of the state would have been supplied with abundant cheap power. It would have made all the difference between marginal living and decent living to a great many people.

But after an elaborate and costly village had been built for the engineers and workers on the job, and after some of the dams had been completed and a great deal of money spent, the whole notion was abandoned. Someone, somewhere, may have a convincing excuse for this waste of your money and mine, but I haven't heard it yet. I don't insist that the dam is necessary. People got along without it for centuries and can still get along without it. But I just don't like things to be started with a lot of ballyhoo and then not finished. It's wasteful and irresponsible, and in this case it worked a real hardship on the whole surrounding territory.

Thousands of workers were attracted to the area by the project. Schools were overcrowded by the children of the Quoddy workers, so they had to be enlarged; and the whole machinery of living everywhere had to be geared up to meet the new demands. Then the project was whimsically abandoned almost overnight, and five thousand men were thrown out of work. Many of them became the problem of the little town of Eastport, which had already bankrupted itself in its attempt to adjust to new conditions for which it was not, primarily, responsible. The result was chaos. There was untold suffering and even starvation; but worst of all, I think, was the loss of hope for the better times that had been promised and the loss of confidence in a power that could do this to its own people.

The last time I saw Quoddy it was a mess. The handsome houses—and there is a whole village full of them—

were empty and falling into disrepair. Today, in view of the ever-increasing energy problem, the Passamaquoddy Power Project is again being discussed and seriously considered as feasible and desirable.

Eastport itself has a magnificently beautiful location, looking out on Passamaquoddy Bay and the islands. The tides here range up to thirty feet, so that sometimes you can step from a wharf into a row boat with the greatest of ease, and six hours later you can't get into it at all without a parachute. Eastport has some of the longest-legged wharves in the world.

The first sardine cannery in the United States was established in Eastport in 1875, and there have been sardine factories there ever since. As everyone undoubtedly knows, sardines are small herring cooked and canned in oil or mustard sauce. Formerly the scales were thrown away, but now they are used in the manufacture of nail polish, artificial pearls, lacquers, and similar products.

In spite of her depressed economy, Eastport is one of the towns to have resisted the blandishments of oil interests and refused to countenance the establishment of refineries on her fine deep-water harbor.

Eastport is as far Down-East as you can go. You've glanced at all of it, now. You'll never really get to know it all, not if you live to be a hundred years old and devote the rest of your life to exploring the coast of Maine. There will always be one more backroad that you never noticed before, one more island that you lacked time to visit, one more deep indentation or long cape that you somehow missed. It's useless to try to become familiar with every inch of this fantastic and beautiful coastline.

It would be better not to try. It would be better, instead, to find one tiny section of it that you like the looks and feeling of, and learn to know that well—its weather and its tides and its rocks and fields and woods, its flowers and wild life, and above all, its people. When you have done that, you can truthfully say that you know the coast of Maine. Knowledge is not a matter of breadth of observation, but of depth of perception and understanding, here as everywhere.

16 · More Islands

ACCORDING to the maps of the U.S. Geological Survey and the charts of the U.S. Coast and Geodetic Survey, there are almost eleven hundred islands along the coast of Maine. This means *real* islands: dry land surrounded by water and supporting some life, even if it's only a few huckleberry bushes growing out of a little patch of starved soil; bits of land worthy of being called islands and of bearing names of their own. Of these eleven hundred, I have tried to give an account of a few of the best-known—for one reason or another—and most easily available: the islands of Casco Bay, Monhegan, Vinalhaven, Mt. Desert and the like. I hope I haven't given the impression that these are the only islands worth visiting, because such is far from being the case. If you like islands—and as I have said, almost everyone likes the *idea* of an island, at least—practically any old island at all is worth a visit. If you can get there. Some of the islands, unfortunately, are very nearly inaccessible.

Matinicus is an island that can be reached by passenger ferry from Rockland, a distance of twenty miles. It lies on the outermost fringe of the islands of Penobscot Bay, with only Ragged Island and Matinicus Rock between it and Portugal. It has the true feeling of an island, remote, sea-washed, self-contained. It is a lovely island, with a harbor on the rugged eastern side, and on the west long fields sloping gently to the sea.

There is one industry today on Matinicus: deep-sea fishing; and this without doubt was the original industry.

Even before the first permanent settlement there, the island was unquestionably used by the European fishermen and before them by the Vikings as a base from which to fish and a place on which to build their stages and dry their catches. Before that, from time immemorial, the Indians regularly made trips out from the mainland in their birch canoes to catch sea birds, collect eggs, kill seals, and fish. There is no way for an island like Matinicus to escape being a fishing community, and nobody on Matinicus wants to escape it. They're fishermen and seamen born and bred.

The island was first settled over two hundred years ago, and at that time and for a century and a half following, there were fine farms there, and thriving herds of cattle, so that the place was completely self-supporting. It had its troubles, of course: troubles with the Indians, troubles with the French, troubles with the English, and troubles with its own absentee government, seated on Vinalhaven, which was suspected of slighting Matinicus in matters of schooling and taxes. But all these things straightened themselves out in time; and in time, with swifter transportation and improved methods of food preservation, it was found to be cheaper and easier to get milk and fresh vegetables and meat from the mainland than to wrastle it out of the island's thin soil. So the people returned to the first means of livelihood, the one for which they were really intended.

Most of the homes on today's Matinicus are comfortable and modern, although there are a few old houses of great interest to remind the visitor of the past. One is the Joseph Young homestead, a Cape Cod type built in 1800, with fascinating doors presenting Biblical motifs and one of the half-dozen old pianos in the United States with mother-of-pearl keys. The children of Matinicus attend school on the mainland now, but there is a church on the island where services are conducted by ministers from the Maine Seacoast Mission.

Five miles south of Matinicus lies Matinicus Rock, bearing the outermost lighthouse on the coast of Maine. It is never called anything but The Rock, locally; and locally it is as important as that other Rock, Gibraltar. There are thirty-two acres of it, rising in sheer cliffs from the Atlantic, with only one possible landing place—if you're lucky. Even on lucky days, the boat must be hauled up on a slip out of reach of the pounding and trampling surf that constantly batters The Rock, and the winds that ceaselessly pour over it.

The members of the Coast Guard who are assigned duty tending the light on The Rock hate it there. Sometimes they write letters—since there's not much else to do on The Rock—to the *Maine Coast Fisherman,* a little trade paper read by everyone on the coast, expressing their feelings. They are rather pathetic letters, in a way, telling how nice it was back in Minnesota, with the wheat fields blowing and one's best girl just down the road, and how bare and awful it is stuck out there in the middle of the ocean. Even for one who likes space and solitude, a year on The Rock might be too much of a good thing.

Once in a while there are visitors, usually ornithologists who come from all over the country to study the puffins, the little sea parrots who breed only on The Rock and on Machias Seal Island along the whole coast of both Americas. Most of the time, after all their time and trouble, they find it impossible to land. This is doubtless disappointing to the bird watchers, but it's downright infuriating to the keepers, who were looking forward to new faces, new voices, and something new to talk about.

Between Matinicus and The Rock lies Criehaven, charted as Ragged Island, but called roughly and affectionately by those who love it Ragged Arse. The Indian name was Racketash, which was corrupted by the early English with their Anglo-Saxon propensity for always finding the earthy word. Criehaven can be reached by passenger ferry from Rockland, and although it's only a small island of about three hundred acres, it's perfectly lovely. There are cool, shady copses of spruce, bravely blooming old orchards, and great ledges of pink granite against which the surf breaks in a frill of white lace. It was settled by young Robert and Harriet Crie in 1848, right after their marriage, and at the end of the next half-century was largely populated by Cries and Crie in-laws. They were a hard-working, self-respecting tribe, and did well with the fisheries, farming, and sheep raising. Later, during the years when summer people went to one place and stayed put, a prosperous summer colony of artists, writers, and others developed. There was a school and a church, and although there was no doctor, one could be summoned in short order from the mainland by carrier pigeon messages. This was a much quicker and more dependable method than sailing over in rough weather.

Now Criehaven has simmered down into a comfortable and pleasant middle age. It's not as busy and bustling as it used to be, but it's still beautiful, and the few summer people who still go there love it more than ever for its sea-girt peace and quiet.

To me, one of the most impressive islands on the Maine coast is Isle au Haut, pronounced either "Ile-a-holt" or "Eel-oh-ho," depending on where you were brought up. The natives favor Ile-a-holt. This is a fair-sized island, about six miles long and three miles wide, and it is very high. Cliffs rise five hundred and fifty feet sheerly from the deep and turbulent water. They give the impression of great age, of having been battered mercilessly for thousands of years by the tremendous seas shouldering in from Spain—which is indeed the case—and of being able to stand the pounding for thousands of years to come. There's a feeling of great and ageless strength about Isle au Haut.

More than this, Isle au Haut is one of the few inhabited islands that has been very little altered by the occupancy of man. From a short distance, it looks exactly as it must have looked to the Vikings and to Champlain, who gave it its name. This is the result of chance. Although it was first settled in 1792 and although there was no reason why a prosperous community shouldn't persist there where the soil was good and the fishing excellent, it was just too lonely, remote, and difficult for most people. They came, but they went away again. So the dense forests were never cut off and the island retained its pristine appearance.

Then a group of wealthy men from Boston, New York, and Philadelphia discovered it, liked its virginal quality, and formed a club, the Point Lookout Club, to improve the island while still preserving its unspoiled natural beauty. During the heyday of the club, roads were built, lakes stocked with game fish, and good landings installed. Then the day of such enterprises passed; but the heirs of some of the members turned over a large part of the island to the Acadia National Park, most of which is on Mt. Desert Island. Under Park administration, Isle au Haut will probably continue to be unspoiled.

The island may be reached by mail and passenger ferry from Stonington, six miles away, and there are simple accommodations to be had on the island. It's a good place to stay for a while.

Swan's Island, between Isle au Haut and Mt. Desert Island, may be reached by car ferry from Bass Harbor. The roads on the large island with its three hamlets—Atlantic, Minturn, and Swan's Island—are good, so it's an advantage to be able to take your car across. This island was originally called by Champlain Brûlé-Côte, which means burned hill or coast, because when he saw it, there had evidently been a recent forest fire, started either by the Indians or by lightning. This name very soon changed to Burnt Coat, and so it appears on most old charts. Then a Massachusetts man named Swan came into possession of the Burnt Coat group, and inevitably the island became Swan's Island. The U.S. Board of Geographical Names and the U.S. Post Office Department frown on the use of the apostrophe; but for some unexplained reason they have made what is almost a unique exception in the case of Swan's Island.

Swan instituted what amounted to a private homesteading plan. He promised—and kept the promise—a hundred acres of land to any man with a family who would settle and build on the island, and after seven years, a deed to the property he had cleared and improved. Very soon a busy and prosperous community came into being. There were lumber mills, grist mills, shipyards, and, of course, farming and fishing. The people who accepted Swan's offer were intelligent and hard-working, and Swan's Island became a desirable place in which to live.

It still is. The main industries now are lobstering and fishing, and the place has the simple charm of the off-the-track fishing village wherever in the world you may find it. The scenery is beautiful, the pace is placid, and the islanders are friendly without exhibiting the overcordiality of the commercial-minded tourist-trapper. Swan's is a very pleasant place to visit or to stay.

Until recently, Beals Island, half a mile off Jonesport across Moosabec Reach, was a true island in the sense that it could be reached only by boat. Now there is a toll bridge across the Reach. I'm of two minds as to whether this is an improvement or not. It's supposed to be of great benefit to the Beals Islanders to be able to go to the mainland easily and safely; but I thought Beals was doing all right in the olden days, when sometimes one couldn't go ashore at all for fairly long periods of rough weather.

In those days, the island—which with the neighboring island of Great Wass constituted the town of Beals—was about as self-sufficient and independent as any company of six hundred people could be. There were five churches on the island—five up-and-coming and prosperous churches, which is something of a record. Everybody worked for his church, because there was almost no other outlet for the instinct of sociability. There were excellent schools, rated Grade-A by the state; and the Beals Island High School basketball team won state and New England trophies year after year. There was no football team. There weren't enough big boys to form one. So they concentrated on basketball; and because there wasn't much to tempt the athlete from training and practice, the team was good.

On Beals Island in those days, Elizabethan English was still spoken, a language with a quaint and sometimes incomprehensible charm. There are still traces of it in the speech of the people; but contact with the mainland is rapidly erasing it, which seems to me rather too bad.

Beals isn't much of a summer place yet, although I suppose that it soon will be, now that we have the bridge. Most of the men are lobstermen or seiners, and many of the women work in the clam-shucking plants. More and more, however, are finding employment across the Reach in Jonesport, especially during the summer season, and this association has changed their manner and speech and, I suppose, their thinking, too, to some extent.

To me, Beals is an odd island. It isn't as beautiful in the conventional sense as some we have mentioned; but it has a peculiar, barren, stark appeal. It is surrounded by reefs and ledges, two of which are marked on old charts as The Virgin's Breasts and The Lecherous Priest. When the tide is out and all these configurations are exposed, the place looks almost like a lunar landscape. I can understand how one might become very much attached to Beals Island.

Although we're supposed to be talking about islands of the Maine coast, I'm going to include three other islands. At this late date, I'm not going to fight the terms of the Webster-Ashburton Treaty of 1842; but I can hold my own opinion, which is that Campobello, Grand Manan, and Deer Islands ought by rights and reason to belong to Maine instead of New Brunswick. That's why I'm including them in this chapter about islands—that and the fact that no island lover should miss them.

Campobello is only two hundred and fifty yards from Maine, and can be reached over a bridge. You pass through customs here, and it seems odd to me to be questioned by members of the Mounties, whom I have always associated with the Northwest. The island is best known, probably, as the summer home of the Franklin Roosevelts. The house is open to the public now and well worth a visit. Further along are several gift shops where it is sometimes possible to pick up bargains in English wool and china.

The island is ten miles long and supports two typical

fishing villages, Welshpool and Wilson's Beach, as well as an almost completely landlocked anchorage, Head Harbor. In between are cliffs and sweeping beaches. The best is two-mile-long Herring Cove Beach, a scavenger's paradise with its treasures of jewel-bright pebbles and fascinating driftwood.

Grand Manan is bigger, almost twenty miles long, and farther out to sea—an hour by car ferry from St. Andrews, N.B., or passenger ferry from Campobello. It's one of those places for which you find yourself feeling vaguely homesick, even if you've visited it only once, and that for a short time. For one thing, the people are so obviously in love with their island, and proud and eager to tell you all about it—about its history and traditions and birds and geology. For another thing, it is stunningly beautiful, with sheer cliffs rising from the sea and broad arcs of beach. For those who are interested, the deep-sea fishing is wonderful here; and at Dark Harbour there is a whole beachful of dulse for the epicures who like to chew it or make it into seaweed pudding.

The other Canadian island, Deer Island, is on the Maine side of Passamaquoddy Bay, very near Eastport, Maine. It's about nine miles long, with a half-dozen or so tiny fishing hamlets nestled into coves. The countryside is delightful. You get there by taking a scow-type ferry across from Eastport; and you can drive completely around the island in a short time—only you won't, as there are too many beaches to comb and things to see—and go back the way you came. Or—and this is more fun—you can take the free car ferry from the other end of the island across to L'Etete, N.B., circle around through St. George, St. Andrews, and St. Stephen, where you cross the border back into the United States. This gives you a chance, if you're interested, to poke around in the Canadian shops, where they have wonderful bargains in wool and china. On Deer Island, in summer—and this seems very much out of the character of the simple place—The Chocolate Cove Playhouse presents excellent plays with Broadway casts on

Tuesdays through Saturdays. A special passenger boat leaves Eastport at around 7:30 P.M. for those who wish to attend.

These, then, are the islands to which public transportation is available, the known and inhabited islands. But the true island fancier won't be satisfied with these. He must have his secret, private island, his own island, if not in terms of deeds and taxes, then in terms of love and knowledge. That's the only way you can own an island anyhow: by knowing and loving it. Everybody has to find his own special island. I can't help you there. But I can outline the procedure for you.

Don't trust names. Being in the business of words, I'm easily seduced by a fine-sounding name. Before I even see it, I'm prepared to find wonderful an island called Pound of Tea or Junk of Pork or Eastern Ear or West Brown Cow. There are some other evocative names: The Hypocrites and The Cuckolds; Ministerial Island and the High Sheriff; Despair, The Shivers, and Jordan's Delight; Bombazeen and Bum Key. Actually some of these are rather dull islands. Two of my favorite private islands are Bar Island and Sheep Island—and there are thirteen Sheep and fifteen Bar Islands in Maine. Names tell nothing. The best way to form a primary opinion of an island is to look at it from the mainland or from a boat; and the next best way is to study a map—if you can really read a map—and decide from it whether the island is rugged and broken and various, or just another piece of land surrounded by water.

Having made up your mind which island you wish to explore, you then must find a way of getting there. The easiest course is to approach a lobsterman with the proposition that he put you ashore on his way out to haul his traps, and pick you up several hours later when he returns to harbor—or even the next day, if you so desire. There's always someone who'll be glad to do it. Or if necessary and the distance isn't too great, you can rent a boat and row yourself over, being sure to pull your craft well up on the shore, or else the tide will float it off and you'll find yourself marooned. Take whatever food you think you'll need, such as a peanut butter sandwich and an apple, or a steak and some potatoes; but food or no food, be sure to take a jug of water. Most of these islands are uninhabited simply because there is no fresh water supply on them; and you can become very thirsty scrambling over rocks in the hot sun and stiff salt breeze.

Being alone on a small island is a marvelous experience. I'm not sure I'd like to live thus forever, but for a day it's wonderful to feel that every inch of the earth under your feet is yours, temporarily at least, and that you have all the time in the world to explore it. Nobody's pushing you or laughing at you for being childish over a tidal pool full of minnows. You discover hidden little beaches and beautiful small coves that you feel sure no one else has ever seen. There are wonderful treasures on the shore—shells, and buoys, and striped pebbles and weathered planks carved intricately by sea worms. You feel yourself relaxing and expanding, feel all the dust of the mainland blowing out of your mind and spirit. When at last it is time to return to the problems and duties that you left behind you across the reach of water, you feel much better able to cope with them.

If your first island isn't quite what you hoped, don't be discouraged. There are loads of others, one of which will be that to which your thoughts return often and often when you are far away. Maybe you'll become a collector of islands, as I suspect I'm becoming. I'm satisfied now with my Sheep and Bar; but I just found a new one on a map, down Buck's Harbor way, which one of these days——

So—Happy island hunting!

17 · My Down-East

You can't say of your own Down-East, "This one thing is why I love it." You love it because of a hundred things, most of them inconsequential, which add up to an essential character. My Down-East is a place called Corea (no, you never heard of it) about eight miles from Winter Harbor, on the Gouldsboro Peninsula; and the quality I love about it is, as nearly as I can explain, its complete lack of pretension, its stripped-down bareness to the bones of use. Neither the country nor the people go in for softness and superficiality, and the result, which could be bleakness, is in fact a great functional beauty, which is in my opinion the only true beauty. Everything in the hamlet, whether put there by man or by nature, is there for a purpose. It is, I am sure, not unique among Maine coast villages. There must be a dozen others just like it, hidden away among the ledges and islands. It just happens to be the one I know. So let me tell you about it.

When first I went there, Corea was entirely a lobster town. Every man except one derived his living directly from the sea, owning his own boat and gear and setting out and tending his own traps. You should have seen the harbor in the late afternoon, when all the boats were in for the night. It's a small harbor, a little basin surrounded by bare ledges and long-legged wharves and connected with the sea by a narrow, winding passage beyond which the surf pounds on the reefs and offshore islands. In the late afternoon there were perhaps thirty boats there, a full harbor, all washed by the declining sun, a soft rose against the sea's sharp blue, all faced into the tide like a herd grazing into the wind. There wouldn't be a single pleasure boat among them, not one mahogany and chrome craft, not one slim white yacht. They were all work boats, designed and built for a hard, specific job. They looked so staunch and competent and purposeful that they made all other boats seem a little silly. I've never seen a harbor like Corea, nor one I liked so well.

The one man not a lobsterman was the storekeeper, and he made his living almost as directly from the sea, since his customers were almost entirely fishermen. There weren't any summer people, except a stray or two like me. There was just this one store, which was also the post office. It served as well as general intelligence, being situated strategically where the two dead-end roads converged on a slight rise overlooking the harbor. Nothing escaped the eye of the storekeeper. If you wanted to know where anybody was at a given moment, you asked him; or if you went away for the day, you told him all about it and he took care of stray callers during your absence, transmitting messages with great accuracy. It was a very efficient system.

Almost everybody owned a car, but then they were less important than the boats, just as the state of the tide was more important than the state of the road. There was— and is—only one leading into the village; and one day as I was returning home, I found it completely covered with rope at a point just a bit above the store. There were a hundred or more lengths of tarred quarter-inch line neatly laid out all over its whole surface, and I couldn't possibly get by without driving over them, which I was loath to do. So I parked the car and went down to ask the storekeeper what was going on.

"Oh, Forrest's gettin' ready to put his traps out tomorrow. He had to have a good long level place to straighten out his lines, and there ain't much better than the road.

Told him you was off and would be wantin' past, but he knew better. He'll have 'em picked up early tomorrow mornin'. Want I should find you a lift down to the Point, or do you want to walk?"

That's what I mean by Corea's being a lobster town. There was no question at all which was more important, Forrest's lines or my convenience. I was summer people, and Corea wasn't in the summer people business. Its business was lobsters.

All this was a long time ago, and Corea like the rest of the coast has changed some since then. The storekeeper has died and the old store now houses lobstering gear. The needs of the populace are met by trips to supermarkets in nearby towns; or by the new little store way down at the end of the road, in a converted lobstershack beside the harbor. It is run by two retired gentlewomen from Away, known locally as the girls-down't-the-store. The post office now occupies an ell of the postmaster's house on the side road leading to Crowley's Island.

Forrest has retired from the sea and no longer uses the highway to straighten his lines. It's just as well. Corea has been discovered and is to some extent now in the summer people business. Old houses have been bought and spruced up by out-of-staters, a few mobile homes have been towed in, and many new cottages have been built. The west shore of Gouldsboro Bay has been developed, and the Navy has a new installation over on the hayth— the local pronunciation of heath. I can't tell you what they do there. It's so highly classified that we're not supposed even to think about it, let alone ask questions. Many of the native men and women now work for the summer people as caretakers or household help, and some have little gift shops in their homes.

These changes make less difference basically than you might think. There are a few pleasure boats in the harbor, but they are so outnumbered that they are inconspicuous. The development is invisible from the road and

village and is nicely laid out anyhow. The Navy base is
way over on the back shore. Actually, there isn't much
difference in the appearance and functioning of Corea
from the old days.

There isn't any fire department, or any policeman, or
any movie house. There is no farming at all. Most people
have a very small vegetable plot for their own use, a few
people keep a few hens, and many women cultivate very
beautiful flower gardens. But no one owns a horse or cow,
and very few have even an apple tree with which to bless
themselves. In fact, there are very few trees of any sort
in the town at all, except some wild stands of stunted
fir and spruce, too small and gnarly for lumber. There is
too little soil over the basic pink granite ledges to support
any form of vegetation except the very sparsest: lichens and
mosses, coarse salt grass, cranberry vines and low blueberry bushes, wild roses and rugosa, and a great variety
of tiny alpine and subarctic types of flowers.

Corea doesn't even have any place in history. Nobody
in the early days was so foolish as to attempt a landing
here, where the coast is guarded by submerged ledges,
clusters of small, offshore islands, a continual tremendous
surf, and truly epic fogs. This is the identical stretch
against which Champlain warned all mariners in such
stringent terms, and all shipping gave it a very wide berth
indeed. It's probably the worst piece of coast in all Maine.

Yet it does have its own local history, simple and representative. As in most small Maine towns, a few names
predominate. In Corea the names happen to be Young
and Crowley. I was talking one day with my favorite lobsterman, George Crowley, an elderly man who has spent
over half a century hauling lobster pots. We were out
in his boat tending his traps, a fascinating occupation if
you don't mind the smell of the decomposed fish that
serves as bait, and if you don't easily become seasick. You
never know what you're going to pull up. Lobsters of
legal size, you hope; but if not, there will be sea urchins
and star fish and squid and crabs and cod and flounders

anyhow. These aren't particularly interesting to an old hand like George Crowley, of course, but they are to me.

As we were bucketing along from buoy to buoy, I asked him how his family happened to settle in Corea in the first place. "Didn't have much choice in the matter," he told me. "My great-great-grandfather was a British seaman. His ship wrecked over yonder on Outer Bar and he was the only one washed ashore. He just never got around to leaving, and none of the rest of us ever see any call to move on either. So here we be." I imagine that's the story behind a great many well-established names along the Maine Coast.

Another seaman was less fortunate than George Crowley's great-great-grandfather. About a hundred years ago his body was washed up on that same Outer Bar, which is in a good position to catch anything afloat, being the outermost of the little string of islands that guards the entrance to the harbor. This man evidently fell or was pushed overboard from a passing ship, since there was no wreck thereabouts at the time. The local authorities made a few inquiries along the coast, but no one seemed to be missing. Since no one was willing to take charge of the body, it was buried in a small orchard on the shore of Crowley Island.

This coast changes very fast, almost from year to year, and within a decade what had been an apple orchard became a sand dune. In the course of the conversion, the skeleton of the stranger came to the surface. He was buried again, and a few years later he again reappeared. By this time, any gruesome associations had evaporated, and he was just a collection of bones; so that it became one of the games of the children to dig up the skeleton and assemble it on the beach. A woman I know remembers vividly playing that game many, many times. When the kids got bored, they collected the pieces and buried them again. Once, during an especially stormy winter when the whole shoreline shifted and old landmarks disappeared, they lost him for a season. Eventually they found him again.

As the years went by, various pieces were lost, until now he is gone forever.

Coreans accept the whole thing as a matter of course, as though it were a part of everyone's growing-up to have a skeleton to put together like a puzzle. But I can't help wondering who he was, where he came from, and most of all, how he'd feel about serving as a game for children playing in the brilliant sun and stiff salt wind. I hope he wouldn't mind. He really shouldn't. He should be pleased.

What is there to love about a place which seems to be distinguished more by what it lacks than by what it has? That's a little hard to answer, because the whole thing hinges on the sort of person you are and on what you need to make you happy. I just like it, that's all; and so the very lacks seem to me to be priceless assets. There aren't very many people, and to me that is a great advantage, because I can know them all. I like them. I like their coastal faces, all lean brown planes, guarded against emotion, not given to quick laughter or grimaces of easy grief —until you come to the eyes, which look out coolly, intelligently, clearly, confidently, ready to give or to withhold. I like that Down-East walk of theirs, a lounging stride that escapes sloppiness by a narrow margin and urgency by a hair, a walk that is almost but not quite studied, and that gets them where they are going. I like the way they treat me, as though I were a reasonably sane human being.

I like the looks of the country itself. Its lack of forests and mountains makes it spacious and bright and clean, a country of moor and great ledges and of the sea. Always the long rollers come piling in from Europe, and always the whole scene, as far as the eye can reach, is lively with leaping spray. Everywhere you look, great fountains play —along the ledges of the shore, against the reefs of the offshore islands, and far out where the submerged rocks lie, and where Titm'nan Light is a magic tower, unreal and faraway and enchanted, catching the sun's full glow after all the rest of the world is steeped in twilight.

Then there are all the lovely sounds that fill the emptiness. I have never been in a place that talks so much, and never with the voice of man. The wind blows constantly, sometimes softly and with a sad sighing, sometimes with a harplike singing in the grasses, sometimes with almost an organ tone. The gulls scream and mew over, flashing bright in the sun, soaring and turning and coasting down invisible hills of air. Flocks of tiny shore birds with a peculiar erratic dipping habit of flight skim along the edge of the water. Some radar of their own keeps each in his exact place in their close formation, in spite of their eccentric course and great speed; and their high, sweet, constant calling is like a rain of chimes.

Because of the extremely dangerous character of the coast, it is well marked with a variety of devices, so that the toll of the bell buoys and the hollow hoot of the whistling buoys sounds continually, now loud and demanding, now ghostly and diminished, depending on the direction of the wind. In the early morning, as soon as the sun is up, there is a cheerful puttering of lobster boats going out to work; and at sunset the swallows under the eaves of the cabin put their children to bed with such a scolding and admonishing that sometimes we knock on the wall to warn them that they are disturbing the neighbors. Then there is a dead silence from them, during which the wind sounds a little louder. In a minute one chirps experimentally, another answers, and shortly they are all twittering away again at full pitch.

And always and forever, above and below and around all the other sounds, is the sound of the sea. Sometimes it is a loud roar, punctuated by pistol shots as a greater breaker than ever crashes on the rocks. Sometimes it is a slow and lazy rumble. Sometimes it sinks to a murmur like a beast's quiet breathing; but it is never still. Even on the rare days when the ocean farther out looks like glass, it is still busy and restless along the shore, filling and emptying little pools, working away at crevices in the ledges, lifting the seaweed gently and combing it with cold, careful fingers.

I like the country's infinite variety. You would think that, given the three simple elements of clean-swept land, open sea, and the weather, there would be a very definite limit to the changes that can be rung. After we had been there for about a week on our first visit, George Crowley, who had taken me under his wing as an obvious inlander who didn't know her way around, came down to Cranberry Point to see how my daughter and I were making out. We were making out fine, I told him. "Every day since we've been here has been different," I said. "We've had a bright day and a foggy day and an in-between day and a rough day and a rainy day—I guess we've had a sample of about every kind of day there is, so we're prepared for anything."

He looked at me, his bright old eyes amused in his weathered face. "There's some surprises yet in store for ye," he informed me in his slow and gentle voice; and he was right. I don't remember one day that was like another. Even if they seemed to start out the same, they were always different by nightfall.

Sometimes the air has a sparkling diamond quality, and sometimes it is as soft and bland as milk; and with the change, the whole world changes. The islands offshore are new islands, and the rutted and grass-grown road leading across the heath to town is a strange route to an unknown destination. Even on a day which is bright and burnished near at hand, so that every coppery blade of grass is distinct and every sea-worn pebble clear-cut, a wall of fog sometimes stands out to sea, concealing Titm'nan Light. Boats chug around behind it and emerge suddenly, looking larger than life. Once in the afternoon, as we were looking at the distant fog wall, three separate rainbows appeared on it, mile-high columns of brilliant color, like great stained-glass windows. Two deer stepped out of the scrub near us and they, too, stood at gaze, entranced and unafraid. It was one of those moments when the world is in accord with itself and everything conspires to miraculous perfection.

Often the fog doesn't stay out at sea, but moves in silently and takes over the land. First you see it a long way off, just a rosy haze in the sun. Then Titm'nan Light is gone, although the sun still shines warmly where you are lying on the springy turf. The next time you look up, Western Island is just a shadow, and then it too is gone. The gulls fly lower and their voices are subdued and anxious. Long streamers reach out high above you to extinguish the sun, and suddenly the air is chilly. The big rugosa bushes among the nearby rocks grow vague and their colors fade; and the next thing you know, you are moving in a luminous whiteness, and then in a dense, damp gray. The eaves drip, the invisible surf sounds loud, and every twig on every bush is beaded with tiny pearls.

It's of days like that that the lobstermen say, "Only reason I found my way back into harbor was that I'd had the foresight to stick my knife in the fog on the way out, to mark the entrance." Those are the days when the boats remain at anchor, and everyone stays at home and knits bait bags and trap heads, or else sits around the store swapping talk.

But even foggy days aren't all alike. They sound drab and monotonous and depressing, and yet one of the lovliest sights I ever saw occurred on a foggy evening, when you couldn't find your hand in front of your face. On fair nights there were always a great many fireflies winking around all over the place. What happened to them on foggy or rainy nights I never thought to wonder. On this foggy night I went out to get a piece of fireplace wood, and brushed a low bush by the door. Immediately it sprang into trembling light, like a Christmas tree, and all the lights, like those of a Christmas tree, were of different colors—green and gold and green-gold and yellow and pinkish and blue, all captured in the foggy web of the bush. The whole thing was like magic and unbelievably beautiful. I shall never forget that little bushful of fireflies.

Then, when you think you have at last seen every face that the country can present—the opalescent look of the sea before dawn, the lavender play of lightning on great green combers during a midnight thunder storm, the breathless hush of high tide at noon—the season changes and you have it all to learn over again. The blueberry bushes turn scarlet, so that the trees look black and the sea so blue it hurts. The wild geese come over in high-flying wedges and foxes bark at night. All distances change subtly in the cool crystal air, and all sounds too. It's then that you realize that one lifetime is not enough, that you will never know all that you would wish to know about this country that you have taken to your heart.

I suppose that every family in Corea owns a clock; but if every clock in town stopped, it wouldn't make the slightest bit of difference in the way of life. The measuring-out of time is determined by more powerful forces than a clock's little ticking. When the tide and the weather are right, the boats all go out together, no matter what the clock says; and when the traps are hauled or the fog moves in, they all come home. People get up when the sun rises and start their work; and after the long day, go to bed when it sets. They eat when they are hungry and rest when they are tired.

It sounds like a very disorganized way to live, but it isn't. A natural routine and discipline is set up, an intrinsic rhythm established, free from the strains and tensions of clock regimentation. You have a sense of abiding by universal laws rather than of being bound by niggling little rules. You feel free of bondage and yet secure in an order that is much greater than anything achieved by man. Relieved of the pressure of clock-watching, your mind expands and opens to take in the world around you. The pendulum of the clock has nothing to do with you, nor has its sweeping hands. Only the great pendulum of the tide can drive you away from the little aquariumlike tidal pool where you have been hunting for sea urchins and anemones; only the slow hand of the declining sun can call you home from blueberry picking on the moor.

Perhaps that is the final and compelling reason why I look on Corea as My Down-East. It is the place where I feel most surely that I am a part of a colossal and perfect plan. Perhaps that is what, in the final analysis, we are all seeking in this world—our own place where we belong, in the understanding of which we will come to know and understand ourselves. When we have found that, we have each arrived safe Down-East, whether it be along the coast of Maine or at the opposite end of the earth.

PART III

The Nickels-Sortwell House in Wiscasset is famed for its Federal-style facade.

Things to See and Do

IT WOULD BE impossible to catalogue all the things there
are to see and do on the coast of Maine; and were it possible, only Methuselah could come anywhere near to seeing
and doing them in a lifetime. So in the list that follows, I'm
confining myself to things of historic, artistic, natural and
—in a few cases—very special interest. I've arranged them
for easier reference according to regions. But before we
go into that, I'd like to make a few suggestions for compil-
ing your own program of activities in accordance with
your own tastes.

First, before you even leave home, write to the State of
Maine Publicity Bureau, 78 Gateway Circle, Portland,
Maine 04102, for their free pamphlets concerning the
area you intend to visit. These will give you an excellent
idea of the facilities and amusements available: the golf
courses and race tracks, for example; or charter boats for
fishing; or cruises along the coast and among the islands;
or public clambakes. Some coastal towns can be reached
only by ferry, and there are so many ferry lines and their
schedules are so subject to change that it would be impractical for me to, try to include them. But the Maine
Publicity Bureau covers the whole subject very adequately.

After you get to Maine, buy on a newsstand for sixty
cents the current copy of the magazine *Down East*. (No,
I am not in their employ, nor do I own stock in the company.) This publication is worth the price. It's interesting

and beautifully printed; and moreover, it contains each month a complete calendar of events along the coast: art exhibits, festivals, flower shows, open houses, lectures, concerts, and recitals, presentations at the various summer theaters, and such sporting events as tuna derbies, boat races, gymkhanas, and archery matches. The advertisements, too, repay study if you are looking for something special in the line of handcrafts or art to take home, or for a house to rent or buy.

Pick up also a copy of *The Coastal Courier,* published weekly during the summer especially for summer visitors by the Rockland (Maine) *Courier-Gazette.* This can be obtained free at such places as airline terminals, railroad stations, and newsstands in hotels. It covers in even greater detail the activities from Kittery to Calais, throwing in for full measure a great deal of incidental information about the industries and communities of the area.

Most towns of any size at all have public information booths. Use them. The attendants are eager to help you find whatever you are looking for, whether it be a scenic picnic spot or the name of a reliable veterinary.

And don't neglect the best of all information sources, the native resident. Talk to him. Ask him questions. You'll find him almost invariably helpful and friendly, whether he's a clerk behind a counter or a lobsterman walking along one of the little roads that lead to the sea. He knows more about the country than anyone else, and he's glad and proud to share the knowledge.

Through these various mediums you'll learn enough to keep you busy and happy for a month of Sundays with very little help from me.

Just a word about my list of things to do and see. The *open* hours of public buildings are as nearly correct as I can make them at the time of writing. However, things change; so if you're going out of your way to visit any of them, you'd better check first. I've indicated, as far as I know, which things are free and which charge admission, but these, too, are subject to change. Fees are usually twenty-five to fifty cents or more for adults, less or nothing for children.

THE WESTERN COAST

Kittery to Cape Elizabeth

KITTERY

Maine Handcrafts. A permanent exhibition of Maine crafts and decorative arts in the lobby of the State of Maine Publicity Bureau building near the entrance to the Maine Turnpike. Free.

First Congregational Church. An excellent example of colonial New England church architecture. The pulpit dates back to 1730. Free.

Lady Pepperell House. Built in 1760; open weekdays in summer 10–4. Fine period furniture and furnishings. Adm.

Sparhawk House. (near Congregational Church), 1742. Home of Mary Sparhawk, who induced the British to spare Portsmouth.

Portsmouth Navy Yard. Apply for pass at gate.

Congregational Church. Though there seems to be some dispute about it, many consider this the oldest church in Maine; said to have been built 1729.

KITTERY POINT

Fort McClary Memorial. Only the original blockhouse remains of the fort built in 1690. The area is now a state park with picnic, swimming, and playground facilities. Free.

Pepperell House. Home of William Pepperell's father; birthplace of William (1682); (see page 125).

SOUTH BERWICK

Hamilton House. Built in 1770; open in summer on Wednesday through Saturday 1–5. Fine Georgian house in lovely riverbank and garden setting, furnished with antiques. Adm.

Sarah Orne Jewett Memorial. Built in 1774; open in summer on Wednesday through Saturday 1–5. The birthplace and home of the famous author of *The Country of the Pointed Firs.* Excellent example of colonial interior with period furnishings. Adm.

Berwick Academy. One of the oldest in Maine.

Warren Garrison House. Former home of Gladys Hasty Carroll.

Spring Hill Recreation Area. Picnic tables, fireplaces, beach. Lodge with clambake and other group equipment. Golf course. In winter, ski slopes, school and tow, trails, toboggan run, skating.

YORK

The Old Gaol Museum. Begun in 1653 as the King's Prison, this is the oldest existing English public building in America; open in summer on weekdays 9:30–5:30, and on Sundays 1:30–5:30. Famous for its dungeons and fine collection of china and furniture. Adm.

Elizabeth Perkins House. Built on the bank of the York River at Sewall's Bridge in 1730; open in summer on weekdays except Monday 10:30–5:30, and Sundays from 1:30. Although colonial, it remains as it was lived in by a Victorian family. Adm.

Sewall's Bridge. A replica of the first pile bridge in America, built in 1761.

Jefferd's Tavern. Built as a hostelry before the Revolution; open weekdays in summer except Monday 10:30–5:30, and Sundays from 1:30. In excellent state of preservation and restoration. Tea is served in the original taproom. Free.

Old York Cemetery. Boulder over witch's grave (see page 132).

Wilcox House. Built in 1740; open weekdays in summer 9:30–5:30 and Sundays from 1:30. The house has served as a tavern, post office, and residence, and contains rare old furniture and interesting art exhibits. **Adm.**

Old Schoolhouse. Original school built in 1745; open weekdays 10–5 and Sunday afternoons. The schoolmaster and children in effigy wear period costumes. **Adm.**

Mount Agamenticus (see pages 119, 135, 136).

Big A Ski and Recreation Area. Chair lift, tow, trails, lodge, ski school.

YORK BEACH

Nubble Light. Established in 1879. One of the most frequently painted and photographed lighthouses in America. Free.

OGUNQUIT

Marginal Way. A beautiful footpath along the cliffs between the river mouth and Perkins Cove. Worth walking. Free, with benches for resting.

WELLS

Joseph Storer Garrison House (see page 139).

Lindsay Tavern (1799). Now run as tourist home (see page 139).

KENNEBUNK

The Brick Store Museum. Open in summer on weekdays except Monday 10:00–4:30. Permanent exhibits of objects relating to colonial times, especially to shipbuilding; changing exhibits of artistic and historical interest; annual August exhibit of contemporary paintings and graphic arts. Free.

First Parish Unitarian Church, 1774; alterations in nineteenth century; bell by Paul Revere.

Storer House, Storer Street. Birthplace of Kenneth Roberts.

Wedding Cake House. Built in 1826; private. Classic example of wooden scrollwork used as ornamentation; supposed to be compensation to a bride who was deprived of her wedding cake when her husband was hastily ordered to sea.

The Lafayette Elm, on Storer Street. Believed to have been set out on the day of the Battle of Concord and Lexington; known to have shaded Lafayette during an outdoor public reception in his honor in 1825.

Perkins Mill (1749) (see page 139).

KENNEBUNKPORT

Seashore Electric Railway, a museum of trolley cars. Open from noon until twilight daily in summer. Here are more than sixty old trolley cars from all over the world, in operating condition. A charge is made for rides.

Booth Tarkington studio and schooner.

Congregational Church (1784).

Historical Society. Open Wednesday afternoons in summer. Special exhibits in restored rural schoolhouse.

GOOSE ROCKS (near Cape Porpoise)

Artists' colony.

Watercolor gallery (summer exhibits).

SACO

Saco Jail (now a museum), 1653 (see page 144).

York Institute. Antiques, art, Indian relics.

Cyrus King House (1807). Now rectory of Catholic Church.

OLD ORCHARD

Animal Fair Game Farm, on Cascade Road near beach. Open daily 11–9. A thirty-acre zoo containing animals from all over the world: camels, swans, kangaroos, buffalo, etc. Adm.

SCARBORO

Black Point Preserve and Game Farm (see page 146).
Prouts Neck Bird Sanctuary (see page 146).
Parson Lancaster House (1766).
Winslow Homer House.
Scarboro Salt Marsh (see page 147).

CAPE ELIZABETH

Two Lights State Park. Picnicking, fishing; scenic and historical.
Crescent Beach State Park. Beautiful beach, bath-house, showers, picnic tables, fireplaces. Open May 30 through September 30.

THE CASCO BAY AREA

Portland to Cape Small

PORTLAND

L. D. M. Sweat Mansion, 111 High Street. Open year round daily except Sunday 10:00–4:30. Interesting Federal-style home in process of restoration. Adm.
Portland Museum of Art, same address, same hours as above. Outstanding permanent collection of painting and sculpture; current shows of contemporary art. The Summer Art Festival, beginning each July, is famous throughout the nation. Free.
Victoria Mansion, Park and Danforth Streets. Built in 1859; open summers daily except Monday 11:00–4:30. This work of Henry Austin, the most distinguished eclectic architect of the Victorian period, is accepted as the finest example of its type in the United States. Superb examples of Victorian art, furnishings, decoration, and way of living. Adm.
Old Tate House, 1270 Westbrook Street. Built in 1775 by George Tate, Mast Agent to the British Crown; open daily except Monday 11–5, Sundays 1–5. A fine

old house, authentically restored, with period furnishings. Adm.

The Wadsworth-Longfellow House, 485 Congress Street. Built in 1785; open in summer daily except Sunday 9:30–4:30. The boyhood home of Henry Wadsworth Longfellow, this beautifully preserved house contains memorabilia of the Wadsworth and Longfellow families and reflects a happy way of life. At the rear is a small, quiet, and lovely walled garden. Adm.

Portland Observatory, off Congress Street. Open daily 10–7. Formerly used to signal townspeople of the arrival of ships; now offers a remarkable view of the city and Casco Bay. Adm.

Kotzschmar Organ Recitals, Portland City Hall (1809–12). Most midweek evenings in summer, but check locally for time and artists. Concerts by the nation's most famous organists on one of America's truly great organs. Free.

Eastern Cemetery, Congress Street at Munjoy Hill. The old, pleasant burial place of Commodore Edward Preble, hero of Tripoli, and of the young captains of the *Boxer* and the *Enterprise.* Free.

Longfellow Square, State and Pine Streets. Monument to Longfellow by Franklin Simmons.

Museum of Maine Historical Society (rear of Wadsworth-Longfellow House). Historical and Indian materials; library.

Wiscasset Atomic Power Plant. Opened in 1972.

St. Luke's Cathedral (1855; Gothic), 137 State Street. By Henry Vaughan. Madonna and Child by John La-Farge.

Portland Club (1805), 162 State Street (Shepley House). Postcolonial; from designs by Parris.

Mellen-Fessenden House (1807), 166 State Street. Now Catholic chapel; was home of Secretary of Treasury under Lincoln, William P. Fessenden.

Society of Natural History, 24 Elm Street. Natural history material, Indian relics.

Cathedral of the Immaculate Conception (1869), 307 Congress Street. Seat of Maine diocese. French Gothic; fine exterior, interior, stained-glass windows; notable Stations of the Cross.

Neal Dow House (1824), 714 Congress Street. Home of author of Maine's prohibition law.

Neal Dow Birthplace, opposite Neal Dow House. In process of being made into a museum.

Fort Allen Park, Fore Street and Eastern Promenade. Site of old forts; view of Casco Bay.

Deering Mansion (1804), 85 Bedford Street. Sea captain's old home; period furniture and relics.

Deering Oaks Park, Deering Avenue. Site of successful stand by Maj. Benjamin Church and his company against Indians, 1689. Largest park in Portland.

Williston Congregational Church, 32–38 Thomas Street. First Christian Endeavor Society.

Thomas B. Reed Monument, Western Promenade. View of White Mountains.

SOUTH PORTLAND
Portland Head Light (1791). First U.S. lighthouse. Over 200 Casco Bay islands can be seen from hurricane deck.

YARMOUTH
Brimstone Hill Meeting House. Built in 1796, restored and preserved by the Village Improvement Society. An excellent example of the period. Free.

Old Baptist Church (1796).

Indian Burial Ground (early 1700's).

POWNAL
Bradbury Mountain State Park. Camp ground, picnic area, fire places, rest rooms; beautiful view of Casco

Bay; old cattle pound (circa 1750); abandoned feldspar quarry of interest to geologists. Free.

FREEPORT

Old Tavern (1779). Allegedly an agreement was signed here making Maine a separate state in 1820.

BRUNSWICK

Bowdoin College Museum of Fine Arts, Walker Art Building. Open weekdays 10–12 and 2–4, and Sunday afternoons. Considered the best small museum in America. Outstanding American paintings and silver; Assyrian and Greek sculpture, coins, and gems; Renaissance drawings; the loaned collection of paintings of the late Sir Harry Oakes. Special summer exhibits. Free.

Pejepscot Historical Society Museum, 12 School Street. Open summer afternoons 1:00–4:30. Local antiquities and interesting regional Americana. Adm.

Harriet Beecher Stowe House, 63 Federal Street. Built in 1806; open all the time. The home of the author of *Uncle Tom's Cabin* is now an inn of thirty rooms. Meals are served.

Gilman Mansion (1789), Union and Oak Streets. By Melcher; remodeled 1840; period furnishings and relics.

Emmons House (1814), 25 Federal Street. Home of Longfellow while professor at Bowdoin.

The Bowdoin Pines, outside town on U.S. 1 toward Bath. This tiny forest reservation of the few remaining mast pines in America is now a picnic area. Free.

HARPSWELL PENINSULA

Old Town House (1788).
Elijah Kellogg Church (1843).

ORR'S ISLAND (Orr's Village)

Pearl of Orr House. Home in Mrs. Stowe's *Pearl of Orr's Island.*

TOPSHAM

Aldrich House (1800). By Samuel Melcher.
Peacock Tavern (circa 1790). Still a hotel.

BATH

Davenport Memorial Museum, City Hall. Open weekdays during business hours. A collection of paintings, ship models, and tools used in early shipbuilding. The bell in the tower was cast by Paul Revere. Free.
Residence of William King, first governor of Maine; Whiskeag Road; 1805.
Peterson House (1770), Washington Street.
Home of Herbert L. Spinney, 75 Court Street.

POPHAM BEACH

Fort Popham Memorial Park. Facilities for picnicking, camping, and swimming. Interesting old abandoned fort to explore. Free.

THE MIDDLE COAST

Georgetown to Thomaston

GEORGETOWN

Reid State Park. Good picnic and swimming facilities on scenic coast.

HALLOWELL

Old Powder House.
Vaughan Mansion.
Worster House (1832). Famous hotel.

AUGUSTA

Fort Western, Bowman Street. Built in 1754 by the Plymouth Company as a defense against the French and Indians; open in summer on weekdays 9–5, Sundays 2–5. The original twenty-room barracks is maintained as a museum depicting colonial living and has several rooms of special exhibits. Adm.

State Capitol and Museum. Seat of state government since 1832. A beautiful new museum has recently been opened in the Capitol Building. Special exhibits. Free.

Reuel Williams House (1810), southwest corner Stone and Cony Streets. Portraits, old furnishings, historical relics.

Kennebec Dam, 1837.

Blaine House (1830), northwest corner Capitol and State Streets. Executive mansion.

Lithgow Library, Winthrop and State Streets. Material on New England.

State Park. A 20-acre tract between Capitol and Union Streets. Arboretum and plant collections of special interest to students of botany and horticulture. Maine Forest Service uses park as experimental station on plant survival in this climate.

Macomber Playground. Between Valley and Center Streets. In 1930, a "children's court" was experimented with here, with children serving as policemen, lawyers, and jury. Its success led to its adoption throughout the country.

WISCASSET

Lincoln County Museum and Old Jail. Built in 1809; open weekdays in summer 9–5 and Sunday afternoons. The exhibits cover two hundred years of Maine arts, crafts, and skills. Adm.

Maine Art Gallery. Built in 1807 as an academy; open during July and August on weekdays 10–5. Two exhibits each year of Maine's best painters. Free.

Nickels-Sortwell House. Built in 1807; open summers on weekdays except Monday 11–5, and Sunday afternoons. A beautiful and imposing Federal-style home, famed for its facade. Period furnishings. Still under restoration. Adm.

Lincoln County Fire Museum. Exhibits pertaining to the history of the Wiscasset Fire Society, believed to have been the first (1801) organization in the United States formed for voluntary community fire-fighting; old fire-fighting equipment.

Castle Tucker (1807), east end of High Street. Unusual architecture; Victorian furnishings and wallpapers; freestanding staircase. Open weekdays July-August 11–4; June and September by request. Adm.

Lee-Payson-Smith House (1792), High Street.

Abiel Wood House (1812), High and Lee Streets.

Lincoln County Courthouse (1824), on common. Oldest functioning courthouse in Maine; Daniel Webster practiced law here.

Meeting House (1909). Reproduction of one destroyed by fire; has Paul Revere bell.

Head Tide. Birthplace of Edwin Arlington Robinson.

Town Library (1805), High Street. Open weekdays 2–5:30 and Mon., Wed., Fri. mornings 9–12.

Fort Edgecomb Memorial Park. An octagonal blockhouse. Picnic sites. Small fee, children free.

PHIPPSBURG
James McCobb House (1774).

BOOTHBAY HARBOR
Sea and Shore Fisheries Aquarium. A varied and interesting sea exhibit including marine growths, crabs, giant lobsters, rays, and many ocean fish, as well as a seal pool. Free.

SEGUIN ISLAND
Seguin Island Lighthouse. Visitors welcome.

NORTH EDGECOMB

Marie Antoinette House. Private, but permission may sometimes be received to inspect. The house prepared in vain to receive Marie Antoinette.

NEWCASTLE

Kavanaugh House (1803).

St. Patrick's Church (1803–08). Very old French altar and painting seized during Mexican War.

DAMARISCOTTA

Indian Shell Heaps, along riverbank. Mounds of oyster shells that record prehistoric Indian feasts and sometimes yield ancient artifacts.

Todd Sanctuary, on Hog Island in Muscongus Bay. The first nature study camp in America, sponsored by the Audubon Society.

PEMAQUID BEACH

Fort William Henry. Built in 1692 and later restored; open in summer daily 9–12 and 1–5. Adm.

Pemaquid Beach Park and *Lighthouse Park.* Swimming and picnic facilities.

WALDOBORO

Old German Lutheran Church. Built about 1750 (perhaps 1795, according to some sources); open weekdays, services at 3 P.M. on Sundays in summer. A historic and very interesting old building. Free.

Old German Cemetery (1750).

Col. Isaac Reed Mansion.

Old Shipyards.

FRIENDSHIP

William H. Hahn Glass Collection. Seen at convenience of owner. About 1,000 pieces of choice early American glass.

SOUTH WARREN

Knox Street Arboretum and Academy of Arts and Sciences. Zoological, botanical, mineral, Indian collections.

THOMASTON

Montpelier. Built in 1795, reproduced in 1929; open June through October 10–6 daily. A really elegant mansion furnished with antiques and containing the personal possessions of the original builder and owner, Major General Henry Knox. Adm.

The Prison Store, Maine State Prison. This shop is maintained and operated by the inmates of the State Prison and offers for sale the products of their various craftsmanships, some of which are superior. Arrangements may be made for the refinishing of your antiques and old furniture. Prices reasonable, workmanship excellent. Browsing free.

Weymouth Boulder. Marks first landing of Capt. George Weymouth, 1605.

PENOBSCOT BAY

Rockland to Stonington

ROCKLAND

William A. Farnsworth Art Museum and *The Homestead,* Elm Street. Museum open year round weekdays except Monday 10–5; Homestead open summer weekdays except Monday 10–5. Drawings, prints, paintings by nineteenth- and twentieth-century European and American artists; frequently changing exhibits of contemporary painting, photography, arts and crafts. Birthplace of Edna St. Vincent Millay. Free.

Owl's Head Lighthouse.

Owl's Head Light and Municipal Park.

Maine Seafoods Festival. Annually on first weekend in August, Thursday night through Sunday evening. An outstanding festival. Lobsters, clams, fish, etc., plus parades and boat rides to inspect Navy and Coast Guard vessels in harbor.

ROCKPORT

Walker Park and Beach. Swimming, picnic tables, rest rooms.

Captain's House and Old Book Shop. Open year round. Wood carvings, figureheads, art books.

CAMDEN

Camden Hills State Park. Well-conducted park area of almost 5,000 acres offering complete camping facilities in summer, skiing in winter.

Bok Amphitheater. Concerts.

Public Beach. Swimming, rest rooms, picnic tables, fireplaces, drinking water. Free.

ISLESBORO

Warren Island State Park. For boating people only. Campsites, picnic tables, fireplaces, drinking water, privies, mooring float. A few minutes by water from Islesboro Village landing. Open May 15 through September 30.

BELFAST

White House (1825), 30 Church Street.

Clay House (1825), 130 Main Street.

Joseph Miller Tavern, Poor Mill Road.

There are also many fine old houses on High Street that are not open to the public but are well worth driving past.

SEARSPORT

Penobscot Marine Museum. Open weekdays in summer 9–5 and Sunday afternoons; in three buildings:

the Old Town Hall, The Captain's House, and the Duncan House. Unusually fine and complete collection of things pertaining to maritime history of area —ship models and half-models, charts, paintings, logs, instruments, photographs, plus an outstanding display of pressed glass. The Captain's House is especially beautiful and interesting. Adm.

Searsport State Park. Camping, boating, and swimming.

PROSPECT

Fort Knox State Park. Impressive old fort of masterly stonework. Subterranean passages fun to explore. Picnic area with fire places, tables, spring water, and rest rooms.

WINTERPORT

Congregational Church (1832). Paul Revere Bell.

Blaisdell House (1786). Attributed to Christopher Wren.

Several other fine old mansions not open to the public.

BUCKSPORT

"Witch's Curse." In cemetery, mark like a severed leg on a gravestone is attributed to a curse put by a condemned woman on Col. Jonathan Buck, for whom town was named; heart-shaped mark now appearing.

Jed Prouty Tavern (1804). Several Presidents of U.S. stayed here, and many stage notables of the early 1900's.

Municipal Swimming Pool. Open July and August.

CASTINE

Wilson Museum. Open during July and August on Wednesdays and Saturdays 2–5. Chiefly archeological, containing objects of the Paleolithic, Neolithic, Bronze, and Iron Ages, many of them European. There is also a collection of very early guns and arms. Free.

Maine Maritime Academy, for the training of midshipmen as officers of the U. S. Merchant Marine and Navy. The 7,000-ton training ship *State of Maine* may be visited and inspected. Free.

Old Meeting House (1790).

Old Courthouse (1800). Now a library.

Blake House (1797; addition 1857). Original furnishings.

Fort Madison (1812).

Fort George (1814). Built by British.

Fort George Memorial. Archeological research and reconstruction project at old fortifications which were occupied by four nations since 1779: French, English, Dutch, and American. Free.

STONINGTON

Ame's Pond. This rather small pond contains over 4,000 pink and white water lilies and is beautiful to see. Free.

Eastern Penobscot Archive Museum. Penobscot Bay area material.

DOWN-EAST

Ellsworth to Calais

BLUE HILL

Parson Fisher House. Built in 1814; open in summer on Tuesdays and Fridays 2–5. This old house is interesting for its several ingenious architectural features, its famous clock, and its old books and paintings. Adm.

Home of Ethelbert Nevin.

Congregational Church (1772).

ELLSWORTH

Colonel Black Mansion. Open May 30–November 1 daily 10–5. Particularly fine brick mansion filled with

period furniture, china, glass, and bric-a-brac; lovely
garden. Adm.

Public Library. Open weekday afternoons. Beautiful
old sea captain's house adapted to library use. Free.

Old Congregational Church. Always open. Classic example of old New England church architecture. Of
this church it is said that it "has given more great
men to the State and the Nation than any other
church of its size in New England." Free.

MT. DESERT ISLAND

Jackson Memorial Laboratory and *Hamilton Station.*
Visiting hours at Laboratory on Tuesdays and Fridays
at 7:30, Wednesdays at 3:30. This is one of the nation's foremost research centers on cancer and other
constitutional diseases. Visiting hours at the Station
by appointment only. Here experiments into animal
behavior are conducted. Free.

Robert Abbe Museum and Sieur de Mont Spring. Indian relics and wild flower garden. Free.

Sawtelle Historical Museum on Little Cranberry Island.
Take ferry from Clark Point or Manset. A collection
of prints, documents, and relics pertaining to the area.
The ferry ride and the lovely island make the trip
worth while. Adm.

Acadia National Park. All facilities here for camping,
but during the season it is wise to reserve space in
advance. There is so much to see and do in this dramatically beautiful national park that a complete catalogue is impossible. The Park rangers will be glad to
answer questions and give suggestions. However—sunrise from the top of Cadillac Mountain is worth getting up for, and you should see the spectacular Thunder Hole spouting salt spray. A special feature is a
series of nature walks and boat trips conducted by
the Park naturalists, and unusual campfire nature programs twice a week at the two public camp grounds
near Bar Harbor and Seawall. The walks range from

easy for the lazy to vigorous mountain climbs for the energetic. These are free. The boat trips involve a fee to the boatman. For details of time and place, ask a ranger or a naturalist for a program. Although roads are not plowed between December and April, certain trails are now open all winter for snowmobile use.

Abby Aldrich Rockefeller Garden at Seal Harbor. Beautiful Chinese garden owned by Rockefeller family; open to public Wed.,10 a.m–5 p.m. Free.

LAMOINE

Lamoine State Park. Camping and beach. Free.

WINTER HARBOR

Schoodic Point, a part of Acadia National Park. Spectacularly beautiful scenery, picnicking, fireplaces, surf fishing (no license required), but no camping. Bring a loaf of bread to feed the gulls. The Navy's Radar and Communications Installation is open to the public on Armed Forces Day only. Free.

PETIT MANAN POINT, *Steuben*

All-Souls-by-the-Sea. This virtually unknown, tiny Episcopal chapel, hidden away on a winding back road, has an indefinable, simple charm that makes it worth a visit. Open all the time and free.

MILBRIDGE

McClellan Park Recreation Area. Tent sites, picnic tables, drinking water, rest rooms. Lovely views.

COLUMBIA FALLS

The Ruggles House. Built in 1818; open weekdays in summer 8:30–4:30. A beautiful house furnished with antiques and particularly noted for the delicate detail of its interior wood carving. It contains probably the finest flying staircase in New England. Adm.

Maude Bucknam House (1820).
Old Lippincott House.

MACHIAS

Burnham Tavern. Built in 1770, restored in 1907; open in summer on Tuesdays and Wednesdays 2–5, and by appointment at other times. The oldest historic building east of the Penobscot, having served as an inn during the Revolution. Relics of the period. Adm.

MACHIASPORT

Jasper Beach, off the Starboard Road. One of the few beaches in the world composed entirely of pure jasper stones. Many collect these bright sea-polished pebbles to make jewelry. Free.

Fort O'Brien Memorial. Picnic grounds at old earthworks of fort.

CUTLER

U. S. Navy Radio Station. Completed 1961; apply at gate for permission to enter, which may or may not be granted. This is the most powerful station of its type in the world, linking the mainland with ships on and under all seven seas. Some of the twenty-seven towers are as tall as the Eiffel Tower in Paris. The Buck Rogers effect can be appreciated from the highway.

Machias Seal Island. (Owned by U.S., operated by Canada.) Noted as breeding ground of rare and peculiar bird, the puffin. In summer fishing boats leave daily from Cutler for the island.

LUBEC (Hamlet of Bailey's Mistake)

Boot Cove. Natural bridge and thunderholes. When surf rushes into the 110-foot gashes in the cliff, a thunderous growl results that can be heard ten miles away. Private property, but owner will give permission, if requested, to drive to the cove. Free.

West Quoddy Head Light Station. Candy-striped lighthouse on most easterly point of the United States. The Coast Guard welcomes visitors. Free.

West Quoddy Head State Park. Picnic tables, fireplaces, rest rooms. Free.

Chaloner Inn (Cleaves Tavern, 1804).

Old Golden Ball Inn. Pre-Revolutionary.

Comstock House and several other fine old houses.

International Bridge to Campobello Island.

DENNYSVILLE

Cobscook Bay State Park. Picnic facilities. Open May 1 through October 1.

PEMBROKE

Reversing Salt Water Falls, off Mahar's Point on Leighton Neck. You must walk two miles over a woods road to reach this impressive half-mile-long set of falls that roar alternately in and out of the bay as the tide rises and ebbs. Fossils found in abundance here. Free.

Old Iron Works (1828).

EASTPORT

Indian Reservation at Pleasant Point. The home of the Passamaquoddy Tribe of the Abanaki Nation, descendants of the Indians encountered by Champlain and du Monts in 1604. Beautifully made baskets and souvenirs may be purchased. Free.

Border Historical Society Museum. Local historical material.

Eastport Camping Area. Rest rooms, tent sites, fireplaces.

PERRY

Halfway Marker on U.S. 1. A red granite stone marking the 45th parallel, halfway between the Equator and the North Pole. This parallel also crosses through

Southern France, Turkey, Mongolia, China, Japan, and Canada.

45th Parallel Picnic Area. Picnic facilities.

CALAIS

International Bridge between the United States and Canada. Under this bridge occurs the greatest rise and fall of tide in the nation, a 28-foot variation.

Moosehorn National Wild Life Refuge. A 22,565-acre tract of woods, fields, ponds, and streams, most of it accessible only by hiking, set aside for the protection of wild life. A wonderful place for naturalists and nature lovers to observe the habits of deer, bear, beavers, otters, seals, and other animals in their natural wild setting. Over 190 species of birds have been reported. Birds and animals are protected, but fishing for trout, pickerel, and bass is allowed. Inquire at Calais Information Booth for descriptive leaflet; or the resident game warden will gladly answer questions and make suggestions. Free.

Index

(Italicized figures denote illustrations.)